FEB

LT
B.
KENNEDY, J. F.

S0-ABB-051

ALL TOO HUMAN

To Dolores
No Other Love

CONTENTS

Sometimes I love you.
Sometimes I hate you.
But when I hate you,
It's 'cause I love you . . .

— *"Sometimes I'm Happy"*
words by Leo Rubin and Clifford Grey
music by Vincent Youmans

ONE

Woman
of the Century

Christmas, 1981

Jackie and I

I first began to see a lot of Jackie in the summer of 1981.

At the time, I was the editor of *The New York Times Magazine* and was bringing out a new novel, an espionage thriller called *The Parachutists.* Jackie was an editor at Doubleday, my publisher, and she liked my novel well enough to make one of her rare public appearances at my book party.

"I am already 100 pages into it and can't put it down," Jackie wrote me shortly after the party. "I am going to be late for dinner tonight and work tomorrow and it will be your fault. . . . They should let you play Alexander [the book's hero] in the movie."

A few days later, I picked up the telephone and called her.

We lunched together twice in the weeks between Labor Day and Thanksgiving, and around Christmas time, she invited me to a party at her home on Fifth Avenue. I was one of the first guests to arrive, and as I stepped off the elevator into the foyer, I was certain that I heard the voice of President Kennedy — then dead for 18 years — coming from somewhere in the apartment.

When I entered the living room, I discovered the source of my confusion. There, standing with a drink in hand and an elbow on the fireplace mantel, was Senator Edward Kennedy. He was talking in a booming voice to Maurice Templesman, the new man in Jackie's life.

The large room soon filled with other familiar voices and faces — Kennedys, Shrivers, Smiths, Bouviers, Auchinclosses, Radziwills, New Frontiersmen, and old New York friends. There were even a few writers, including John Phillips Marquand Jr., who, I later came to learn, was the first great love of Jackie's life.

Antique silver frames stood on the grand piano. They displayed photographs of Jackie's family, though none, I noted with some puzzlement, of its most illustrious member, John Fitzgerald Kennedy.

Before I met her, I had formed a picture in my mind of Jackie as a remote figure moving across a small black-and-white television screen — the poised young woman conducting a tour of the White House, the stylish First Lady dressed in a blood-caked suit in the cabin of Air Force One, the veiled widow striding down Pennsylvania Avenue behind her husband's coffin. When Jackie suddenly materialized in my life in the year she turned 5'2", I was unprepared to meet the liberated New York career woman in all her living color.

At one point during the party, I found myself alone in the crowd with Jackie.

"Oh, Ed," she said, "I'm so glad you could come. Journalists are the most interesting people in the whole world!"

I was won over.

Her eyes were her most arresting feature. A dark luminescent brown, they were set deep in their sockets, and one of them was larger than the other. Under that big, brilliant right eye, there was a tan spot on her cheek. But other than that one tiny blemish, time had done little to dim her beauty. She looked as willowy as a young girl — slightly over 5'7" tall and 125 pounds, give or take a pound or two. Jacqueline

Kennedy Onassis was about the same size as Greta Garbo, her only close rival for the title of The Most Famous Woman of the Twentieth Century.

At our lunches, she dressed very simply: a cashmere pullover, a wide belt, and slacks. She wore just a touch of mascara and lip gloss, but she always managed to look like a woman who took extravagant care of herself. Twice-a-week facials at Nardi Salon on East 57th Street helped. So did a recent face lift, which was performed by a Park Avenue surgeon named Dr. Michael Hogan. Still, I came to realize that when Jackie peered in the mirror, she reacted no differently than other women her age. She was critical of her own looks. To console her, a friend once pointed out that old trees are more beautiful than young ones.

"I see what you mean," she said, "but it's still very difficult to take."

I always received the full Jackie Treatment. She fixed me with those widely spaced, asymmetrical brown eyes in a gaze that could only be described as adoring. She punctuated her phrases with girlish words like *gosh* and *golly* and *gee* — sometimes all three in one sentence. But her famous Jackie mask hid a complicated personality. She was still biting her nails well into middle age. She chain-smoked when she thought no one was watching. And sometimes, when she sensed the absence of approval, her voice trailed off into that familiar little-girl whisper, and I would catch the suggestion of a childhood stutter.

After one of our lunches, I offered to help Jackie catch a cab. She was wearing a trench coat cinched with a knotted belt, a scarf worn like a babushka and pulled forward to shield the sides of her face, and her Jackie O sunglasses.

As we strolled down the crowded street, I asked her about her children. She replied that Caroline was working at the Metropolitan Museum of Art and living in a West Side apartment with two other young women. John — whom she never called John-John — was a junior at Brown University. We were approaching the corner when she turned to me and said, "Sometimes I can't help but feel concerned about them."

I wasn't sure I had heard her correctly.

"Them?" I asked.

"The children," she responded.

It was totally unlike her to blurt out something so private. I didn't know what to say. We stood there for a moment in silence. Then she explained: she was concerned that her children were being influenced in their judgment by people who wrote warped accounts of JFK's years in the White House and of her relationship with their father.

For as long as I could remember, I had been intensely curious about the bonds that united Jack and Jackie. Were they the bonds of money and political convenience, or were they the bonds of love?

Like many others, I read everything about Jack and Jackie that I could lay my hands on. A new biography of Jackie was published practically every year, and Jackie profiles were a magazine staple. The *Readers' Guide to Periodical Literature* had more listings for Jacqueline Lee Bouvier Kennedy Onassis than for any other living American woman. Books on John Fitzgerald Kennedy and his martyrdom numbered in the thousands.

Curiously, however, I could not find

a single volume devoted to Jack and Jackie's life together.

"What do you tell your children about the relationship between you and President Kennedy?" I asked her.

"I'd rather not think about the past," she said.

Her mood had abruptly changed, and the window into her soul was shut tight again.

"Please, let's not talk about the past," she went on. "I have to remain alive for myself. I don't want to dredge up the past."

I stumbled over an apology, but before I could get out more than a few words, Jackie had flagged down a cab, climbed in, pulled off her scarf, and was waving good-bye.

The Dreaded Klieg Lights

For several years during the early 1980s, Jackie threw open the doors of her Fifth Avenue apartment to a large group of friends for her annual Christmas party. She would begin to draw up the guest list shortly after Thanksgiving, and send out as many as 50 engraved Tiffany invitations.

She expressed mixed feelings about holding the yearly affair. When people asked her why she didn't just cancel the party and forget the whole thing, Jackie replied that she didn't want to offend her friends and family, who had come to count on this evening. Although she didn't say so, she knew that for many of her guests, the party was the high point of their winter social calendar.

That was only part of the reason. As the daughter of an alcoholic father and temperamental mother who were frequently locked in combat, Jackie did not have many happy memories of her childhood Christmases in New York

City. Later, at Merrywood, where she spent her teen-age years, Christmas was a difficult time for the household's seven children, who came from three different mothers. One Christmas at Merrywood, Jackie wrote a Nativity play in which her stepbrother Yusha played Joseph, her sister Lee was a Wise Man, her half brother Jamie was baby Jesus, and Jackie herself was Mary.

Then, of course, there was that bleak Christmas of 1963, when Jackie, just 34 years old, celebrated the holiday with her two young children a month after JFK's assassination.

"Can anyone understand," she asked a friend, "how it is to have lived in the White House and then, suddenly, to be living alone?"

Nonetheless, since then, she had resolved to make the holiday a joyous time for Caroline and John. This was especially important to her in 1981, a year that was full of unnerving news about assassins and assassinations. Lee Harvey Oswald's body was exhumed from its Dallas tomb at the request of his wife and the conspiracy buffs, who refused to believe that a lone gunman had killed President Kennedy.

Both President Ronald Reagan and Pope John Paul II were hit by bullets, barely escaping with their lives, and Anwar Sadat was murdered by Islamic fundamentalists. It appeared as though the bloody madness of the '60s was starting up all over again.

Until then, Jackie seemed to have managed the impossible — keeping herself and her children out of sight and out of the public's mind. But in 1981, the dreaded klieg lights of attention began snapping on again, threatening her family's peace and security. A deranged California law-school graduate by the name of Kevin King was arrested for stalking Caroline — following her to the very doorstep of her West Side apartment building. Even more disturbing, the Manhattan district attorney revealed that Mark David Chapman had Jackie's name on his hit list when he gunned down John Lennon a few months earlier.

By 1981, moreover, the heroic legend of John F. Kennedy had begun to sink into the sludge of gossip and innuendo. Once a mythical figure, Kennedy was being portrayed as a coarse, shallow, morally deficient, power-hungry man.

His successes were traced to his nice teeth and good hair; his failures, to a character that was insufficiently good.

The desanctification of JFK went beyond the bounds of historical revisionism. It raised profound questions about the very authenticity of the image of JFK, as well as the value of his 1,000 days in office. And it tainted all those around him, especially his wife, who was often depicted in books and in the supermarket tabloids as the snooty, spiteful, greedy, needy Jackie, the original material girl.

And so it was probably no mere coincidence that, while reviewing her Christmas party list, Jackie's eye fell on the name of an old and trusted family friend, Abraham Ribicoff. A former governor of Connecticut and an ex–U.S. senator, Ribicoff had known Jack Kennedy from his earliest days in Congress. He had been among the first to promote the idea of Kennedy for president. Jackie picked up the phone, and dialed the Connecticut number of Ribicoff and his wife, Casey.

"Governor, this is Jackie," Ribicoff recalled her saying.

"How are you, Jackie?"

"Governor," she said, "you and Casey will be receiving an invitation to come to the Christmas party we are having in my apartment, but that isn't why I'm calling you. My children will be coming home to spend the week with me between Christmas and New Year's, and I would like very much for you and Casey to have lunch with me. I'll tell you why. My children never knew their father, and the person who knew Jack best was you. And I'd like you to come and talk with them, so they can understand who their father was and what he was."

"I'm deeply touched," Ribicoff said. "Name the day, and we'll be there."

Those Who Were Truly Great

At noon on Tuesday, December 29, 1981, Abe and Casey Ribicoff entered the sedate lobby of 1040 Fifth Avenue. Jackie's building was one of those Art Deco limestone towers that had sprung up in the 1920s and early '30s along Park and Fifth Avenues. It had been designed for wealthy clients by Rosario Candela, the leading apartment architect of his day, who had also designed 740 Park Avenue, where Jackie had lived as a child. Jackie had bought her 14-room apartment for $200,000 in the spring of 1964, just four months after the bloody day in Dallas.

The Ribicoffs had been here before, and they knew their way. They stepped off the elevator on the fifteenth floor directly into Jackie's small foyer. A black-and-white marble floor led into a long, wide gallery that contained a console and antique gilt mirror flanked by tall Chinese porcelain vases filled with branches of white quince. The walls of the living room were covered in gray silk fabric, and they were hung with antique engravings of dogs, the elaborate frames linked by gray ribbons.

While the Ribicoffs waited for Jackie to appear, Casey looked out of one of the tall French windows. The apartment commanded spectacular views to the north, south, and west onto the reservoir, Central Park, and the Metropolitan Museum of Art. Paint was peeling from the ceiling over the windows, which were covered in gray draperies that pooled on the polished, dark wood floor.

Jackie came into the room. She was dressed in a silk shirt and slacks and was accompanied by John and Caroline. The Kennedy children had just celebrated their birthdays — John his twenty-first on November 25, and Caroline her twenty-fourth two days later. They had last seen the Ribicoffs two years before at the dedication of the John F. Kennedy Library in Boston, where John had stirred the emotions of an audience of several thousand by reciting a poem by Stephen Spender:

I think continually of those who
    were truly great.
Who, from the womb, remembered

the soul's history
Through corridors of light where
the hours are suns,
Endless and singing. Whose lovely
ambition
Was that their lips, still touched by
fire,
Should tell of the Spirit, clothed
from head to foot in song.
And who hoarded from the Spring
branches
The desires falling across the bodies
like blossoms.

Cocktails of tomato juice were served by Marta, Jackie's Italian housekeeper. Then, the party moved into the library, whose walls were papered in red. On a beautifully set round table, silver caught the light from a roaring blaze in the fireplace.

"We're going to have a very good lunch," Jackie told Abe Ribicoff, "and you're going to be the only one not to eat."

And, indeed, over the lamb chops, the children started asking questions.

"How did you get along with my father when he was in the Senate?" Caroline asked.

"Whenever I went to Washington," Ribicoff replied, "I went to your father's office, and your mother would be there. She would always bring him his lunch. He loved Boston clam chowder, and she always brought a pot. He had a lot of health problems, and he had to be careful what he ate. She was the type of wife who'd come with a picnic basket, and there'd always be enough for both him and me. And while we were eating, she'd tell him, 'You're lucky, Jack. If Abe weren't Jewish, *he'd* be running for president, not *you.*' "

The questions and answers went on for three hours. The fire died. Jackie said almost nothing.

"Do you think my father was popular?"

"Do you think my father accomplished something in his programs?"

"Do you think he was liked by his colleagues?"

"Was he in pain a lot?"

Ribicoff told them the truth as he saw it. He found it one of the most touching experiences he had ever had, and he was especially moved by the scene of the mother sitting there with her two children. Only a few years before, Judith Campbell Exner had scandalized the country with revelations of her White House love trysts with President Kennedy and her simultaneous affair with Chicago Mafia boss Sam Giancana. But the children never mentioned her name, and Ribicoff never alluded to the subject.

"You know," Ribicoff told the young Kennedys, "your father had many parts. He gave different parts to different people. He often shared some of the most intimate things with me. But did I know him completely? The total person? No. No one got the total person — except your mother."

He then turned to their mother and said, "Only Jack and Jackie really knew each other."

ALL TOO HUMAN

*The Love Story of
Jack and Jackie Kennedy*

EDWARD KLEIN

Thorndike Press • **Chivers Press**
Thorndike, Maine USA   **Bath, England**

ALAMEDA FREE LIBRARY
2264 Santa Clara Avenue
Alameda, CA 94501

This Large Print edition is published by Thorndike Press, USA and by Chivers Press, England.

Published in 1997 in the U.S. by arrangement with Pocket Books, a division of Simon & Schuster, Inc.

Published in 1997 in the U.K. by arrangement with Simon & Schuster Ltd.

U.S.　Hardcover　0-7862-0890-2 (Basic Series Edition)
U.S.　Softcover　0-7862-0889-9
U.K.　Hardcover　0-7451-5435-2 (Windsor Large Print)
U.K.　Softcover　0-7451-8743-9 (Paragon Large Print)

Copyright © 1996 by Edward Klein

Acknowledgments may be found on page 663.

All rights reserved.

The text of this Large Print edition is unabridged.
Other aspects of the book may vary from the original edition.

Set in 16 pt. Bookman Old Style by Minnie B. Raven.

Printed in the United States on permanent paper.

British Library Cataloguing in Publication Data available

Library of Congress Cataloging in Publication Data

Klein, Edward, 1936–
　　All too human : the love story of Jack and Jackie Kennedy / Edward Klein.
　　　　p.　　cm.
　　　ISBN 0-7862-0890-2 (lg. print : hc)
　　　ISBN 0-7862-0889-9 (lg. print : sc)
　　　1. Presidents — United States — Biography.　2. Presidents' spouses — United States — Biography.　3. Large type books. I. Kennedy, John F. (John Fitzgerald), 1917–1963.　II. Onassis, Jacqueline Kennedy, 1929–　　.　III. Title.
　　[E842.K54　　1997]
　　973.922′092′2—dc20
　　[B]　　　　　　　　　　　　　　　　　　　　　96-38780

TWO

Fawn in the Woods

May, 1951

Bongo, Bongo, Bongo

Mounted on Sagebrush, her show jumper, Jacqueline Bouvier was charging across a field aflame with dogwood, rhododendron, and wild violets. Spring had arrived late in Virginia in 1951, and although it was the middle of May, the meadows and trails of Merrywood were just then coming into bloom. At a full gallop, with all four of Sagebrush's feet flying off the ground, Jackie appeared to be standing erect in her stirrups, leaning forward, as motionless as a statue.

From the stable door, Herman Butler, the groom, watched as Jackie signaled Sagebrush, and the large gray Anglo-Arab mare leapt over a stone wall. Horse and rider seemed to hang in midair for a breathtaking moment before landing on the other side without breaking stride. Sagebrush let out a grunt, and her flanks quivered with excitement. Jackie urged her on, and they sped across a broad green pasture in one final breakneck gallop.

Jackie dismounted and handed off her sweat-slick horse to Butler. They chatted about her morning ride while she petted Butler's dog, a tricolor collie named Fuddy II. Since childhood, Jackie had been schooled in dressage — the art of guiding a horse with barely perceptible movements of hands, legs, and body weight — and she never tired of talking about horsemanship. She loved riding because it required discipline and physical courage and, perhaps most important of all, because it satisfied something deep in her aesthetic nature. Properly mounted on a fine horse, a woman always looked her best.

She walked to the main house, the country seat of the Auchincloss family, and went to her third-floor bedroom. The ceiling of the room slanted sharply beneath a gambrel roof, which gave the space a tight, claustrophobic feeling. The furnishings were simple — a few pieces of painted furniture, twin beds, and fleur-de-lis wallpaper that also ran across the low ceiling. On the dresser, there were scrapbooks bulging with newspaper clippings, society columns, and hundreds of photos of Jackie.

She liked to be photographed in different costumes and settings, and she never took a bad picture. The scope of her face was her father's — fleshy, sensuous, and Mediterranean. But the dark Bouvier eyes and voluptuous lips existed side by side with the sharp nose and arched aristocratic eyebrows she had inherited from her mother.

"I am tall, 5'7"," Jackie wrote in an unpublished self-portrait that she composed that spring, "with brown hair, a square face, and eyes so unfortunately far apart that it takes three weeks to have a pair of glasses made with a bridge wide enough to fit over my nose. I do not have a sensational figure but can look slim if I pick the right clothes."

In the reflection of her bedroom mirror, she looked elegant in riding breeches, top boots, and a man's dress shirt. When she removed her hunt cap, tendrils of thick, wavy hair clung to the sides of her face, accentuating her exotic, delicate looks. She had not yet developed into a great beauty; that would come later. But at the age of 21, she was already an astonishing sight to behold. People were often at a loss how to describe her; some even went so far as to compare her to a forest creature, a fawn in the woods.

She lit up a Pall Mall, and pulled off her boots with a bootjack. As she undressed, she slipped a 45-rpm disk onto her portable record player, which was shaped like a cookie box with a handle on top. It had been given to her by an aristocratic Russian emigré named Arkadi Gerney, whom she had met in Paris during her junior year abroad. She began to sing along with the record:

"Bongo, bongo, bongo, I don't want to leave the Congo. Oh, no, no, no, no, no! . . ."

She laid out two separate sets of clothing on a bed — one for lunch, the other for a supper party that was being given that evening in Georgetown by Charles Bartlett, the gifted young correspondent of *The Chattanooga Times*, who was well connected in the worlds of Washington society and politics. Charlie and his wife, Martha, had arranged the Sunday-night supper with the purpose of introducing Jackie to John Kennedy.

She had met Jack Kennedy casually a couple of years before at a wedding reception on Long Island, and like everyone else, she knew of his reputation as a war hero, a playboy, and a rising politician. The Kennedys of Massachusetts were a famous family, and photos of the Kennedy children with their father, who was America's prewar ambassador in London, had appeared in practically every Sunday supplement in America. Until the early 1940's, Joseph P. Kennedy had been mentioned prominently as a possible presidential nominee of the Democratic Party, but respectable people wouldn't have anything to do with him, because they said that he had amassed his fortune as a bootlegger and stock manipulator. Most people in Jackie's circle spoke of the Kennedys as coarse, loud "Irish micks."

At first, Jackie had tried to beg off from attending the Bartletts' supper, explaining that she already had a date that night. But the Bartletts wouldn't take no for an answer.

"You *must* come," Martha told Jackie. "You can leave early and still make your date."

Jackie couldn't understand what the fuss was all about. After all, the Sunday-night supper had become a kind of Washington institution, a chance for young movers and shakers to get together and debate the issues of the day, especially the mounting fear of Soviet Communism. There would be plenty of other suppers at which she could meet John Kennedy.

But Charlie Bartlett was insistent.

"Please come, Jackie," he begged. *"Please!"*

Jackie thought that Charlie was becoming quite a bore. But she finally agreed to make an appearance at the supper, have a quick bite, say hello to Jack Kennedy, and leave for her date.

". . . Bingle, bangle, bungle, I'm so happy in the jungle. I refuse to go . . ."

She started the record all over again, then continued dressing.

Jackie wasn't that interested in meeting Jack Kennedy — or any new man, for that matter — because she was secretly carrying the torch for someone else.

Last year, during her junior year abroad, she had danced to "Bongo, Bongo, Bongo" at L'Elephant Blanc, a fashionable Paris nightclub, which was the place to go for elegant young people after the war. It was a wonderful time to be an American in Paris. The city was aswarm with socially prominent young men from the States — George Plimpton, Cass Canfield Jr., John Phillips Marquand Jr. — and Jackie knew them all. She was happy to be away from her warring parents. She was speaking French, which brought out the uninhibited side of her nature. And she was falling in love for the first time — with John Marquand.

Marquand was tall and slim and somewhat stooped, had sandy hair and bright blue eyes, and he dressed casually in tweed jackets from J. Press and oxford shirts from Brooks Brothers. His family came from Boston, and he had a close but troubled relationship with his father, a domineering man whose best-selling novels, *The Late George Apley* and *H. M. Pulham, Esquire,* chronicled aristocratic WASP manners.

Young Marquand went to Harvard, and at the end of World War II, he was in the second wave of the U.S. Army unit that liberated Paris, which made him something of a war hero. He had a wonderful dry wit, and after a few drinks, he did hilarious imitations to amuse his friends.

Everyone called him Jack.

Jackie fell head over heels for Jack Marquand. A hint of how she felt was contained in a letter she sent to her stepbrother Yusha.

"I sort of feel you are miserably in love," she wrote, "and I know just how you feel."

Jackie and Jack Marquand went everywhere together in Paris. They ate at Chez Allard and La Grenouille, two little bistros on the Left Bank. They spent evenings at L'Elephant Blanc, where Jackie chain-smoked aromatic French cigarettes, drank grasshoppers — a cocktail consisting of crème de menthe, crème de cacao, and cream — and listened to Jack talk about his novel in progress, *The Second Happiest Day*, which he was writing under the pseudonym John Phillips. Everyone got very drunk. Arkadi Gerney, who was 6'2" and spoke half a dozen languages, tore off his shirt and danced bare chested to "Bongo, Bongo, Bongo."

In the hours before dawn, Jackie and Jack Marquand strolled along the banks of the Seine, past young couples making love in the shadows. They often ended up at Marquand's apartment on the Left Bank.

They made love in the fashion of the day, groping and fumbling and going almost all the way. It left Marquand, as the American saying went, "with blue balls." It left Jackie, as the French put it with more delicacy, *une demi-vierge,* a half-virgin.

Then one night, after a few too many grasshoppers, as they were going up to Marquand's apartment on the slow, creaky French elevator, Jackie let herself get carried away. She was in Marquand's arms, her skirt bunched above her hips, the backs of her thighs pressed against the decorative open grillwork. And when the elevator jolted to a stop, she was no longer a *demi-vierge.*

The Unforgivable Sin

At Merrywood, Jackie looked out her bedroom window over a vast green lawn running steeply down to the shore of the Potomac River. A group of small islands divided the water. On her side of the river, the Virginia side, there were rapids. On the far shore, along the old C & O Canal that skirted the Washington, D.C., border, the water was muddy and smooth.

She often expressed the thought that her life was like the river outside her window. "There is rough water on one side of my life, and calm water on the other," she said. "But eventually, the two sides of the river meet, as they do in my life, which is both turbulent at times and calm at others."

Merrywood was the calm side of Jackie's life. It stood on the Potomac Palisades on land once surveyed by George Washington. Visitors approached it from Chain Bridge Road by way of a long gravel driveway that passed a clay tennis court, the greenhouse, and the paddock where Jackie exercised Sagebrush. An Olympic-size swimming pool — the only private pool for miles around — stood in front of a bathhouse that was designed to look like a rustic fairy-tale cottage. At the bottom of the hill, the driveway formed a graceful circle that led visitors to the front of a large, imposing house.

The original structure, a copy of an eighteenth-century Georgian mansion, was built in 1919 by Newbold Noyes, the editor of the *Washington Star*. He sold the property in the early 1930s to Hugh Dudley Auchincloss Jr., an heir to the Standard Oil fortune, who later became Jackie's stepfather. Over the years, the surface of the red brick had calcified to a chalky white, which made the mansion look as though it had stood among the first-growth beach, oak, and chestnut trees for the previous couple of centuries.

Jackie had come to Merrywood almost 10 years earlier, when her mother married "Hughdie" Auchincloss. In the large Auchincloss household, with its seven children from three different mothers, Jackie was waited on hand and foot by a small army of servants. Though baptized and confirmed as a Catholic, she came of age at Merrywood, which was a bastion of WASP old money.

Most Americans were only vaguely aware of the hereditary ruling class that existed in their midst. But the power of the WASP ascendancy had endured in America for three centuries. It was made up of several hundred wealthy families whose male members advanced from exclusive private schools like St. Mark's and Groton to Yale, Princeton, and Harvard, and then on to the top of Wall Street partnerships, large banks, powerful law firms, and, with the outbreak of the Cold War, to the upper echelons of the CIA.

They could identify each other by their accents, and the words they used in everyday conversation. Jackie grew up in a household where the word *tomatoes* was actually pronounced "tomahtoes," and a girl was called a "gale." Windows had curtains, not drapes or draperies. One lived in a house, not a home.

In the Auchinclosses' social circle, there was an unofficial dress code. Women were encouraged to sport huge heirloom diamond engagement rings and brooches, but the frocks they bought at Bergdorf Goodman had to be drab and dowdy. Men wore bespoke suits from London's Savile Row or from Charvet and Sulka in Paris, but their neckties were stained with food and their socks drooped over their ankles.

Everyone drank to excess. They amused one another with long, alcohol-fueled anecdotes about eccentric cousins and dotty aunts. They lived near each another in mansions smelling of beeswax in Virginia's Fairfax County, on the East Side of Manhattan, Boston's Nob Hill and the north shore of Long Island. They liked to impress each other with their wealth. Back at the turn of the century, William K. Vanderbilt had spent the equivalent of $365 million in today's money to build Marble House, his "summer cottage" in Newport. Those whose fortunes approached that of the Vanderbilts had manor houses along one of Newport's main strips: Bellevue Avenue, Ochre Point, or Ocean Drive.

Above all, it was their confident manners — "the sheer restfulness of good breeding," as one of them put it — that marked the Auchinclosses and their peers. This set them apart and allowed them to look down their patrician noses at the newly rich — those awkward, sweaty non-Anglo-Saxons whose wealth had begun to eclipse old WASP fortunes.

In the early 1950s, the United States was in the midst of the greatest economic boom in its history. It was also at the zenith of its global power. Out of long habit, WASPs clung to the consoling myth that they had been chosen to carry out America's mission to civilize the world. After all, they reasoned, it was their innate courtesy, charm, honesty, good sportsmanship, and sense of duty — not something as crass as money — that made them better than everyone else.

When Jackie was a young woman, WASPs were still so exclusionary that they discriminated even against each other. Jackie's mother, the third Mrs. Hugh Dudley Auchincloss Jr., was the daughter of a pudgy, cigar-chomping character by the name of James T. Lee, who had made his money in real estate and banking. There was talk that Janet had invented her illustrious Southern background, and that in reality her ancestors were Levys, not Lees. No one ever produced a shred of evidence that she was Jewish, but she was never fully accepted in high WASP circles.

Her friends whispered that Janet was nouveau, that wealth and position didn't rest easily on her shoulders and, what was even worse, that she had to *strive* to keep up appearances.

"I flatter myself on being able at times to walk out of the house looking like a poor man's Paris copy," Jackie once commented, "but often my mother will run up to inform me that my left stocking seam is crooked or the right-hand top coat button about to fall off. This, I realize, is the Unforgivable Sin."

The Auchinclosses, true to their class, could be the worst kind of snobs and bigots. The writer Gore Vidal, who was distantly related to Jackie and spent part of his own childhood at Merrywood, caught the Auchinclosses well when he observed, "You have no idea what a muddled view of things the American aristocracy had in those days, with their ferocious anti-Semitism, hatred of the lower orders, and fierce will to protect their property from any encroachment."

In many ways, Jackie tried to rise above all this. But as much as she yearned to be emancipated from the Auchinclosses and their narrow-minded attitudes, she felt an acute longing to return to Merrywood whenever she was away. Once, while on a summer trip in Italy between her sophomore and junior years, she wrote her stepfather: "I began to feel terribly homesick as I was driving — just like a dream — I started thinking of things like the path leading to the stable at Merrywood with the stones slipping as you ran up it . . . all the places and feelings and happiness that bind you to a family you love — something that you take with you no matter how far you go."

During her junior year abroad, while she was falling in love with Jack Marquand, she heard from her stepbrother Yusha that the family was thinking of selling Merrywood. It was becoming too heavy a financial burden. This was the first inkling Jackie had that the Auchinclosses were living beyond their means. Like many WASPs, they were running out of money and entering the twilight of their influence and power.

The news affected her profoundly. In a subsequent letter, however, Yusha reassured her that plans to place the family home on the market had been put off for the time being.

"I'm so thrilled," she said, "that we aren't selling Merrywood."

But the thought of losing Merrywood continued to haunt her. To Jackie, Merrywood was more than a plot of land with a river running through it. It existed in her mind as a golden place of idealized beauty, peacefulness, and enlightenment.

Merrywood was her original Camelot.

The Mistress of Merrywood

Jackie came down the broad, carpeted stairs at Merrywood just as the grandfather clock struck half past 12. A large, almost life-size portrait of Hughdie Auchincloss as a young boy dressed in knickerbockers hung on the second-floor landing. The house was filled with the aroma of roast beef and Yorkshire pudding. The clink and chime of crystal and china could be heard coming from the dining room, where Jake Owen, the butler, and his wife, Marie, were bustling about, setting the table for 11. The cook, Nellie Curtin, was issuing orders in the kitchen.

It was Mother's Day — May 13, 1951 — but in all other respects, it was like any other Sunday afternoon at Merrywood, an occasion for the large Auchincloss clan to gather for luncheon with their rich and powerful Washington friends. In the distance, Jackie could hear the echoing *boom-boom-boom* of 12-gauge shotguns as Hughdie and his lunch guests shot clay pigeons on the trapshooting range up on the hill by the barn.

As she reached the bottom of the stairs, Jackie heard a different kind of sound — a sudden sharp noise coming from a room on the ground floor. For an instant, the servants stopped what they were doing and the whole house fell silent. Then there was a second noise — this one a hard, dull thump — which was quickly followed by a stream of shouts and shrill curses.

Jackie rushed from the central hall-way, across the living room, and into the adjoining card room. At the same moment, her stepbrother Yusha arrived from a different part of the house.

They found Jackie's mother, Janet Auchincloss, and their 11-year-old stepsister Nini circling each other like a pair of crouched wrestlers. Bright red finger marks were visible on the young girl's left cheek where Janet had struck her across the face.

"I'm going to kick you!" Janet shouted, aiming her foot at Nini's shins.

"And I'm going to kick *you*," Nini yelled back, lashing out with her foot at Janet.

Jackie stepped between them, and the fighting stopped. Nini burst into tears and ran from the room. Jackie turned to Janet, who stood with an impassive expression on her face in front of an oil painting of herself mounted on Danseuse, her old show jumper.

"Oh, Mummy," she said, *"honestly!"*

The mistress of Merrywood, Janet Norton Lee Bouvier Auchincloss, was a force to be reckoned with. Even when she wasn't erupting in cyclonic displays of temper, she dominated her surroundings. She had lovely pink-and-white skin and dark eyes framed by a thick head of hair. Men found her sexy. They were fascinated by the way Janet slid her lips over her teeth, barely parting them, as though she harbored some naughty secret that she dared not disclose. She always left them wanting more.

Women were a different story. They thought that Janet was mad with the desire for money. They were right — but only up to a point. Actually, Janet did not hunger after furs, expensive clothes, and jewels as much as she did after a certain kind of perfection. She was interested in the surface of things — the hem stitching on her Porthault sheets, the punctuality of the service at her meals, the drape of her ball gowns. She loved money because it made perfection possible.

She was out practically every night of the week at black-tie society dinners, yet she found time to volunteer as a nurse's aide at a Washington hospital and to oversee the wardrobes, French lessons, and social lives of her seven children and stepchildren. In addition to Merrywood, she ran a large summer estate in Newport. It was called Hammersmith Farm, and along with its vast gardens, hothouses, livestock, and 16 staff members (including three nannies and one governess), it was the setting for an endless round of parties from June to September.

All this took a great deal of discipline and organization, and woe to anyone who got in the way of Janet's juggernaut, including her husband. Hughdie was a good-natured bear of a man, the opposite of Janet's first husband, John Vernou Bouvier III. Whereas Jack Bouvier was a compulsive womanizer, capable of sleeping with two or three women in an evening, Hughdie suffered from chronic impotency. Even after years of psychiatric help, Hughdie could achieve only a partial erection, and then only with the help of pornographic books and photographs, which he collected in large numbers.

Whenever Janet threw one of her temper tantrums, Hughdie would simply turn off his hearing aid and remark, "Your mother's menopause is going on too long, and it's making her argumentative."

The children were not so tolerant. The oldest, Hugh Dudley III, known as Yusha, was the son of Hughdie's first wife, a volatile Russian named Maria Chrapovitsky who had been partially scalped in an airplane propeller accident. Nina ("Nini") and Thomas were from Hughdie's second marriage, to a sadistic alcoholic named Nina Gore (who was also the mother, through a previous marriage, of novelist Gore Vidal). Next in the pecking order came Jackie and her younger sister, Caroline Lee Bouvier. And finally, there were the two children — Janet Jr. and James — who were born to Janet and Hughdie following their marriage in 1942, the year Hughdie came into his full inheritance.

None of the children was spared Janet's outbursts — not even Jackie.

"I have seen Janet strafe Jackie across both cheeks," said a member of the family.

Jackie embodied all the virtues that Janet Auchincloss admired most. Like her mother, who had broken her nose three times in riding accidents, Jackie was a fearless horsewoman. She once fell off Sagebrush and was in a state of semiconsciousness for three days. Both mother and daughter had a passion for art, and they had recently been given a special tour of the Gulbenkian collection at the National Gallery by its director, John Walker. While Janet watched in amazement, Jackie and Walker gossiped about the intimate lives of the famous European artists whose works were on display.

Of all the children, Jackie was the most talented. She was not an intellectual, but she was a voracious reader who expressed herself wonderfully and had a literary wit. Letter writing was an art form much prized by Janet Auchincloss, and Jackie wrote the most memorable letters in the family. They were

often read out loud at cocktail hour —
such as the one Jackie sent in 1950
describing a trip she took to the south
of France.

I just can't tell you what it is like
to come down from the mountains
of Grenoble to this flat, blazing
plain where seven-eighths of all you
can see is hot blue sky — and there
are rows of poplars at the edge of
every field to protect the crops from
the mistral and spiky short palm
trees with blazing red flowers growing at their feet.

Jackie drew amusing pictures, which
were given as presents at Christmas.
She spoke good schoolgirl French,
which was the only language permitted
at the dinner table during the week.
And she composed witty verses — such
as this poem, which was written on the
occasion of the engagement of her Vassar classmate Ellen Gates, whose nick-
name was Puffin, to Russell "Derry"
D'Oench.

Puffin and Derry in wedded bliss
   soon will be,

Vassar will miss her and so will we.
But watch yo' step, honey, on that
    path of roses,
There's mo' thorns 'neath them
    there leaves than you knowsis . . .

But then Puffin stops and thinks
    over each friend
And how they've all come to some
    sad end.
Jackie skinny and underpaid
Is earning her living as the French
    maid . . .

Like most women in society, Janet
Auchincloss was an accomplished actress. She pretended that she was the
product of a socially superior background when, in fact, she came from
low-class Irish stock. She taught Jackie
everything she knew about the life of
high society.

"Darling," she told her daughter, "the
best way to attract boys at a dance is
to pay attention to whoever you're dancing with. I don't care if he's two inches
tall, if he's a fat tub of lard, if he's eight
feet tall — you look as though you're
having the best time with him, and you
laugh at his stupid jokes even though

you know they're stupid, and before you know it, you'll make him believe that he is everything that you're conveying to him. But you will also catch the eye of all those boys who are watching you."

Growing up, Jackie made fun of her mother. But she felt a grudging love for her and was deeply dependent on her. She was also more like Janet than she ever cared to admit. Like Janet, Jackie had a ferocious temper. She once kicked in the slats of her sister Lee's bedroom door.

"Aunt Janet was like the rest of us," Yusha said. "She was a bit in awe of Jackie."

Her mother believed that if there was any hope for Jackie, she had to marry into money. Five of the seven children at Merrywood were the direct descendants of Hughdie Auchincloss; they bore his family name and had received trust funds from the matriarch of the family, Grandmother Auchincloss. But Jackie and Lee were impecunious Bouviers whose only inheritance had been the $3,000 they had each received in 1948 upon the death of their paternal grandfather. Jackie didn't even have a piece of serious jewelry to call her own.

The notion of money, if not the actual word itself, was never absent from Janet's conversations with Jackie. Money was the measure of every man, woman, and child who entered Janet's circle. "He doesn't have any *real* money" was Janet's ultimate put-down.

But Jackie did not want to end up like her mother — a society clubwoman married to a rich but dull man. In her class yearbook at Miss Porter's School, the private all-girls boarding school she had attended, Jackie had written next to "ambition in life": "Not to be a house-wife."

"I knew I didn't want to marry any of the young men I grew up with," she said on another occasion, "not because of them, but because of their life."

Coming from her background, where she experienced the daily humiliation of being the poor relative, it was natural for her to crave a life that would be cushioned by a great deal of money. But for Jackie, as for her mother, money was a means to a larger end.

All through her childhood, Jackie had spent hours alone with books, spinning fantasies in which she was the protagonist of her own romantic stories, and she did not want an ordinary existence. She wanted to *do* something — something smart and stylish and exciting. She wanted to live on her own. She wanted to go to the ballet and art galleries and concerts and plays. She wanted to hunt with Sagebrush. She wanted to go out and dance all night with Jack Marquand, the way she had in Paris. She wanted . . .

"I didn't know what I wanted," she confessed. "I was still floundering."

THREE

The Way
of the World

May, 1951

Sexual Confidants

Shortly before lunch, Jackie picked up an extension phone at Merrywood and asked the long-distance operator to place a call to Rhinelander 6-0744 in New York City.

"And please reverse the charges," she told the operator.

"Whom should I say is calling?"

"His daughter."

It was almost one o'clock in the afternoon, but Jackie could always tell as soon as her father answered the phone whether she had gotten him out of bed. His normally rich and mellow voice was rough and grating as he greeted her with his favorite endearment.

"Hello, Jacks," he said.

It was a familiar sound to Jackie — the raspy voice of a man being roused from a drunken stupor. And it made her heartsick.

Her father had recently been discharged from Silver Hill, an exclusive sanitarium in New Canaan, Connecticut, where wealthy alcoholics sought treatment. This was not his first attempt to overcome his dependency on drink. He had checked himself into drying-out places before. But this time was supposed to be different. He would turn 60 in a few days and was filled with dread that he would end up like his older brother, William Sergeant Bouvier, dead of alcoholism.

During Jack Bouvier's six-week stay at Silver Hill, the director, William B. Terhune, encouraged him to drink a lot of water, have regular bowel movements, and walk off his alcohol dependency by strolling through the trails on the property, which resembled an exclusive country club. Alcoholism was still a taboo subject in the early 1950s, and Silver Hill's treatment program, which was heavily influenced by the tenets of Christian Science, advocated denying the existence of the illness as a way of weakening its hold over the mind and body. Upon Jack Bouvier's release, Terhune instructed him not to discuss his drinking with anybody, not even with close members of his family. That, he warned, would only focus attention on his problem.

No sooner had Jack Bouvier arrived

home, however, than he went back to the bottle.

All her life, Jackie had tried to deny the painful reality of her father's condition. As a child, she often saw him sprawled drunk on the living-room sofa. Dressed in nothing but his underwear, socks, and shoes, he would rant against "kikes" and "micks" and "wops," and curse the world for the unfair way it had treated him. Before he passed out, Jackie and her mother would carry him to the bedroom, undress him, and clean up his vomit and urine. The next morning, she would witness his tearful apologies as he begged his wife and daughters to forgive him and pleaded for one more chance.

When her mother married John Vernou Bouvier III in 1928, he looked like money, breeding, and power. He was a 37-year-old bachelor and at least 15 years older than Janet, though it was hard to be sure, since she always kept the exact date of her birth a secret. Tall, with icy blue eyes, he had an animal magnetism that made him irresistible to women. He was as handsome as Clark Gable, black-haired and swarthy and, thanks to repeated exposure to a sun lamp, as dark as the Sheik of Araby, a fact that accounted for his various nicknames: "Jack the Sheik," "The Black Orchid," "Black Jack."

But beneath the good-looking surface, there was very little substance. Jack Bouvier was a pale imitation of his imposing father, a mustachioed Victorian gentleman known as The Major. Rather than try to compete with his successful father, Black Jack played the part of the spoiled, profligate, guilt-ridden son.

His wide-lapelled suits came from Bell, his shirts and paisley ties from Tripler. He tooled around New York City in a black Mercury convertible, shuttling between dinner at 21, prize fights at Madison Square Garden, and late cocktails at the Racquet Club with his most recent female conquest.

His impeccable credentials had appealed to the social climber in Janet. After all, Jack Bouvier was a member of the Sons of the American Revolution and the Society of the Cincinnati; he was both listed in the Social Register and counted among "the Four Hundred."

Soon after their marriage, however, Janet learned that Jack Bouvier was, like herself, a fantasist who had created the illusion of a grand lineage. As it turned out, the Bouviers were not, as he liked to claim, related to French nobility. And if they had once been fabulously wealthy, they were no longer.

What was worse, Black Jack turned out to be a violent drunk. He frequently beat Janet in front of the children. Janet fought back, hurling plates and curses at her husband.

Early in life, Jackie found various ways to escape from these ugly family brawls. "I read a lot when I was little," she explained, "much of which was too old for me. There were Chekhov and Shaw in the room where I had to take naps, and I never slept but sat on the window sill reading, then scrubbed the soles of my feet so the nurse would not see I had been out of bed. My heroes were Byron, Mowgli, Robin Hood, Little Lord Fauntleroy's grandfather, and Scarlett O'Hara."

After Jack Bouvier lost most of his money in the Depression, Janet's father let the family live rent free in an apartment in one of the buildings he owned — a large duplex at 740 Park Avenue, which had been designed by the architect Rosario Candela. "Remember, you're living in my house," he barked at his son-in-law, humiliating him in public. But there was nothing Big Jim Lee could do to save the marriage, and Janet and Jack Bouvier divorced when Jackie was 11 years old.

Things had only gotten worse between them in recent years. Though Janet enjoyed the good life with Hughdie at Merrywood, that didn't stop her from continuing to blame Black Jack for all her disappointments and unhappiness. She was consumed with hatred for him. Jackie could not remember hearing her mother say a single kind word about her father. Ten years after the divorce, she still called him "that no-good drunk."

He reciprocated her sentiments.

"My whole life has been ruined by that bitch," Black Jack said. "I should have stood up to her from the beginning."

The previous week, Jackie had been invited to attend a dinner at New York's Cosmopolitan Club for the top contestants in *Vogue* magazine's annual Prix de Paris. Jackie was among the dozen finalists, and she had arranged to stay with her father.

His apartment at 125 East 74th Street was a light, airy bachelor flat. The living room had a marble fireplace with a walnut mantel. Large glass French doors opened onto a smaller room that was used for dining. There were two day beds in the guest bedroom for Jackie and Lee.

Whenever she spent time with her father, Jackie became aware again of his desperate financial plight. Watching him go broke had produced in her a sense of permanent panic about money. He tried to hide the depressing facts from his daughter, but his stratagems never worked. He had been forced to give up his limousine and chauffeur, but he pretended he didn't care because he still had his convertible. "He would have his daughters' portraits done by the top New York photographers for an outrageous price," recalled a relative, "then save money by limiting the number of prints he ordered, hanging studio proofs instead."

He used Jackie's visit as an opportunity to tutor her in the way of the world, delivering lectures on fashion, antiques, and interior decoration. But his favorite subject was the eternal mating game between men and women. Pay attention to everything a man says, he told her. "Fasten your eyes on him like you were staring into the sun." Be inaccessible, untouchable, mysterious. Once a man possesses you, her father warned, he automatically loses interest.

In many ways, they were more like sexual confidants than father and daughter. From the time Jackie was old enough to understand the difference between men and women, her father engaged her in sexually stimulating conversations. One of Jackie's favorite stories, which she had heard firsthand from her father, was how he had misbehaved on his honeymoon with her mother. On his way over to England with Janet on the *Aquitania*, he had slipped away from his bride and slept with tobacco heiress Doris Duke.

When Jackie was a teen-ager, her father visited her frequently at boarding school in Farmington, Connecticut. Arriving in front of her dormitory in his convertible, he would announce his presence with a special honk of the horn. Jackie would burst out of the door, fly into his arms, and kiss him on the lips.

"My God," one of the new pupils at the school once observed, "why on earth is that girl kissing that Negro?!"

At Farmington, Jackie and her father played a game in which she would point to the mothers of her classmates.

"That one, Daddy?" she would ask.

And if Jack Bouvier had not slept with the woman in question, he would reply to his daughter, "Not yet."

And Jackie would point to another and ask: "That one, Daddy?"

"Oh, yes," he would say, "I've already had her."

"And that one, Daddy?"

"Yes."

"And that one, Daddy?"

"Yes."

One time, a few years later, when Jackie was a sophomore at Vassar, she telephoned her father's Wall Street office and told his secretary that she was getting a poodle cut at the hairdresser's.

"The news was brought out to Jack on the floor of the Exchange," recalled

Kathleen Bouvier, a niece by marriage. "By one in the afternoon, he had grown quite anxious. By closing time, he was a nervous wreck. He tried calming down [over cocktails] at the Yale Club, but he was too excited to concentrate on relaxing. Giving up, he raced home.

"Jack just couldn't wait to see what it would look like on her," Kathleen continued. "In fact, he was really extremely worried that it wouldn't suit her in the least. . . .

"I found myself earnestly reassuring him, clucking like a mother hen — until it occurred to me that there was an element of the ridiculous in his exaggerated apprehension. If the poodle cut did not become Jackie, it would not, after all, mean the end of the universe.

"But Jack couldn't see that for a second. He was as obsessed with Jackie's poodle cut as he had ever been with the pursuit of a woman. . . .

"It must have seemed like a strange tableau to the young girl as she bounced in, when we all together breathed a sigh of relief. Of course, it was a terribly disappointing denouement. The poodle cut looked great, and Jackie looked radiant.

"The grin on Jack's face was a delight to see."

As a guest in her father's apartment, Jackie had to contend with his morning hangovers.

"Jack would force himself out of bed — as a rule, quite groggy and in not too good a mood," Kathleen Bouvier recalled. "In anticipation of this, Esther Lindstrom [his maid] would set out his coffee on the kitchen table, with the good sense to let a surly man have his cup of coffee by himself. Immediately after downing that first draught, Jack headed into the bathroom and drew a steaming hot bath while he shaved."

When Jackie came into the dining room for breakfast, she could hear her father splashing about like a sea lion, letting out an occasional groan and growl. Without fail, most of the tub water landed on the floor, so Esther always had a mop in hand.

After selecting a Brooks Brothers' button-down shirt and a club tie to complement it, Jack would join Jackie at the dining-room table, dressed in shirtsleeves and tie — but nothing below his waist except a pair of baby-blue boxer shorts, socks, and garters.

"Sitting with regal formality and cavalierly oblivious to his state of undress, Jack would read the *New York Herald-Tribune* for news, the *Daily News* for the latest sporting events, and his indispensable *Wall Street Journal*," Kathleen Bouvier said. "But never did Jack find the slightest use for *The New York Times*."

The phone rang constantly with calls from women pleading to speak with Jack. Although he had a more-or-less steady girlfriend at the time — a Canadian beauty named Pam Vanderhurst who was not much older than Jackie — he would speak to Pam and the other women about each other, and treat them all like members of his harem.

Yet Jackie never felt pushed aside by her father's paramours. They came and went, but she was the special one, the constant in his life — "my best girl," as he liked to say.

It did not bother Jackie that her father was a great roué. She adored him, doted on him, felt sorry for him. And she sided with him when he complained that her mother was to blame for the loss of his money, his esteem in society, and the respect of his Bouvier relatives, especially his father. If Jackie had been the mistress of such a man, she would have been able to rescue him from himself.

Jackie's complex relationship with her father was the source of her greatest pleasure, but it always left her feeling that she had something to hide. In the summer of 1950, during her junior year abroad, Jackie had gone to England on her Christmas vacation and visited a woman who had been very close to her father when she lived in America.

"Jackie knew the lady had twins shortly after her return, but she never had been told whose children they were," John H. Davis, a Bouvier relative, recalled. "Now, on her vacation jaunt to England, Jackie came face to face with the twins and to her utter consternation saw that they were almost exact replicas of herself! The same broad faces, the same wide-apart eyes, the same prominent chins, the same dark hair, the same complexion. They were Bouviers, all right; they were *her* brother and sister."

Overall Art Director of the Twentieth Century

When she emerged from her father's apartment shortly after seven o'clock, Jackie was running half an hour late. She turned south on Lexington Avenue toward the Cosmopolitan Club, where *Vogue* was holding its Prix de Paris dinner. She smoked a Pall Mall as she strode down the street. By the time she arrived at the club, the reception room was filled with nearly a hundred women, almost all of them mildly intoxicated.

Large crowds always made Jackie anxious. Before she ventured out to a party, she would spend hours in front of the mirror, fussing with her hair and makeup, changing outfits again and again, trying to bolster her shaky self-confidence. The results were always the same: she was late for every appointment, which made her even more nervous.

At the door, a *Vogue* secretary in white gloves pinned a corsage on Jackie's left shoulder, and a waiter offered her a drink from a tray of aperitif glasses half filled with Dubonnet. She was escorted around the crowded room by Carol Phillips, a tall, blond writer for *Vogue*, who introduced her to Iva Patcevitch, the publisher, and Mary Jessica Davis, the editor in chief. They stopped to talk with editors from *House and Garden*, *Glamour*, and *Vogue Pattern Book*.

At one point, Carol Phillips turned to Jackie and whispered in her ear, "Are you nervous?"

"Just look," Jackie replied, holding out her trembling hands.

"That girl was so tense," Carol Phillips told a friend later, "that when she put on her nail polish, she'd smeared it all over her fingers."

Jackie was not the confident young woman that she often appeared to be. More than at any time in her life, she needed guidance then from her parents. But as usual, they could not agree on anything, least of all what she should do after she graduated from George Washington University, where she had transferred for her senior year.

That spring, *Vogue* featured a full-page layout of "the Misses Bouvier." Lee posed in yellow-and-white tulle. Jackie modeled a white silk organdie Gibson girl dancing dress with a bright sash of red faille. Fashion magazines did not make a clear distinction between pretty society girls and professional models, and Jackie took such delight in seeing her own picture on the large glossy page that she toyed for a brief time with the notion of becoming a photographer's model.

The trouble was, the range of opportunities open to female college graduates was limited. Women with careers were looked at askance; they were considered hard and aggressive creatures and were treated as virtual social outcasts. Those who had to work were encouraged to take jobs that carried no prestige — as nurses, teachers, secretaries — and that would not put them into direct competition with men.

Jackie was determined to break the mold, and thanks to her connections, she had an interesting job offer. A friend of her stepfather, Allen Dulles, the deputy director for plans of the CIA, had lined up an entry-level post for her at the CIA. She was also one of 12 finalists in *Vogue*'s Prix de Paris.

It was Jackie's mother who had seen the announcement of the contest and had urged her daughter to apply. "I think I was under a dryer in a beauty parlor," Janet Auchincloss said, recalling how she had come upon the announcement in a dog-eared copy of *Vogue*. After Jackie entered the contest, however, her mother developed second thoughts.

"She feels terrifically strongly about keeping me 'in the home,' " Jackie confided in a letter that she wrote at this time. "I see her point a little — as I have been away at school and abroad so much and have lived between here and New York without ever having a home base, which Mummy seems to feel is important."

Her father, on the other hand, saw her graduation as a chance to woo his daughter away from the hated Auchinclosses — "those so-called blue-blood Newport snobs," as he called them. He would enjoy having his best girl live near him during her six months at *Vogue*'s offices in New York.

Jackie was caught between her parents and didn't know what to do.

Part of her — the tough, Irish, common sense part — agreed with her mother: she should stick close to home and get on with the essential business of finding a rich husband. But another part — the glamorous French part — sided with her father: she should return to Paris, the City of Light, which in her mind represented independence and romance and Jack Marquand.

She was seriously leaning toward taking the Prix, if she won.

"I would rather work at what interests me than have a home base," she said.

At times, the pressure from her mother and father got so unbearable that Jackie felt as though she were falling apart, and she wished that she could run away. It was at these times that she would have a dream that had been recurring since childhood. In it, she was on a train, on her way to some unknown destination, and when she arrived, she was crowned as the queen of the traveling circus.

After a typical Cosmopolitan dinner of chicken tetrazzini, Mary Jessica Davis rose to make a short speech. She compared life to a ship at sea: it wasn't the direction the wind blew; it was how you trimmed your sails. *"Vogue,"* she said, "has a policy of finding young women with the best minds and grooming them for the top posts in magazine journalism. You Prix de Paris finalists are the chosen few. But what you make of your opportunity is up to you. If you trim your sails correctly, your careers will be set for life."

It was hardly necessary to remind the 12 finalists how fortunate they were to be chosen from among the 1,280 college seniors who had applied for the Prix that year. At a time when women college graduates were lucky to find office jobs as secretaries, each of the *Vogue* finalists could count herself as, literally, one young woman in a hundred.

The first-prize winner would get a trial year as a junior editor on French *Vogue* and New York *Vogue* and a permanent position on the staff if she made good. The second-prize winner would get a six-month tryout and the same consideration for becoming a permanent member of the staff. In addition, 10 awards of merit were given to the runners-up, and these young women were considered for jobs on other Condé Nast publications.

Mademoiselle, a non–Condé Nast magazine and the most popular publication in America among the college set, also conducted a contest for graduating seniors. Lord & Taylor and B. Altman had training programs that prepared women graduates for careers in fashion and retailing. But the *Vogue* Prix was the most significant avenue of advancement for young women in the business of fashion journalism, and Jackie thought she was up to the challenge.

"Being away from home gave me a chance to look at myself with a jaundiced eye," she remarked. "I learned not to be ashamed of a real hunger for knowledge, something I had always tried to hide. . . . A career on a magazine is what I have always had in mind, and [the Prix] seems the perfect way to start trying for it."

Along with the other finalists, she had sat for a portrait by Richard Rutledge, the well-known *Vogue* fashion photographer. Rutledge caught her full face, with her dark hair parted in the middle and pulled back from her forehead. It was a copy of her father's hair style, and she looked so much like Jack Bouvier in the photo that the resemblance seemed to be a conscious effort at imitation.

At this critical juncture in her life, when she was struggling to break away from home and develop her own identity, Jackie felt a stronger empathy with her father than with her mother. To the rest of the world, Jack Bouvier might appear to be a self-absorbed dandy who was sinking under the weight of booze, debt, and old age. But to his daughter, he was still a man of great style and sophistication. He was also, in her eyes, a sensitive, misunderstood soul.

Her identification with her father was reflected in her Prix de Paris application. She had been asked to write an essay on "People I Wish I Had Known." Other applicants might have chosen Madame Curie, Eleanor Roosevelt, or Sarah Bernhardt, but Jackie was not so conventional. She chose three decadent artists: the French poet Charles Baudelaire, the Irish author Oscar Wilde, and the Russian ballet impresario Sergei Diaghilev. All three were notorious for smashing bourgeois conventions: Diaghilev and Wilde were homosexuals, and Baudelaire wrote erotic poetry about lesbians.

Jackie described them in terms that she could easily have applied to her father, who always talked about raising life to an art form. Baudelaire and Wilde, she wrote, "both were poets and idealists who could paint sinfulness with honesty and still believe in something higher." As for Diaghilev, "though not an artist himself, he possessed what is rarer than artistic genius in any one field: the sensitivity to take the best of each man and incorporate it into a masterpiece all the more precious because it lives only in the minds of those who have seen it and disintegrates as soon as he is gone."

And what was it that she hoped to learn from these men?

"If I could be a sort of Overall Art Director of the Twentieth Century, watching everything from a chair hanging in space," she wrote, "it is [the theories of Baudelaire, Wilde, and Diaghilev] that I would apply to my period, their poems that I would have music and painting and ballets composed to."

"I was crazy about her writing," Carol

Phillips said. "I was keen to have her on my writing staff eventually. I was especially touched by the paper she had written, as part of her Prix de Paris application, on her grandfather's death."

All her life, Jackie had a morbid fascination with death, and she had written an autobiographical short story about the funeral of her grandfather, John Vernou Bouvier Jr., a man she admired as much or more than her own father. The Major wore beautifully tailored double-breasted suits and high, stiff collars. He lived in gracious surroundings on Park Avenue and in East Hampton, quoted from Plato, Shakespeare, and the British historian Thomas Babington Macaulay, and acquired a mistress in his seventies. He and Jackie were kindred spirits in their love of literature and luxury and the pride they took in the Bouvier family history.

Jackie's short story began with a scene of her seated next to her grandfather's open coffin.

A Christmas Story
The Violets

The front door opened and closed

in the hall and I heard my aunt speaking with someone: another caller I supposed. "No, I'll go in alone," a voice said in the doorway. There were steps on the rug behind me. They passed my chair and I saw a short man with white hair stand in front of the coffin. He was holding a bunch of violets.

He stood there for about 3 minutes then leaned forward and placed the violets between my grandfather's hands. As he stepped back he looked over at me . . . "I couldn't get any flowers. All the shops are closed. But I got these from a woman on the corner. I remember Dick always liked violets." He stopped self-consciously and left the room.

I heard my aunt taking him to the door. She came back and went over to the coffin. "What are these doing here?" She picked up the violets. "That man left them," I told her. "They don't belong there," she said and put them next to a sheaf of gladioli on the floor.

And then, in an uncanny scene that

foreshadowed her behavior 12 years later at the funeral of President Kennedy, Jackie described how she slipped a memento into the coffin.

I picked up the violets and put them to my face. They smelled cool and raindrops were still on them. They were a Christmas present to my grandfather from someone who had really cared about him. I stood listening to the swish of traffic in the rain outside and feeling the wind blow through the window. . . .

I knelt on the bench beside the coffin and put the violets down inside, beneath my grandfather's elbow, where the people who came to close the coffin would not see them.

"Despite how she talked and wrote, I felt that, deep down, Jackie was vacillating about the *Vogue* Prix de Paris," Carol Phillips said. "I could tell that she was wavering about her plans. She was unsure of herself and her future direction."

Carol Phillips arranged to have lunch with Jackie two days later in the Grill Room of Schrafft's on the ground floor of the Chrysler Building. The room was decorated in the Art Deco style with floor-to-ceiling mirrors, black iron-and-crystal chandeliers, and a red carpet.

Jackie sat across the table from Mary E. Campbell, the formidable personnel director of Condé Nast. Mary Campbell was a large, heavy-set woman with dark hair and eyes and pale skin who had been a gym instructor at Barnard College before coming to work for Condé Montrose Nast, the founder of the publishing empire. A lapsed Catholic, Condé Nast often joked that he counted on Mary Campbell to make a good recommendation for him to God. Shortly after he died in 1946, she became the director of the Prix de Paris — the final authority on who won the top prize.

She had kept an eye on Jacqueline Bouvier ever since Jackie was named Debutante of the Year three years before by Igor Cassini, who wrote a widely syndicated gossip column under the pseudonym Cholly Knickerbocker.

America is a country of traditions [Cassini wrote]. Every four years we elect a President, every two years our congressmen. And every year a new Queen of Debutantes is crowned. . . . The Queen Deb of the year for 1947 is Jacqueline Bouvier, a regal brunette who has classic features and the daintiness of Dresden porcelain. She has poise, is soft-spoken and intelligent, everything the leading debutante should be. Her background is strictly "Old Guard."

Jackie was dressed that day in a black-and-white tweed skirt, Beth Levine platform pumps, and a silk crepe blouse. She wore a piece of costume jewelry pinned to a velvet ribbon that ran diagonally from under the collar of her blouse to her waist. She fit Mary Campbell's definition of the perfect *Vogue* employee: *trés chic* — pronounced "tray chick," so it wouldn't sound pretentiously French.

"This was before Jackie had discovered Kenneth [the hairdresser], so her hair was frizzy," Carol Phillips said. "Her wide-set eyes were peculiar. And she was aware of these things. She had an attractive quality of a certain shyness, which she projected. She didn't have monumental self-confidence. She wasn't nuts about herself. Her manners were so exquisite that you couldn't tell what was on her mind. She had excellent presence, but she was aware of her faults and concerned about them."

A waitress in a black dress with white stockings and white shoes approached the table and asked if they were ready to order. After studying the menu, Jackie ordered a chicken salad. Carol Phillips and Mary Campbell ordered sandwiches with the crust removed.

"For dessert, you have to try their famous hot fudge sundae with almonds and ladyfingers," Carol Phillips told her.

Jackie was familiar with the menu at Schrafft's, a 40-restaurant chain that had become a kind of New York cultural icon associated with respectability and prim elegance. Her father had frequently brought Jackie and Lee to Schrafft's on their shopping expeditions.

Over lunch, Jackie explained how her father had helped her develop a sense of flair and individual style. As a lady's man, Jack Bouvier cultivated an interest in women's clothes, and he would spend hours shopping with Jackie and Lee at Saks Fifth Avenue, Bonwit Teller,

Bergdorf Goodman, and DePinna, giving them the benefit of his eye for fashion. The girls would vie for their father's attention, teasing him unmercifully, seducing him with shameless flattery.

"Oh, Daddy," Jackie would say to her swarthy father, "you are so café au lait."

Lee had a more ample bosom than Jackie, and she would try on dresses that emphasized her voluptuous figure. Though Jackie was jealous, she always felt that she, not her sister, was her father's true favorite.

He had very definite views on how a woman should look. "Hideous dress," he might say of a mannequin in a Fifth Avenue window. "It might work if it were belted." Or, "Now there's a beautiful outfit if it were worn by the right woman."

When Jackie finished her monologue about her shopping expeditions with her father, Mary Campbell leaned her boxy torso across the table and smiled. The Prix de Paris, she told Jackie, was hers for the asking.

FOUR

"These Charming People"

May–June, 1951

Real Money

Jackie returned to Merrywood from New York on the evening of Saturday, May 12, and went to her mother's bedroom suite, which occupied an entire wing of the second floor. She found Janet Auchincloss in her dressing room, preparing to go out to a black-tie society dinner.

The small, cozy space off the master bedroom was decorated in pale colors and was one of Janet's favorite rooms. Along one wall, there was a large, framed cork board that hung by a golden rope. On it were displayed dozens of snapshots of her family, showing them horseback riding in East Hampton, picnicking at Bailey's Beach in Newport, and attending garden parties in Georgetown.

"Mummy," Jackie said, "I'm going to ask Mr. Dulles to let me out of my commitment to the CIA job so that I can accept the Prix de Paris."

Janet had been anticipating this, and she told Jackie that she and Hughdie had decided to send her to Europe this summer, along with her 17-year-old sister Lee. It would be a dual present from Uncle Hughdie, Janet explained, celebrating Jackie's graduation from George Washington University, and Lee's graduation from Miss Porter's School in Farmington. At the end of the summer, Lee would enter college at Sarah Lawrence in Bronxville, and Jackie would take Mr. Dulles's nice little job at the CIA and live at home with her mother and stepfather.

Everything had been settled.

Jackie didn't know what to say. She was deeply dependent on her mother and hardly ever ignored her wishes. On those rare occasions when she planned to disobey her mother, she would disguise her true intentions until it was too late for her mother to stop her.

She tried this tactic now. She told her mother that she needed time to think over Uncle Hughdie's offer.

But Janet wasn't so easily fooled.

"I know what's on your mind," she said. "Jack Marquand. But Jack Marquand is a writer, and writers never have any *real* money. Need I remind you of that, Jahk-*leen?*"

The Krock Connection

"Isn't it wonderful?" Janet Auchincloss said the next afternoon as she led her lunch guests into the living room at Merrywood. "Jackie and Lee are going to Europe together this summer."

The high-ceilinged room smelled of furniture polish, old books, and pinewood fires. Hughdie, who was wearing his shooting jacket with a worn leather patch over the right shoulder, took up his usual position, his back to the low fire burning in the hearth. A sweet, aimless smile seemed to be a permanent part of his face.

Lee fluttered around the room in a dress that showed off her figure, expressing enthusiasm for the trip, which would be her first to Europe. But Jackie sulked in a chair. She did not want to chaperone her sister through a lot of musty old churches and museums.

"What shall we drink today?" Yusha asked. "I can whip up a batch of Daiquiris, if you'd like."

Everyone agreed that Daiquiris were

a splendid idea. A long, boozy cocktail before Sunday-afternoon lunch was an Auchincloss tradition.

"I use three kinds of rum," Yusha said as he began preparing his concoction. "A dark Bacardi, a reddish Mount Gay, a light Bacardi, a bit of Myers's, fresh lemon juice and fresh lime juice, sugar, and after I shake it all up, I put in a little bit of fresh orange juice. . . ."

As Yusha continued to explain how he made his Daiquiris, the other Auchincloss children wandered into the room, all of them dressed in new spring outfits selected by Janet, except for Nini, who was wearing a drab hand-me-down skirt, wool socks, and heavy shoes.

The children had met the guests before, but Janet insisted on making formal introductions. One by one, they were presented to Arthur Krock, the chief Washington correspondent of *The New York Times*. In his early sixties, Krock was a short, stubby man of great formality who walked with his head flung back and always had a big cigar in his mouth. When Janet presented Jackie to him, he held her hand longer than he did the others'. He had an eye for beautiful young women, and he saw himself in the role of the matchmaker between Jackie and some powerful Washington bachelor.

Krock was an anomaly in this WASP setting. A poor Jewish boy from Kentucky, he had attended Princeton University, but because of his religion, he had not been taken into a good club. His lifelong ambition was to become the editor of *The New York Times*, but the Jewish owner, Adolph Ochs, and his son-in-law, Arthur Hays Sulzberger, feared an anti-Semitic backlash against their newspaper. They decreed that all their top editors had to be gentiles.

Krock arrived in Washington in 1932, the year Franklin Roosevelt was elected president, and soon became the most powerful journalist of his day. In all his years in Washington, no one ever heard him allude to his Jewish background. In fact, he was the only Jew invited to the Dancing Class, an exclusive series of subscription gala balls. And he was one of two Jewish members of the Metropolitan Club (the other was columnist Walter Lippmann), where he ate lunch every noon at the center members' table with Hughdie Auchincloss.

"A young man would come into the room," recalled a Metropolitan Club friend, "and Arthur would say, 'He made Ivy at Princeton,' which, of course, was *the* club to make. And I would say, 'Arthur, how in the hell would you know that? That man is 40 years younger than you.' And he'd say, 'Oh, I keep tabs on everybody.' And that was the funny thing, because with his brilliance of mind, he was mixing with all of the playboys in Washington."

Just that day, Krock had published one of his ponderous front-page pieces about President Truman's dismissal of General Douglas MacArthur as United Nations commander in Korea, where America had already suffered more than 60,000 casualties. Truman was trying to limit the scope of the conflict to avoid a larger war with the Communists, but MacArthur had advocated bombing enemy sanctuaries inside Red China. The tumultuous debate that ensued over the proper conduct of the war was tearing America apart, and upon his return to America, MacArthur had been given a hero's ticker-tape parade in New York City and an invitation to address a joint session of the United States Congress.

"The nature of the dispute between the Administration and General MacArthur over the best policy to assure national security is as old as recorded history," Krock said, quoting almost verbatim from his article. "The Roman Senate openly debated, and Fabius Maximus, the Cunctator, unsuccessfully resisted the demand of Scipio. . . ."

Krock's wife, Martha, was also a journalist of sorts. She wrote a society column for the local Hearst paper, *The Washington Times-Herald*, called "These Charming People." Born Martha Granger in Lake Forest, a wealthy suburb of Chicago, she was a good-looking woman who regularly made Mr. Blackwell's annual list of the best-dressed women in America.

Yusha offered Martha a Daiquiri.

"We've just come back from the farm in Berryville," Martha said, referring to the Krocks' weekend house in the Shenandoah Valley of Virginia.

It was apparent from the way she slurred her words that Martha was already tipsy. Her custom was to have her first drink of the day with breakfast and take a nip now and then from a bottle she carried in her handbag. Krock was so grateful to have a trophy WASP wife that he would never criticize Martha's drinking, even when she turned nasty.

"You have no idea how those birds in Berryville chirp in the morning," Martha said. "They so irritate Arthur. He thinks he hears them singing, 'Jew, Jew, Jew.' "

At lunch, as Hughdie went through the elaborate ritual of decanting a bottle of his favorite Burgundy, Jackie listened to her mother and Martha Krock discuss the new exhibit of Raoul Dufy's paintings that had been praised by a reviewer in that morning's *Washington Post.* On Jackie's other side, Arthur Krock was commenting on an amazing picture that had appeared in that day's *Post* showing General MacArthur dressed in civvies for the first time since World War II. Krock was a staunch supporter of Dwight Eisenhower, and he was upset by signs that the MacArthur hero worshippers in the right wing of the Republican Party were planning to block the nomination of Eisenhower for president in 1952.

"Will Truman run again?" Hughdie asked Krock, who had won a Pulitzer Citation on the basis of an interview he had conducted with the Democratic president.

"Joe Kennedy thinks Truman will step aside and that the Democrats will nominate either Kefauver or Stevenson," Krock said.

Joseph P. Kennedy was the twelfth richest man in America — *Fortune* estimated his worth at $400 million, the equivalent of several billion dollars in today's money — and he and Krock spoke on the telephone practically every day. Their relationship went back to the early 1930s, when Kennedy first began to indulge his dream of becoming president of the United States and Krock spotted him as a comer.

"I wanted power," Joseph Kennedy told Krock in his characteristically blunt way. "I thought money would give me power, so I made money, only to discover that it was politics — not money — that really gave a man power. So I went into politics."

As a former Hollywood producer, Kennedy understood the importance of publicity, and he saw politics as another form of show business. He courted powerful figures in the press, including Henry Luce, one of the founders of *Time* magazine, William Randolph Hearst Jr., and Arthur Krock, who was the most trusted journalist of his time.

In Joseph Kennedy's cynical view of the world, every man had his price. He showered Arthur Krock with lavish gifts and large sums of money, invited him to his home in Palm Beach, Florida, and even paid for his first-class fare to Europe on luxury ocean liners. Prior to the outbreak of World War II, when Kennedy served as the United States ambassador to the Court of St. James's, Krock was a frequent guest at the American residence in London.

In return, Krock performed so many favors for Kennedy that he became known as an "honorary Kennedy." In the mid-1930s, he promoted the appointment of Kennedy, a notorious stock swindler, as head of the Securities and Exchange Commission. When Joe's son, Jack, fell ill during his first year of college, Krock arranged for him to recuperate on a ranch in Arizona owned by one of his friends. After Joe became ambassador in London, Krock helped him hire a *New York Times* reporter named Harold Hinton as his press secretary and speechwriter.

And it didn't stop there. Krock edited and rewrote large chunks of Jack Kennedy's senior thesis at Harvard, found him a literary agent, and came up with a title for the subsequent book — *Why England Slept.* He was the ghost writer for Joe Kennedy's 1936 campaign manifesto, *I'm for Roosevelt.* He offered to let his Negro valet, George Thomas, go to work for Jack Kennedy. And after Joe Kennedy had all but destroyed his political reputation by advocating the appeasement of Nazi Germany, Krock floated trial balloons in *The Times* on behalf of Joe's candidacy for the Democratic presidential nomination.

"Kennedy knew the human race pretty well," Krock explained, "and he knew its weaknesses and strengths and pretensions and hypocrisy, and he went right to the nut. He would have made a hell of a president."

As a Jew, Krock identified with Kennedy's efforts to overcome the prejudice against his ethnic background. For that reason, perhaps, Krock's conscience never seemed to be bothered by Joe Kennedy's immoral behavior.

"I was not shocked in the least," Krock said. "I expected, and still do, that politicians and big-business men don't have any morals."

By the time the roast beef and Yorkshire pudding arrived, Krock had launched into a monologue about the impact of modern communications on American politics.

The recent Senate investigation of organized crime, led by Senator Estes Kefauver of Tennessee, was the first government hearing ever to be broadcast nationally on television. Mobsters Joe Adonis, Frank Erickson, and Frank Costello (who allowed only his fidgety hands to be televised) had appeared before the cameras, creating a sensation. Almost overnight, Kefauver had become a national celebrity.

"More than fifty percent of the homes in the New York metropolitan area now have television sets," Krock said. "That's a sure sign that the political future belongs to the men who can learn to master this powerful new medium of communications. In that regard, I believe that one of the most interesting contests to watch next year will be the Senate race in Massachusetts between Henry Cabot Lodge and either Paul Dever, the governor, or Congressman John Kennedy."

Jackie, who was invariably bored by talk of politics, was intrigued by the mention of the name John Kennedy, the man she was going to meet later that night at the home of Charlie and Martha Bartlett.

"Oh, *you* know Jack Kennedy," she cooed in a throaty way, flirting with Krock. "Tell us about him."

Young Kennedy had definitely decided to seek higher office, and he had a lot going in his favor, Krock said. He had been voted "the best-looking man in the House" by the Washington female correspondents, and he possessed the kind of boyish good looks that were tailor-made for television. By contrast, Cabot Lodge, though a strappingly handsome man with a trademark name through the state, had the stiff aura of an aristocrat, not at all the quality that would go over well on television. Kennedy's other advantage was money. The

Kennedys' money might be nouveau, Krock said, but it was far more plentiful than Cabot Lodge's old money.

"Joe Kennedy has a saying," Krock said. " 'It takes three things to win in politics. The first is money, the second is money, and the third is money.' "

What Krock did not say was that Joe Kennedy believed that Jack needed a wife and family if he was going to move up from the House to the Senate, establish a national reputation, and fulfill the Kennedy dream of capturing the White House.

Krock, the "honorary Kennedy," had volunteered to help find a suitable mate for Jack, and he had turned to his own wife for help. Her society column, "These Charming People," gave Martha Krock special knowledge of the daughters of the best Washington families. Everyone agreed that the most eligible young woman around was Jackie Bouvier, the daughter of Martha's good friend Janet Auchincloss.

However, when Martha raised the subject, Janet expressed serious reservations about "those vulgar Kennedys." Janet hadn't struggled all these years to secure a place for herself in the WASP world only to see one of her daughters go off and marry Irish riffraff. She wanted Jackie to have the social prestige that came with marrying into society.

Martha understood Janet's aspirations for Jackie. But society, as she and Janet understood it, was in the last stages of disintegration at Newport, Bar Harbor, Southampton, and along Fifth and Park Avenues. Whether they liked it or not, representatives of the old WASP order, with their standards of duty, honor, and right and wrong and their good and bad manners, were being swept away. In their place, new men were emerging — young, vital, profoundly modern men who, in the words of historian Arthur Schlesinger Jr., "were beyond the definitions of class and race, region and religion." John Kennedy was such a man.

Meanwhile, Krock raised the name of Jackie Bouvier in his daily phone conversations with Joe Kennedy. The young woman was Catholic. She was beautiful. She was brainy. And she exuded upper-class breeding. She embodied just the right image that Joe, the old Hollywood public-relations expert, was seeking for his son Jack. The idea appealed to Joe Kennedy, and he gave Krock the green light to proceed.

It didn't take the resourceful Krock and his wife long to find the ideal co-conspirator in their marital plot. His name was Charles Bartlett. He was a young man whose wealthy family Martha had known back in Lake Forest and was one of Arthur's journalistic protégés in Washington. Bartlett had agreed to give a supper party that night at his Georgetown home to introduce Jackie Bouvier to Jack Kennedy.

The Matchmakers

Later that evening, the temperature dropped into the midforties, and Jackie put up the top on her 1947 black Mercury convertible before leaving Merrywood. She drove across the Chain Bridge and turned onto Reservoir Road. A few minutes later, she pulled up in front of 3419 Q Street in the heart of Georgetown, the oldest neighborhood in Washington, D.C.

It was a typical row house, just 16 feet wide. Three narrow steps, flanked by wrought-iron handrails, led up to the front door. Jackie announced herself with the brass knocker, and the door swung open to reveal the smiling face of her friend Charles Bartlett.

"Come on in," he said. "You're the first."

The small house did not have a hallway, and Jackie walked directly into the living room. It was decorated with a pair of antique Sheraton armchairs and a few pieces of cheap furniture. Landscape prints hung on off-white walls. A green rug covered the floor. Jackie could hear Martha Bartlett in the kitchen giving instructions to the help, a Negro woman, who was being paid the going rate of $6 for the entire evening of cooking, serving, and cleaning up.

Charlie put on a Tommy Dorsey record and offered Jackie a drink. She asked for an old-fashioned, and they sat and chatted in the facing Sheraton armchairs. With his shaggy hair and plain face, Charlie looked more like a Midwestern farmer than a Yale man from a prominent Lake Forest investment-banking family. But as Jackie was well aware, there was a sparkling mind at work beneath those homely features.

Two and a half years earlier, when he was only 27, Charlie had been entrusted with the job of opening the first Washington bureau for *The Chattanooga Times*, a paper run by the same family that owned *The New York Times*. Thanks to his mentors, Arthur and Martha Krock, Charlie was introduced to all the right people, and he soon became a player in the power circles of Washington.

"During the war, Washington had really jumped at the seams, and it was still lively when I arrived in January 1949," he said. "It was a small place, and if you had a few connections, you knew everybody very quickly. There were a lot of dinner parties, a lot of bright people, a lot of communication among staffers in Congress, artists, musicians, and journalists. Until then, it had been rare for people from my background — what you might call the wealthy class — to go into journalism. But after the war, everything changed, and journalism was no longer a class thing — it sort of transcended class — and it became an acceptable, even desirable way to spend your life."

Shortly after Charlie's arrival in Washington, the Krocks arranged for him to be invited by the Auchinclosses to one of their parties at Merrywood, and it was there that he met Jackie Bouvier.

"She was a wonderful-looking girl," Charlie said. "She was enormous fun and imaginative. Her status in the house, I think, was a rather tenuous one. She never talked about it, but I had the feeling there were all kinds of Auchincloss children, and I don't know where Jackie stood in the scale of things."

Jackie was an insecure 19-year-old young woman, but she was already sharpening her skills as a femme fatale. With her adoring gaze and breathless *gollies* and *gees*, she made Charlie feel as though he were the most important young journalist in Washington. At first, he was flattered by her attention, but as time wore on, he began to feel uncomfortable under the spotlight of Jackie's adulation.

"I was a homely boy from the Middle West, and I didn't have the cachet to provide Jackie with the glamorous life she desired," he said. "I never felt that Jackie and I were really meant for each other."

Charlie's problem went deeper than that. He was a devoutly religious Catholic, and he felt conscience-stricken over his secret sexual longing for Jackie. He was plagued by so much guilt that he could not even bring himself to kiss Jackie good night after their frequent dates. He agonized over what to do and finally decided that the wisest course of action would be to introduce her to a more appropriate suitor.

That summer, Black Jack Bouvier, who was dead broke, brought Jackie and Lee to East Hampton, where Charlie was staying with friends. Charlie took Jackie to the Maidstone Club, where they drove their car onto the beach and ate bread and spaghetti for lunch. He also invited Jackie to accompany him to his brother David's wedding to Gladys Peggy Pulitzer, the daughter of "One-Eyed" Pulitzer, a man who held the record for the most trans-Atlantic crossings by ocean liner.

As Charlie and Jackie drove to Puddle Duck Farm in Syosset, on the north shore of Long Island, Charlie did not bother to mention to Jackie that his friend Jack Kennedy would also be a guest at the wedding.

Charlie and Jack were both navy veterans, and they had met right after the war when a girl named Dodo Potter took Charlie to a well-known Palm Beach night spot called El Patio. Charlie had heard horrendous stories about the Kennedy children, how noisy they were and how they were impossible to have around. But over drinks in the tropical atmosphere of El Patio, he discovered a kindred spirit in Jack Kennedy.

They were both shy young men with an instinct for guarding their privacy and concealing their emotions. And they were also two rich Catholic boys making their way in the upper reaches of the WASP world. They immediately hit it off.

Jack had been working as a roving correspondent for the Hearst newspapers, but he had just made a decision to leave journalism and run for Congress.

"The newspaper business is great fun," Jack told Charlie that night at El Patio, "but I don't feel that I'll be able to have much leverage as a journalist. I'm going into politics where I can get something done."

Their friendship flowered in Washington during the late 1940s. While Charlie was learning his trade as a political journalist, Jack was serving in the House of Representatives from the 11th Congressional District of Massachusetts. They also saw a lot of each other on weekends in Florida, where Charlie made a valiant but fruitless effort to emulate Jack's winning ways with women.

"In the winter of '49, I was staying with Charlie Bartlett's family in Hobe Sound," recalled Taylor Chewning, the descendant of a wealthy Newport family, "and we went down to Palm Beach and had lunch with the Kennedys. A bunch of us were rather mischievous in those days, and Charlie was so sincere and lovable, and he really didn't have much success with the ladies. I think his religion held him back.

"There was a very, very good-looking woman who went out fishing with us one day," Chewning continued. "And Jack came along, and there was my wife, and Charlie, and this very pretty girl. So we told Charlie that the way to get this girl was to mix up a batch of martinis and get her a little tight, and perhaps some inhibitions might leave, and then he might just move in for the kill. And, of course, the inevitable happened. Charlie got absolutely plastered, and Jack walked off the boat with the girl."

Jack was devoted to pleasure, and his "girling," as he called it, was an open secret in Washington. But Charlie was a prude — too inhibited to participate in his friend's nocturnal adventures.

"I wasn't part of that scene," he said. "I wasn't invited."

Most of their time together was spent gossiping about politics.

"Jack used to love to sit around and talk about [House Speaker] Sam Rayburn and make fun of the senior figures in Congress," Charlie said. "He wasn't an enormously hard worker. He went to Palm Beach on weekends during the winter. I mean, every weekend, he'd hit that plane on Friday. He had a very good life. He didn't have any great desire to travel. I never felt that he was driven by a desire to be something that he wasn't."

Charlie did not harbor any illusions about the kind of man he planned to introduce to Jackie.

"Jack was very spoiled," Charlie said. "I mean, he could not ever have been easy as a husband. He was spoiled, and he was always on the prowl. If there was something he wanted to do, he just did it. He was bored very quickly. If you were talking about something that really didn't grab him, a sort of veil would come over his eyes. He was not an easy personality. You always felt you had to be up for him

— amuse him, interest him, engage him."

Jack's lack of interest in the give and take of legislative life led him to compile one of the worst attendance records in the history of the House of Representatives, and none of his colleagues took him very seriously. When he showed up at the Syosset wedding of Charlie's brother to One-Eyed Pulitzer's daughter, Jack was far better known as a playboy than he was as a politician.

"There was a big crowd at the wedding," Charlie said, "and it was hard to bring Jack and Jackie together, because Jack was like a trout in a stream, and Jackie was always surrounded by people. I introduced her to Gene Tunney, the former heavyweight champ, who was a great friend of my father's. And she got sort of involved talking to him. I just couldn't tear her away. And although they may have said hello to each other, they missed the chance to meet."

Over the next two years, Charlie was involved in building his career and courting Martha Buck, the daughter of a wealthy steel magnate. By the time he married Martha in December, 1950, Charlie had forgotten all about fixing up Jack and Jackie. And there the matter might have rested, if it hadn't been for Charlie's old mentor, Arthur Krock.

"When I came to Washington," Charlie explained, "I had a tiny office, and Mr. Krock was very kind and said I could use the facilities of his bureau any time. I said, 'Well, I can't offer you very much in return.' "

In the spring of 1951, however, Krock indicated that he would be pleased if the Bartletts arranged a supper party to introduce Jack and Jackie. Martha Bartlett was well aware of her husband's debt to Krock, and she had her own reasons for playing matchmaker.

"Jackie had made no secret of her disappointment when Charlie married Martha," Jackie's stepsister Nini said. "Even though Jackie and Charlie weren't really suited for each other, Jackie had designs on Charlie and had wanted to marry him herself. When Charlie married Martha instead, Jackie told me, 'When the minister asks if anyone has any objections to their being husband and wife, I want to stand up in the back of the church and shout, "I do!" ' "

"Martha was the one who finally got Jack and Jackie together," said Lewis Buck, Martha's uncle and her father's business partner. "She did it because Charlie was still interested in Jackie. He'd take her out to lunch and then bring her home for dinner. Charlie and Jackie would be drinking in the living room while Martha, slightly pregnant, was in the kitchen preparing dinner. Martha eventually got fed up with the arrangement and called her father and said, 'What am I going to do?'

"Her father said, 'Bring home somebody for Jackie. Introduce her to some guy.' And that's what happened. It was John F. Kennedy. She arranged that now-historic dinner party, invited Jack and Jackie and several other couples so it wouldn't look too contrived."

At 7:30, a group of guests arrived all at once at the Bartletts' front door, and Martha came out of the kitchen to greet them. She was an attractive redhead, about five months' pregnant, and she carried a cigarette in one hand and a drink in the other.

Each guest had been invited by Martha for a specific purpose.

There was Patricia Murray Roche, a perky blonde and one of the famous 52 first cousins of the Murray-McDonald clan, the crème de la crème of the Catholic aristocracy. Her father had died when Pat was a child, and she had been raised on trust funds from her grandfather Murray, whose major claim to fame was that he had been a partner of Thomas Edison's and held the patent rights on the radiators in the Empire State Building. As a youngster, Pat and her sister Jean had competed in the Pairs Class at East Hampton horse shows against Jackie and Lee Bouvier. Pat had been invited to talk horses with Jackie.

Pat's husband, Jeffrey Roche, had graduated from St. George's and Princeton and had grown up with the Kennedy children in Palm Beach. He had been invited to gossip with Jack about Palm Beach society.

Then there was Loretta Sumers, a slim, beautiful young woman with light-brown hair. "Hickey," as she was known, had gone to private high school on the north shore of Long Island with

Martha Buck, and had made her debut in New York City. Her father was the head of the Curb Exchange and took his family to Palm Beach every winter, where they socialized with the Kennedys. Hickey had become an accessories editor at *Glamour* magazine. She had been invited as the extra woman, just in case Jack Kennedy — who at that moment was coming through the Bartletts' front door — failed to take a shine to Jackie.

The Game

Six feet tall and 150 pounds, John Fitzgerald Kennedy was as skinny as a growing adolescent boy. His tousled reddish brown hair, protruding ears, and flashing white teeth added to the impression of immaturity, as did his attire, which consisted this evening of a baggy sports jacket and trousers with cuffs that stopped several inches above the top of his shoes. It was hard to believe that he was a three-term congressman who would be celebrating his thirty-fourth birthday in 16 days.

As he greeted the roomful of friends, he caught sight of himself in a wall mirror. He was conscious of his appearance and was constantly touching himself — his hair, his necktie, the flaps on his jacket pockets. He was aware that his complexion changed with the state of his health; one day he looked pasty, the next, he had a sickly yellowish hue. He had recently been to Palm Beach working on his tan, and tonight he gleamed with health and vigor.

"It's not only that I want to look that way," Jack told a friend, who had chided him good-naturedly about his narcissistic pursuit of a perpetual tan, "but it makes me feel that way. It gives me confidence, it makes me feel healthy. It makes me feel strong, healthy, attractive."

Yet, curiously, a large part of his pull had nothing to do with his looks.

"It was his nonchalance," said a friend, Gloria Emerson. "He seemed indifferent. And of course you have only to be in the presence of a very attractive man who's indifferent, and his charm magnifies. And so it wasn't just the beauty of his face or the coloring of his eyes that made him so striking. It was his detachment, his distance, that wonderful carelessness of his. Add to that his sense of self-entitlement, which you sometimes find among the rich and very beautiful. He expected people to pick up after him, take notes for him, get him tables at restaurants, make sure that he had clean towels, help him accomplish whatever he wanted. That is a very alluring quality in a man."

"I tried not to pay him any special attention on purpose," Pat Roche recalled. "I knew the reason for the party, and I didn't want to give off that feeling of a set-up romance."

"How's your Uncle Tom," Jack immediately asked Pat, referring to Thomas E. Murray, who was a member of the Atomic Energy Commission. "What's he doing? Did he go out to see the atomic test in New Mexico?"

Jack knew how to work a room. He remembered the names of relatives and had memorized funny little anecdotes about mutual friends. In a few moments, he had everyone charmed and laughing at his wry jokes.

"Jack had a wonderful, inquisitive mind," Pat Roche said. "He was always asking questions. He was fascinated by everything, especially people in politics. He was a real networker and loved to mingle at parties. He was fun and loved a good joke."

Jack accepted a drink from Charlie and then made it a point to sit on the sofa next to Jackie. Up close, his gray-blue eyes were set off by the gleaming tan of his face. He had beautifully tapered fingers. He was supple, almost feline in his gestures, and he looked like money, breeding, and power.

Jackie fixed him with her widely spaced eyes and seemed to hang on his every word. She was different from the women he was used to. She wasn't boisterous like his sisters, or blatantly sexy like his girlfriends. There was a strange otherness about her. She had large, masculine hands, and a flat-chested, thin-hipped boyish body. But her face was the face of an exotic beauty.

"I've never met anyone like her," Jack told a friend later. "She's different from any girl I know."

They were a perfect match: two masters of seduction.

The cook brought out large white pottery bowls filled with chicken casserole, peas, and rice, and placed them on a small table in the corner of the living room. Martha directed each person to his and her place at the table, which was set with inexpensive china and imitation crystal.

"So, Charlie," Jack said, as Charlie struggled to open a bottle of white wine, "what's the latest with Joe McCarthy?"

"Oh, Charlie," Jackie cooed flirtatiously, "*you* know Joe McCarthy?"

"Joe's an old family friend of *ours*," Jack said, competing for Jackie's attention with Charlie.

Two of Jack's sisters, Pat and Eunice, had dated Joseph McCarthy, the Republican senator from Wisconsin who was whipping the country into a state of paranoid hysteria over the Communist threat. McCarthy was a welcome guest at Jack's house in Georgetown, and he had frequently visited Jack's father on Cape Cod and in Palm Beach. Jack had been tutored in Communism by a Maryknoll priest named Father Edward Duffy, who, like many Catholics, opposed the Communists as much on theological grounds as on political ones. For Jack at this stage of his life, the Cold War was a holy crusade, and Joe McCarthy, for all his excesses, was doing the Lord's work.

"Joe McCarthy has proved to one and all that Communist-baiting is politically rewarding," said Charlie. "And so the Democrats are out to get their fair share of the glory. I hear that the Un-American Activities Committee may move to Hollywood, because it would be cheaper than bringing the testifiers to Washington."

"Speaking of hearings, what sort of a guy is Kefauver?" Jack asked.

"Friendly, ambitious, confident," said Charlie, who had just written a column about Tennessee's Senator Estes Kefauver for *The Chattanooga Times*. "But he's self-conscious, shy, more gracious than responsive. He's also a big ham."

"I've been following his crime hearings on television," said Jack. "I loved it when Kefauver asked Willie Moretti how he operated politically, and Moretti said," — and here Jack tried to imitate the gangster — " 'Senata, I don' opuhrate pull-iticle. If it wasn't for my foist conviction, I'd be sittin' where you are today.' "

His humor reminds me of my father's humor, Jackie later recalled thinking.

After dinner, they played The Game, a form of charades, and Martha made sure that Jack and Jackie ended up on opposing teams.

Jack loved any kind of competition, and when it was Jackie's turn, he scrawled something on a piece of paper and handed it to her with a mischievous gleam in his eyes. At the time, he happened to be reading *The Raven*, Marquis

James's Pulitzer Prize–winning biography of Sam Houston, and as Jackie unfolded the piece of paper, she saw the name Sam Houston.

"Oh, Gaahd!" she said.

She thought for a moment, then came up with an idea. She acted out the shape of an hourglass, and a member of her team shouted, "Sand," and Jackie made a cutting motion across her wrist, and someone else shouted, "San — Sam — *Sam* —"

Jackie nodded vigorously.

Then she pantomimed the act of cutting wood with an ax, and someone on her team shouted, "Cut," and someone else said, "Strike . . . cleave . . . hew . . ." And Jackie nodded again.

"Sam Hew — *Sam Houston!*"

And Jackie yelled, "Yes, that's *it!*"

And Jack looked at her and smiled appreciatively.

When it came time for Jackie to leave for her late date, Charlie offered to escort her to her car. She made the round of good-nights, coming to Jack, and she shook his hand. He seemed genuinely surprised — and disappointed — to see her go so early. She and Charlie walked out the door, and Josie, the Bartletts' fox terrier, scurried after them.

"Jackie had opened the car door, and we were saying our final good-nights in the middle of Q Street," Charlie recalled, "when all of a sudden Jack appeared at our side and mumbled something to Jackie along the lines of 'Say, Jackie, can I take you someplace to have a drink?' Just then, our dog hopped through the opened door into the car and started yapping. And a good-looking young man, who had been hiding in the back seat of the convertible, popped up his head. It was too dark to tell who he was."

It was Jackie's date.

"Perhaps some other time," she said to Jack.

The sight of the man in the back seat punctured Jack's ego, and, in a rare moment for him, he was at a complete loss for words.

"Sure," he muttered, "some other time."

Where the Boys Are

Jack telephoned Jackie the next day.

He could not have been more charming. He made wickedly funny comments about each person who had been at the Bartletts' party, rating their social skills at dinner and their performance at charades. He asked her about her college exams, which she had just completed. He gossiped about mutual friends.

But he did not ask her for a date.

Curious, Jackie telephoned Charlie Bartlett.

"Jack thought you were very interesting," Charlie told her.

"How do you know?" she asked.

"Jack and I have the same taste in women," Charlie said.

"He hasn't called again," she said.

"He's busy campaigning in Massachusetts," Charlie explained.

"Well, if he's interested," Jackie said, "he can find me in New York."

A few days later, Jackie stepped off *The Congressional* at Pennsylvania Station. Lugging a heavy suitcase, she hailed a taxi and made her way uptown to her father's apartment on East 74th Street. As she got out, she was trembling with excitement. In the face of vehement objections from her mother, Jackie had summoned up all her courage and come to New York to accept *Vogue*'s Prix de Paris.

Her father greeted her at the door, tears streaming down his cheeks. At first, Jackie thought that he was drunk. But she soon realized that these were genuine tears of joy. He was ecstatic that she was removing herself from the clutches of the dreaded Auchinclosses while she spent six months as a *Vogue* intern in New York and then another six months in *Vogue*'s Paris office. He had achieved the ambition of his life — to have his "best girl" near him as he entered old age.

The following morning, Monday, May 21, Jackie went to the Graybar Building on Lexington Avenue. Both *Vogue* and *Glamour* occupied offices on the nineteenth floor. The broad reception area was on two levels, and Jackie stepped up into a room decorated like a cozy sun parlor with white wicker furniture and large green plants. Enormous windows faced north, letting in flattering light. An elegant young woman sat behind the Chinese Chippendale reception desk. Impeccably dressed editors streamed by, trailing fragrant eaux de cologne. Jackie sat on an enormous sofa and filled out the application form for employment. For a moment, she looked down and noticed small gold stars sparkling up at her from the black floor.

"Are you a Communist?" the application form asked.

"No," Jackie wrote.

"Are you affiliated with any organization which advocates the overthrow of our Government by force or by illegal or unconstitutional methods?"

"No."

She left the line blank after "Soc. Sec. No." She did not have a Social Security number, because until now she had never worked a day in her life.

When she was done filling out the application, a secretary escorted her to the office of Carol Phillips, the managing editor.

"Let me show you around," Carol said.

They stopped by to say hello to Mary

Campbell, the personnel director who ran the Prix de Paris. Then Carol introduced Jackie to Alexander Liberman, the magazine's elegant art director, who was laying out the annual college issue for the August 15 edition. Liberman was tinkering with a nine-page photo essay by Irving Penn on seventy-three famous Washington personalities, including Senator Henry Cabot Lodge, Arthur Krock, and Senator Estes Kefauver. On a cork board above his desk were several versions of the August 1 and the August 15 covers (*Vogue* came out twice a month), including one showing a model in a brown Vera Maxwell coat-weight tweed suit with a very wide skirt. The cover girl was a brunette, and the courtly Liberman commented that Jackie bore a striking resemblance to the model.

At lunch, Carol Phillips asked Jackie for her first impressions.

"Where are all the boys?" Jackie asked.

"Jackie was horrified at what she found," said Kate Rand Lloyd, a *Vogue* writer who had won the Prix back in 1945. "Except for Alex Liberman and a couple of other men, there were only women in the office. *Vogue* did not employ any eligible bachelors."

That very day, Janet Auchincloss telephoned her daughter.

"What are the young men like at *Vogue*?" her mother asked.

"There aren't any," Jackie said.

"Mark my words, you're making the biggest mistake of your life," Janet told Jackie. "You're going to be twenty-two years old in July, and you're not engaged yet. You don't have time to rattle around in a mare's nest."

The next day, Lee telephoned. She had obtained a passport for the trip to Europe with Jackie. Now there wasn't going to be any trip, and she was distraught.

"I was seventeen," Lee recalled, "and my greatest dream was to go abroad as soon as I graduated from school. The main reason was that Jackie had taken her junior year from Vassar to study at the Sorbonne and had lived with a French family in Paris. Her letters to me, of which there were many, were so full of detailed descriptions of where she had been and what she had done, other countries she had visited, how fascinated she was by the history of the places she'd seen, that I was filled with curiosity and a longing to see everything she had been writing me about."

Jackie loved going to work at *Vogue*. The light as she got off the elevator, the perfume in the hallways, the stars twinkling up at her from the floor — everything about it thrilled her. And what was even better, in a matter of a few months, she would be on a great ocean liner, sailing back into the arms of John Marquand Jr. But as her first week at *Vogue* wore on, the barrage of calls from Merrywood never let up. Her mother wanted her to come home. When Jackie insisted that she would not abandon her dream of journalism, Janet put Jackie's stepfather on the phone.

"Hi, it's Unk," the amiable Hughdie said.

"Hi, Unk," Jackie said.

"I've spoken to Arthur Krock," he said, "and he's arranged for you to have an interview with Frank Waldrop, the editor of *The Times-Herald*. They've got some openings on the paper. Mr. Krock thinks he can get you a job."

Jackie told her father about the job that Krock was lining up for her in Washington, and Black Jack countered with an offer of his own. She could come to work for him on Wall Street. There were a lot of young men *there.*

By midweek, Jackie was in a state of deep distress.

"If you come home now," Janet Auchincloss said during another phone call, "you and Lee can leave for France at the beginning of next month. You won't have to wait for six months. You can be in Paris in two weeks."

Jackie spoke with Carol Phillips about her dilemma.

"She raised the subject of Washington," Carol recalled, "and I said to her, 'Go to Washington. That's where the boys are.' "

On Friday, Jackie decided to return to Merrywood for a family conclave. Her father accompanied her to Pennsylvania Station, where she found a seat in the parlor bar lounge car of *The Senator.* As the conductor announced the departure for Washington, she threw open the window and searched for her father.

He was standing alone at the end of the long platform, dressed in an exquisite wasp-waisted spring suit that had been made for him years before by his tailors at Bell. It was now too tight for his thickset body. He looked like a ruined old man. The train pulled out, and his figure grew smaller and smaller in the distance.

Jackie was in tears all day Saturday. On Sunday, she went up to her bedroom at Merrywood and took out a piece of pale-blue stationery.

Dear Miss Campbell,
  I won't be able to come to work for you . . .
  I will stay here [in Merrywood] . . . and then in January if I still want to work for *Vogue* I can move to New York . . . I don't think Mummy realizes that! I will just *have to gamble* on there being an opening and I do so hope there will be.
                    Very Sincerely,
                    Jackie Bouvier

Watching Burt Lancaster

It was a little before 8:00 on the evening of June 7 when Jackie and Lee arrived in a De Soto taxi at Pier 90 in New York City. The largest passenger ship in the world was brilliantly floodlit against the evening sky, and the massive white letters of its name — QUEEN ELIZABETH — sprawled 68 feet across its bow. At the top of the gangway, a bellboy dressed in a tight red tunic and matching pants directed the Bouvier sisters to their cabin in tourist class, for which Hughdie Auchincloss had shelled out $336.56 apiece for the roundtrip fare.

There was a distinctive odor to their room — an evocative blend of tea, flowers, floor wax, and whatever stern antiseptic the British had used to keep the ocean liner clean during its service as a troop ship during the war. Jackie gave the longshoreman who brought their luggage a $4 tip, then sought out the steward and booked two deck chairs on the starboard side — the side that got the most sun and the least wind on the

140

five-day eastbound crossing to Southampton, England.

They joined the crowds on the deck. Many of the passengers were in evening dress, sipping cocktails with friends who had come to see them off. A band played in a nearby lounge. Everyone seemed mesmerized by the vast height of the ship and the dramatic perspective of the Manhattan skyline.

When it was time to go, the bellboy came around ringing a Chinese gong, and shouting, "All ashore." But most people ignored the first gong and waited for the unmistakable final call — the ship's thundering whistle.

After the ship was at sea, Jackie and Lee discovered that they had an unexpected cabinmate, an eccentric spinster named Miss Coones.

"She frightened me enough with her clothes on," Lee recalled, "but when she turned out the light . . . I threw back my bed curtain and was horrified to see Miss Coones's bony naked body. After that, I decided I didn't want to know what was going on in that cabin. Telegrams arrived for us between six and seven A.M., and Miss Coones would stand by the door shouting, 'For

Jaclyn — for Lee.' "

Eventually, the sisters managed to switch to another cabin. Free of their chaperone, they began to explore the huge ocean liner. Jackie could feel the surge of the enormous engines and hear the ship creak — *duh-duh, duh-duh* — as it rolled through the Atlantic waters. She had heard that young people from first class were permitted to "descend" to tourist to do a little slumming, but that tourist class passengers like themselves were forbidden to "ascend" to first. Naturally, the sisters decided to circumvent the rules.

"We tore across the [tourist] class deck," recalled Lee, "leapt over a large fence, whizzed down one flight of stairs, leapt over another fence — and finally we were there."

They found themselves on the balcony overlooking the gymnasium on the starboard side of the sun deck. A large group had gathered along the railing to watch the activity below. Among the spectators, Jackie spotted two friends — Sharman Douglas, the daughter of the former United States ambassador to the Court of St. James's, and Minnie Farrell Cassat, who had been with

Jackie at The Chapin School in New York City.

They greeted each other with shrieks of joy.

"What are you doing here . . . ?"

"What are *you* doing here . . . ?"

Sharman was returning to London, where she was a leader of the "bright young things" known as the "Princess Margaret set," and a frequent companion of the suave British actor Peter Lawford.

"Minnie, what about you?" Jackie asked.

Minnie pointed to the gym below, and said, "I'm watching Burt Lancaster."

Jackie leaned over the balcony, and recognized the famous movie star.

Dressed in a leotard, Lancaster was practicing acrobatic routines with Nick Cravat, his pint-sized sidekick who had been his partner in the Ringling Brothers and Barnum & Bailey Circus before they began making movies together. They had just completed shooting *The Flame and the Arrow* and were on their way to Europe to film *The Crimson Pirate*. They were working out on the horizontal bars to Les Paul and Mary Ford's "How High the Moon."

Lancaster was at the peak of his physical prowess, a tall, broad-shouldered Adonis with blue eyes, a toothy grin, and a thick mane of hair. He swung gracefully from one horizontal bar to another, performing twists, flyovers, and somersaults. He landed lightly on his feet, threw open his arms, and flashed his legendary smile in the direction of Jackie.

Over and over again throughout her life, Jackie had dreamed of running away from home and joining the traveling circus. In her dream, she was a performer who never had to speak but who made herself understood without using words. She would emerge from the shadows beneath the big tent and appear in the center ring dressed in a beautiful beaded costume that shimmered and sparkled under the floodlights. She would stand there, arms thrust out toward the audience, the focus of the everyone's rapt attention, the queen of the circus. . . .

FIVE

A Rendezvous with Death

June, 1951–February, 1952

All or Nothing at All

"I don't want to marry a girl who's an experienced voyager," Jack Kennedy was saying. "And I'm not referring to travel on land and sea. I mean, I don't want to marry a girl who's traveled sexually — who's sexually experienced."

He was soaking his back in a hot bath and talking to a friend about his future. Jack had been a passionate reader all his life, and *experienced voyager* — an obscure metaphor from Lord Byron — was one of those literary phrases that cropped up in his conversation almost as often as four-letter words and scatalogical references to bodily functions.

If it hadn't been for his father, Jack would have been content to remain a bachelor for the rest of his life. But Joseph Kennedy kept telling him that a politician with aspirations for high office had to have a wife and that a Catholic politician had to have a Catholic wife. And so in the summer of 1951, matrimony was very much on Jack's mind.

"There are too many complications with a girl who's an experienced voyager," he said, splashing around in the tub. "They make comparisons between you and other men. I want someone young and fresh. I want to marry a virgin."

His friend, Langdon Marvin, had been sitting on the edge of the toilet seat cover for the past half-hour, listening to Jack mull over the qualities he was looking for in a wife. Few girls seemed to meet his demanding standards.

"But Jackie Bouvier's different," Jack kept saying. "She's definitely different."

A cloud of steam filled the room, and Langdon could just barely make out Jack's hairy arm and chest above the rim of the bathtub. The strains of Frank Sinatra singing "All or Nothing at All" — Jack's favorite record — could be heard coming from his bedroom on the third floor of the house he rented with his sister Eunice on 31st Street in Georgetown.

Langdon came from a prominent New York family — he was a godson of Franklin Delano Roosevelt — and he and Jack had been at Harvard together, where Langdon had been voted by his classmates as the man most likely to succeed. Witty, handsome, and urbane, he had also been featured in the pages of *Life* magazine as a comer in Washington. He worked for Jack on an informal basis, making arrangements for his congressional office, doing some research, occasionally acting as an advance man, and procuring girls for him.

He was the kind of macho intellectual who always appealed to Jack — a tough talker, a big boozer, and an accomplished athlete (he had been a member of the Harvard squash team). Like K. LeMoyne Billings, another of Jack's devoted chums, he worshiped the ground Jack walked on.

Langdon resembled Lem Billings in one other respect: they were both closet homosexuals. In the 1950s, homosexuals were regarded with loathing and repugnance by most Americans, who considered them the worst kind of moral degenerates. Jack often joked that the real reason his father wanted him to marry was so the voters of Massachusetts would not mistake him for a "fairy."

Over the years, Langdon had witnessed many of Jack's bouts with his bad back, and he could tell from the way his friend was biting off his words today that he was in a lot of pain.

For long stretches of time, Jack's back would cause him no trouble at all; then, without warning, he would be struck by excruciating pain. Like everyone outside the Kennedy family, Langdon accepted the story that Jack's bad back was the result of a football injury at Harvard and that the condition had been exacerbated by Jack's PT boat accident during the war. There was a hole in Jack's back that had never entirely healed after his operation, and Langdon had looked into that savage wound and seen the metal plate imbedded in his friend's spine.

What Langdon did not know was that Jack had been born with a congenital malformation of his spinal column and had been an invalid all his life.

Jack raised himself out of the tub and put on a terry-cloth robe. Dripping wet, he limped into his bedroom.

The room was a mess. Clothes were strewn over the bed and chairs. Shoes and socks were scattered across the floor. Underwear and shirts hung from open dresser drawers. All his life, someone had picked up after Jack, and that function was performed in Georgetown by George Thomas, the Negro valet who had once worked for Arthur Krock. That day, however, was Sunday, George Thomas's day off.

From the doorway, Langdon observed Jack run his fingers through his thick, coarse hair and examine himself in the mirror. Jack enjoyed being the object of attention. His perpetual tan, his careless dress, his tousled hair — all this was calculated to draw admiring gazes and to impress people with his healthful glow.

As Langdon watched, Jack put on an eight-inch-wide cloth back brace. Few people knew that Jack wore a corset or that his left shoe was fitted with an orthopedic lift because that leg was shorter than the other. These were closely guarded secrets, as were the facts about his other ailments.

"[H]e used (and carried with him about the country) more pills, potions, poultices, and other paraphernalia than would be found in a small dispensary," said Theodore Sorensen, who went to work writing speeches for Jack the following year.

"He was highly allergic to dogs, horses, and certain kinds of dust and suffered coughing and sneezing attacks, skin rashes, and swollen glands as a result of these allergies," wrote a Kennedy biographer. "He was also periodically asthmatic and had a weak stomach; in his later years, he could not tolerate anything but bland foods. In addition . . . he was slightly deaf in one ear. Chronically underweight through his first thirty-five years . . . he was fed in his youth a diet of milk, cream, butter, creamed soups, chowders, and sirloin steaks, baked potatoes with butter, ice cream, chocolate malteds, and hot chocolate made from milk and topped with whipped cream, all of which he ate in large quantities without ever putting on so much as an extra pound."

"We used to laugh," his brother Bobby said, "about the great risks a mosquito took in biting Jack Kennedy — with some of his blood, the mosquito was almost sure to die."

Since childhood, Jack had been the victim of high fevers, seizures, and collapses. Like many men whose formative years had been scarred by serious illness, Jack was ashamed of physical weakness. He feared that if the truth ever came out, it would be his personal and political undoing.

His illnesses sapped his strength and undermined him psychologically, for he had never understood their ultimate cause. As a child, he was sorely puzzled by his afflictions and wondered why his prayers to St. Jude — the patron saint of impossible causes — went unanswered. As he grew older, he began to accept his fate, and he lived for the moment, defying the odds, recklessly seeking pleasure, never taking himself too seriously. He did not expect to live beyond his forties.

He had spent a good part of his life sick in bed, reading and thinking about death. His Catholic upbringing with its emphasis on life after death, his lifelong illnesses, and his hairbreadth escape from death in his PT boat in the Solomon Islands had all focused his mind on mortality.

He liked to quote from John Buchan's *Pilgrim's Way*, a requiem for the generation lost in the trenches of World

War I. He saw a reflection of himself in Buchan's portrait of lost youth.

He loved his youth, and his youth has become eternal. Debonair and brilliant and brave, he is now part of that immortal England which knows not age or weariness or defeat.

Or he would recite from a poem by Alan Seeger:

I have a rendezvous with Death
At some disputed barricade,
When spring comes back with
rustling shade
And apple blossoms fill the air . . .

Langdon watched as Jack got out a portable blood-pressure machine and stethoscope. With quick, sure movements, he took his own blood pressure and determined that it had not dropped as a result of the stress of the past weekend's campaigning. Then he took a hypodermic needle from a drawer and filled it from a small bottle with a rubber top.

Langdon could not make out the writing on the bottle.

Sitting on the edge of the unmade bed, Jack stuck the needle into his thigh and depressed the plunger, sending the mysterious drug coursing through his veins.

"O Lord, Make Me Good, but Not Yet . . ."

Summer gave way to fall, and Jack stepped up his hectic pace — politicking in Washington, mending fences in Massachusetts, playing around in Palm Beach.

But he still did not call Jackie.

In early October, he set off on an around-the-world trip aimed at rousing press interest in his coming run for the Senate. None of Joe Kennedy's children ever traveled alone. They had grown up in a big, noisy, competitive, interdependent family, and they needed to have people around all the time to admire them, amuse them, and take care of their needs. And so Jack was accompanied on the seven-week journey by two people — his sister Pat and his scrappy younger brother Bobby, with whom he began to develop his first close bonds during their stops in Israel, India, and Southeast Asia.

At Tan Son Nhut Airport in Saigon, they were greeted by Edmund Gullion, the tall, dark-haired American chargé d'affaires. The heat was hellish, and Jack's tropical-weight trousers clung to his thighs as he climbed into the back seat of Gullion's waiting limousine.

"What's that noise?" Jack asked Gullion as they made their way toward the center of the city.

"Small-arms fire," Gullion explained. "Another attack by the Vietminh Communists."

At first glance, Saigon looked like any other French colonial capital. It was laid out with wide, tree-lined boulevards, grand public buildings, theaters, shops, and fine restaurants. The streets swarmed with cars, rickshaws, and willowy Vietnamese women on bicycles, their silk trousers floating behind them like petals in the heavy heat. A huge poster of Bao Dai, the country's emperor, peered down from the façade of the National Assembly building.

But on closer inspection, it became clear that Saigon was a city under siege. The lower floors of the Caravelle Hotel were barricaded behind sandbags, and the entrances of sidewalk cafés were covered by mesh screens used to ward off grenades tossed by passing terrorists.

Their limousine pulled up in front of the American embassy residence, a palm-shaded stucco villa built in the Provençal style of architecture. Jack was shown to his room. A mosquito net hung over his bed, and tiny lizards tapped on his window panes with their tails.

He showered and changed, then went out onto the terrace. Gullion handed him a gimlet, which was made of Rose's lime juice and gin, and they sat and watched the night sky throb with flashes from the Vietminh guns that ringed the beleaguered city.

Gullion did not know what to expect from the young congressman. He knew of Ambassador Kennedy's reputation as a staunch supporter of Joe McCarthy, and he assumed that Jack would see the world in the same one-dimensional terms.

"There's a lot of tension within our embassy as to whether the French can handle the situation here," Gullion said. "Personally, I think they can. But they've got to fix a date for Vietnam's independence. The real opponent the French are fighting here is nationalism, not Communist subversion."

As he listened, Jack tapped his front teeth with his index finger.

The trip had made a major impression on him; he had been profoundly affected by his discovery of the underdeveloped world. For the first time, he began to see the complexities behind the global conflict. It wasn't just a fight between the forces of democracy and the Commies. There was a great conflict going on between new nations that were striving to be born and old ones struggling desperately to hold on to what they had. He identified with the nationalist revolt against unyielding paternal authority.

The next day, Jack met with the commander in chief of French forces in Indochina, General Jean-Marie de Lattre de Tassigny, an imposing, theatrical figure in immaculate white gloves. They got into the general's personal airplane and flew over the broad, flat rice paddies of the Mekong Delta, where the French were bogged down in a bloody struggle against the Vietminh.

"Why should the Vietnamese people be expected to fight the Vietminh Communists to keep their country part of

France?" Jack challenged the general.

After they parted, the outraged de Lattre fired off a formal letter of complaint to the American embassy, charging that Congressman Kennedy was trying to undermine French policy.

"I am," the general sniffed, "far from overestimating the importance of this young man."

Later that afternoon, Jack went to the Cercle Sportif, the exclusive French bathing club in the middle of the city. While he sunned himself on a chaise longue, he watched waiflike Eurasian women in bikinis plunge off the diving board into the emerald water and emerge like mermaids with their long black hair streaming over their shoulders.

In the evening, he was driven through the darkened streets, past shuttered shops, to Cholon, the Chinese section of Saigon, where he visited an expensive house of prostitution. He was presented with a selection of women from various regions of China and Southeast Asia, as well as with a number of Eurasians who resembled the slim women he had seen earlier that day at the Cercle Sportif.

Jack had an enormous sexual appetite and gorged on women like food. He achieved his greatest sexual satisfaction when he was in bed with two women at the same time. Prostitutes were not his normal fare. But he was not a lady's man, either. He never spent any time romancing women with sweet words and sentimental gestures. And once he had made a sexual conquest, he usually lost interest and moved on to the next woman.

"I'm not interested — once I get a woman, I'm not interested in carrying on, for the most part," Jack told his friends. "I like the conquest. That's the challenge. I like the contest between male and female — that's what I like. It's the chase I like — not the kill!"

He resembled his literary hero Lord Byron in this regard, cultivating the image of a promiscuous sinner who indulged in wild debaucheries.

" 'O Lord,' " Jack often said, paraphrasing a favorite prayer, " 'make me good,' but not yet, O Lord, not just yet."

Jack's sexual education started at an early age. When he was 12 years old, his father brought home his mistress,

Gloria Swanson, the most glamorous movie star of the day. At the time, Rose Kennedy was away from Hyannis Port on one of her frequent shopping trips in Paris, and Joe and Gloria went for a sail on his yacht, which was named the *Rose Elizabeth* after his wife.

Young Jack stowed away below deck. When he peeked up and saw his father making love to Gloria Swanson, the bewildered young boy panicked and jumped into the sea. His father had to dive in and save him.

As Jack grew older, his father continued to tutor him in sexual matters in equally unconventional ways. On one occasion, when Jack came home from Choate, he found his bed covered with pornographic magazines that his father had left for his inspection.

"I think it's Dad's idea of a joke," Jack commented.

Later, Joe Kennedy would amuse his son by describing in clinical detail his sexual conquests of showgirls and other floozies. He offered to share his girls with his son and expected his son to reciprocate.

Jack adopted many of his father's attitudes toward women, including the habit of talking about the opposite sex in the most disparaging way. Once, when a friend showed Jack a teary letter that he had received from a girlfriend, Jack shocked him with his response.

"It may be romantic to you," said Jack, "but it's shit to me!"

And yet, Jack may have escaped the worst of his father's influences because he was not the apple of Joseph Kennedy's eye. That heavy burden fell on the shoulders of the eldest son in the family, Joe Junior, a tall, handsome chip off the old block who embodied all of his father's values.

"Joe Junior was clearly the kind of man his father would have liked to have been," said Harvey Klemmer, who was Ambassador Kennedy's aide in London. "Joe was no intellectual, but he was sharper than Jack, brighter, quicker, the kind of witty extrovert who made a party by entering a room."

Toward the end of World War II, when Joe Junior heard that Jack's exploits on PT-109 had made front-page headlines in all the major newspapers, he was so upset that he broke down and cried. He could not accept being less than the best in the family, and his jealousy drove him to volunteer for the fateful bombing mission against a German submarine base that led to his death.

For months afterward, Joseph Kennedy was inconsolable. Any chance that Jack might have had to vanquish his brother in life now seemed gone forever.

"I'm shadowboxing in a match that the shadow is always going to win," Jack complained to Lem Billings.

Then in 1948, Jack's favorite sister, Kathleen, and her English fiancé, Peter Milton, Lord Fitzwilliam, were killed in a plane crash in France. The news of Kick's violent death reached Jack at home in Georgetown, where he was lying on a couch listening to a recording of the musical comedy *Finian's Rainbow*.

"He was in terrible pain," recalled Lem Billings, describing Jack's feelings of confusion and guilt at being left alive after the deaths of Joe and Kick. "He told me he couldn't get through the days without thinking of Kathleen at the most inappropriate times. He'd be sitting at a congressional hearing and he'd find his mind drifting uncontrollably back to all the things he and Kathleen had done together and all the friends they had had in common. He thought of her now as his best friend, the one person in the family with whom he could confide his deepest thoughts, his complex feelings about young Joe, his questions about God, and his doubts about the future. And now she was dead. . . .

"After Kathleen's death," Billings went on, "Jack had terrible problems falling asleep at night. Just as he started to close his eyes, he would be awakened by the image of Kathleen sitting up with him late at night talking about their parties and dates. He would try to close his eyes again, but he couldn't shake the image. It was better, he said, when he had a girl in bed with him, for then he could fantasize that the girl was Kathleen's friend and that when morning came the three of them would go for breakfast together."

The only thing that made sense to Jack was to live for the moment, treating each day as if it were his last, demanding of life constant intensity, adventure, and pleasure.

This attitude helped explain Jack's compulsive need to sleep with as many women as possible. As long as he desired yet another woman, responded with an erection, and performed in bed, he could make himself believe that all was well. For the brief time that sexual intercourse lasted — and with Jack, it never lasted very long — he was relieved of his feelings of isolation and anxiety.

Still, his fear of impotency and infertility always returned. He had contracted venereal disease in 1940, when he was 23 years old, and by the fall of 1951, he was suffering from recurrent symptoms — burning urine, prostate pain, secretion of pus, and anxiety about the effect on his fertility.

His "nongonococcal urethritis," as it was euphemistically called on his medical charts, had become a serious problem. According to Dr. William P. Herbst, a venereal specialist who took over Jack's treatment from the Lahey Clinic in Boston, the congressman was suffering "intermittent slight burning on urination and on examination at that time I found only a mild, chronic, nonspecific prostatitis. Studies of the urine for acid-fast bacilli were all negative. He was treated by periodic massage [of the penis and prostate], sitz baths, and later, the sulfonamide mixture Gantrisin and various antibiotics." But he was never entirely cured.

The Reprieve

By the time Jack arrived in Tokyo, he was exhausted from the stress and strain of traveling. On the way in from the airport, he could barely summon the energy to look out the window at the Japanese capital — a sprawling, filthy landscape of bedraggled wooden buildings populated by drably clothed, undernourished people. The Kennedys checked into the Imperial Hotel, which had been designed by Frank Lloyd Wright and was one of the few structures to survive the American fire-bombings of Tokyo.

In his suite, Jack took his blood pressure and found that it had dropped distressingly. His doctors had warned him about that. When his blood pressure was low, his body tissue could not easily absorb the life-saving cortisone that he carried with him wherever he went.

Drained and weary, Jack took out a hypodermic needle and stuck himself in the thigh. He then went off to the headquarters of the American occupation in Japan, where he had a meeting with General Matthew Ridgway, who had replaced Douglas MacArthur as the supreme commander of Allied forces in the Pacific.

The next day, Jack collapsed.

Bobby had been assuming more and more responsibility for organizing things on the trip, and he responded quickly to the crisis. He booked seats on an airplane, and the three Kennedys flew to Okinawa, where there was a large, well-staffed naval hospital. During the short flight, the radio operator on Pan American World Airways Clipper N1024V received a cable for Jack from General Ridgway.

Am sorry to learn that illness has interrupted your trip. I extend to you my best wishes for a speedy recovery with a pleasant and profitable continuance of your trip.

Ridgway

At the naval hospital in Okinawa, Jack went into shock. His fever rose to 105 degrees. He was packed in ice and put on intravenous feeding. He became delirious. The navy doctors found it impossible to say exactly what was wrong with him. Was it malaria? Jaundice? Hepatitis? The Kennedys had hidden the true nature of Jack's illness, and even as Jack lay in bed, Bobby was figuring out how he could expunge the hospital record of his brother's stay.

Meanwhile, Jack's temperature continued to rise until it was over 106. His condition was listed as critical. Bobby cabled their father back in America.

There was little hope for Jack's survival.

It was an exact replay of Jack's collapse in England in 1947.

Then, he had been rushed to the London Clinic, where he was treated by Sir Daniel Davis, the doctor of the famous press baron Lord Beaverbrook. Sir Daniel was the first doctor to inform Jack that he was suffering from Addison's disease, a failure of the adrenal glands.

The symptoms of Addison's disease matched all the debilitating conditions that had plagued Jack during his lifetime — chronic exhaustion, weight loss, poor appetite, low blood pressure, brown pigmentation of the skin, dizzy spells, vomiting, chills, and stomach pains. When it was discovered in 1855 by Thomas Addison, a British physician, the disease was considered fatal, as it gradually destroyed the adrenal glands and the body's immune system, leaving the patient mortally vulnerable to the slightest infection.

"That American friend of yours, he hasn't got a year to live," Dr. Davis told Winston Churchill's daughter-in-law, Pamela.

At first, the diagnosis of Addison's disease only seemed to deepen Jack's sense of personal doom. Before him lay the indolent life of a sickly son of a rich man. Thanks to his father's money, Jack never had to earn a living, please a boss, or postpone a gratification. When he turned 21, he had begun to receive the income from several trust funds that totaled $10 million. Measured in terms of today's money, he had an annual income in the early 1950s of about $4 million.

Eventually, his Addison's disease was treated with a synthetic substance called desoxycorticosterone acetate (Doca), which was administered in the form of pellets implanted in the muscles of his thighs and back. The pellets had to be replaced every two or three months, and Joseph Kennedy bought up huge amounts of the scarce drug and hoarded it in safe-deposit boxes all over America so that his son would never run short while traveling. Eventually, cortisone was developed as a treatment for Addison's disease, and it began to be used in conjunction with Doca pellets.

By 1950, Jack's condition had dramatically improved. He had more stamina and endurance, and he experienced a markedly increased sense of well-being. The combination of cortisone and Doca actually boosted his libido, increasing his already extraordinary sex drive.

The change in his overall outlook was evident in the fall of 1950, when he visited his aged grandfather, the former mayor of Boston, "Honey Fitz" Fitzgerald.

"You are my namesake," his grandfather told him. "You are the one to carry on our family name. And mark my word, you will walk on a far larger canvas than I."

Shortly after their emotional meeting, his grandfather died.

"There was something in the pageantry and the richness of [Honey Fitz's funeral] that really got Jack," Lem Billings recalled. "It made him realize the extraordinary impact a politician can have on the emotions of ordinary people, an impact often forgotten in the corridors of Capitol Hill. It was as if he were seeing for the first time that he really might be able to touch people as a politician and that if he could, then they could give him something back. . . ."

With Jack's physical revival, his father began to take his son's political prospects more seriously. For the first time since Joe Junior's death, Joe senior dared to dream again of a Kennedy in the White House.

"It was like being drafted," Jack told reporter Bob Considine. "My father wanted his eldest son in politics. *Wanted* isn't the right word. He demanded it. You know my father."

There were dangers associated with the administration of cortisone. In a healthy body, the adrenal glands produced natural cortisone, and the pituitary glands regulated its concentration in the blood stream. But in a patient suffering from Addison's disease, physicians were unable to fine tune the level of laboratory-produced cortisone.

Excess cortisone led to Cushing syndrome, and Jack suffered at times from many of its symptoms: a full red face, headaches, back pain, and muscular weakness. He also displayed the psychological symptoms associated with Cushing syndrome, including feelings of grandiosity and invulnerability. He became even more brazen and reckless than before.

As long as he didn't allow himself to become exhausted, however, cortisone was truly a miracle drug for Jack. It gave him a reprieve from death.

During his recovery at the hospital in Okinawa, Jack spent long hours talking with Bobby. The brothers were separated in age by eight years, which had made a big difference while they were growing up. But by that point, Bobby was a married man and the father of a baby daughter, and their age difference no longer seemed to matter.

Hour after hour, Bobby sat beside Jack's hospital bed, speaking in low tones to his sick brother, trying to rally his spirits. After Jack got well, Bobby said, he would go back to America and "knock Lodge's block off" and find himself a wife.

Jack smiled wanly from his pillow. Time and again on their long, grueling trip together, Bobby had proved his unswerving loyalty. He was willing to put his own ego aside and serve the interests of his older brother. He would stop at nothing to carry out any task, no matter how disagreeable, if Jack asked him. Jack had grown extremely fond of his little brother. Bobby had become his alter ego.

Nothing beat having your own kids, Bobby said. They gave you hope for the future.

Jack listened to Bobby. His brother was making a lot of sense.

More Salisbury Than Smith

After he returned to America, Jack flew up to Massachusetts to test the political waters. His father had become convinced, on the basis of privately financed polls, that the long WASP ascendancy in New England politics was at last coming to an end. He believed that a handsome Catholic war hero like Jack now had a real chance of unseating the junior senator from Massachusetts, Henry Cabot Lodge, the quintessential WASP politician.

"When you've beaten Lodge," his father told Jack, "you've beaten the best. Why try for something less?"

Every weekend, Jack crisscrossed the Bay State's bumpy roads in the back of his father's Cadillac limousine. He hadn't lived in Boston since he was 10 years old, when his father moved the family to Bronxville, New York, to escape the rampant anti-Irish snobbery prevalent in New England. His accent still marked him as an Irish Bostonian — "When Jack spoke, I would hear his mother's voice," said a friend — but in fact, he departed considerably from the ethnic stereotype.

"He was," wrote Arthur Schlesinger Jr., "reticent, patrician, bookish, urbane — much closer, indeed, to a young Lord Salisbury than to a young Al Smith."

Once he set out on the campaign trail, the frail, aristocratic congressman learned how to husband his energy. He slept in late, took regular naps, showered and changed his shirt and socks as many as four times a day, and retired early to bed. In that way, Jack fooled everyone into believing that he possessed virtually inexhaustible stamina.

"Jack told me to let everybody know he was available as a speaker on weekends," Dave Powers, one of his lieutenants, recalled, "and I talked to the local Elks, VFWs, Am Vets, Holy Name Societies, and volunteer fire departments wherever I went. No town was too small or too Republican for him."

At night, he often ended up, as John Galvin, another aide recalled, "sleeping in a crummy small-town hotel with a single electric bulb hanging from the ceiling over the bed and a questionable

bathtub down at the far end of the hall."
After a day of campaigning, he would
sink into the tub, seeking relief for his
back in its therapeutic hot water.

Jack's friend George Smathers, who
had left the House of Representatives
two years earlier to run successfully for
the Senate from Florida, warned him
that 1952 was shaping up as a Republican year. Jack couldn't beat the illustrious Lodge, who was the driving force
behind the Eisenhower-for-president
bandwagon.

"Oh, yes I can," Jack said.

"I don't think so," Smathers said.

"Well, I don't give a damn whether I
win or not, because I don't like this
business of being just a congressman,"
Jack said. "I don't like being in the
House, really. So, if I lose, okay — I'm
out. And if I win, then I'm out of the
House and I'm in the Senate, which is
a hell of a lot better than being in the
House."

The only person, other than his father, who believed in Jack's destiny was
Abraham Ribicoff.

"I was elected to the House of Representatives in 1948, two years after John
Kennedy," said Ribicoff. "He was from

Massachusetts, and I was from Connecticut, and we became friends. I always felt that Kennedy had greatness in him. It became apparent to me that his personality was strong and that people fell in love with Jack, especially women. The chairman of the Democratic Party in Connecticut, John Baily, and I started to talk about Jack and his future. And we both felt all the way back then in the early 1950s that Jack Kennedy could become president of the United States."

In early February, 1952, Jack began to lay plans for the formal announcement of his candidacy for the Senate. When he returned to Washington, he picked up the phone and called Jackie. They had not spoken in nine months.

"What's new?" he asked. "How about drinks tonight?"

"I'm sorry, Jack," Jackie said. "I got engaged to be married two weeks ago."

SIX

From This Moment On

February–April, 1952

No Great Catch

A few weeks later, Jackie stepped out of a taxi in front of the Cannon House Office Building on Independence Avenue. She had on a skirt and a short fur jacket and was carrying a Speed Graphic, a boxy wooden camera trimmed in leather and weighing a hefty four pounds. Her two-inch pumps made sharp clicking sounds as she headed across the broad marble lobby.

She got off the elevator on the third floor. Each of the mahogany doors along the high-ceilinged hallway was flanked by a state flag and the Stars and Stripes. The room she was looking for — No. 322 — was almost at the end of the block-long hall. She paused to look at the brass nameplate.

JOHN FITZGERALD KENNEDY
MEMBER OF CONGRESS

She had called Jack and, using her inquiring-photographer column as an excuse, asked to see him. The receptionist escorted her into an inner office, where Mary Barelli Gallagher, Jack's appointments secretary, greeted Jackie warmly, as though she was accustomed to welcoming strange young women in the middle of the day. Without knocking, she opened the door to Jack's personal office and showed Jackie in.

Jack was sitting in a plush leather chair under a cone of yellowish light from a floor lamp. He was still recuperating from his recent brush with death in Tokyo, and his appearance had changed dramatically since Jackie had last seen him. His gray-blue eyes were hidden in the shadows of their sockets. His complexion was pale and lifeless. And the shoulder seams on his white shirt drooped from his bony frame.

"Oh, hi, Jackie," Jack said, looking up.

For an instant, Jackie was unaware of the presence of a third person in the room. Then she saw the woman sitting a few feet away from Jack.

"You know Flo Smith, don't you?" Jack asked.

Florence Pritchett Smith got up from her chair. She was a short, slender woman in her early thirties. She had a

184

tiny button nose and wore her hair piled on top of her head to give her a couple of inches of additional height. Before the war, she and Jack had been an item in all the New York gossip columns. She had married Earl T. Smith, a wealthy stockbroker, who had a home near the Kennedys in Palm Beach. Flo and Jack were still great friends. Some people said they were still mad about each other.

"Flo's been filling me in on the gossip from New York," Jack said. "She knows all the latest jokes and tells them better than anybody I know."

"That's one talent I don't have — remembering jokes," Jackie said, looking at Flo. "The jokes I hear seem to fly right out of my head."

"I've got to go, Jack," Flo said. Then, rather stiffly, she added: "It was nice to meet you, Jackie."

"Nice to meet you, too, Flo," Jackie said, giving the other woman the once-over.

Jack raised himself from the chair with some difficulty and showed Flo out of the office. He then came over and stood next to Jackie.

During her trip to Europe the previous summer, she had cut her hair short and frosted it with blond highlights. She looked more sophisticated and grown up.

Jack asked about her fingernails, which were green.

She explained that she had recently started working at *The Washington Times-Herald* as the newspaper's inquiring photographer and that her fingernails had turned green from repeated contact with developing fluid in the darkroom. She was being paid the munificent sum of $42.50 a week to photograph and interview people on a human-interest question of the day.

"What kind of questions?" Jack asked.

Jackie took out a clipping of her "Inquiring Photographer" column and handed it to him.

Jack read the question: "What is your secret ambition?"

"Look at the first answer," Jackie said.

"Arthur Krock," Jack said, registering surprise. He read Krock's answer out loud: " 'Just once before I die I'd like to turn out an article in which every sentence would be clear, well-balanced, and well-written.' "

Jack turned to Jackie, and said, "For all our sakes, I hope Mr. Krock gets his wish."

They laughed.

Then Jack pointed to the big sapphire-and-diamond engagement ring on Jackie's left hand.

"So," he asked, "who's the lucky fella?"

Jackie took out another "Inquiring Photographer" column, this one dated February 10, and pointed to a picture of one of the people she had interviewed. His name was John Husted.

"I've found the man of my dreams," she said.

In Paris that past summer, Jackie had dreamed of a different man.

Shortly after she and Lee arrived in France, Jackie had resumed her old love affair with Jack Marquand. It was not primarily sex that drew her to Marquand. He had a keen mind and a wicked sense of humor and was always great fun to be with. He also kept Jackie on her toes, something she liked in a man. Though he was drinking more heavily than ever, she considered becoming Mrs. John Marquand Jr.

Her feelings for Marquand were strengthened during a short visit that she and Lee paid to Bernard Berenson, the famed American art dealer and Renaissance scholar, at his villa near Florence. The slight, white-bearded aesthete lectured the Bouvier sisters on his philosophy of love, marriage, and life.

"Never follow your senses," Berenson advised them. "Marry someone who will constantly stimulate you — and you him . . . Don't waste your life with diminishing people who aren't stimulating. Be with life-enhancing people."

Upon her return to America, Jackie went riding with her mother at Merrywood, and when they dismounted to cool down their horses, she took the opportunity to disclose her feelings for Jack Marquand.

Holding her horse's reins, Janet turned to face Jackie. "Jack Marquand is a drunk, and he doesn't have any real money," she said.

Jackie never knew when her mother's violent temper would come upon her. But she could see it when it started, because her mother's face would change, a dark cloud would fall over it, and suddenly she would erupt and be out of control.

Under no circumstances, Janet said, her voice rising, was Jackie to see Jack Marquand again or have any communication with him.

"Mummy," Jackie said, "I'm a grown woman. You can't tell me who I can see and who I can't."

And Janet struck Jackie across both cheeks.

"After that, I started getting a lot of agitated phone calls from Jackie," recalled John "Demi" Gates, a young CIA operative and one of Jackie's former beaus.

Jackie wanted to get back together as friends with Demi. But he had been obsessed with her for years and was still too much in love with her to settle for a platonic relationship. So he stopped taking her calls.

"And then she started writing me all kinds of crazy letters," Demi said. "She was off her pins, unbalanced, not acting herself. She was being kicked out of the Auchincloss nest, where she had lived in the lap of luxury, and she had absolutely no money. She told me this story about what happened to her mother and father on their honeymoon, which they spent in Guethary, near Biarritz. Black Jack went to the casino and lost virtually everything. And he came back to the room and told Janet that he had gambled away their money and blown their honeymoon. And Janet went to the casino and won the money all back. It was the condensed story of Jackie's life — her father lost all his money, and her mother rescued her by marrying Auchincloss.

"So when her mother refused to let her marry Marquand," Demi continued, "Jackie became desperate. She didn't know where to turn or what to do. And it was at this highly vulnerable moment in her life — when she was on the rebound from Marquand — that she thought she had found protection in the arms of Johnny Husted."

In background and breeding, John G. W. Husted Jr., who sold stocks and bonds on Wall Street, resembled the young men Jackie had grown up with — the very type she said she did not want to marry. He was a tall, attractive Yale man who had served in the war with an American field service unit attached to the British forces. He came from the crème de la crème of WASP society: his sisters had gone to school with Jackie at Miss Porter's in Farmington; his mother was distantly related to the ultrarich Harknesses; and his father, who was a great friend of Hughdie Auchincloss, was a partner in Brown Shipley, the London affiliate of the Wall Street firm of Brown Brothers Harriman.

"I am not a Catholic," Husted recalled, "but Jackie and I had an agreement with a priest in Washington that it was all right with the Church for us to marry so long as we brought up the children as Catholics. Of course, I assumed that Jackie was a virgin. All the girls at that time saved that for their wedding night. If they weren't a virgin, they were considered tarnished goods."

On January 21, 1952 — barely one month after Jacqueline Bouvier and John Husted had their first date — *The New York Times* carried a notice that they were engaged to be married the following June.

Jackie's father was in favor of the marriage, largely because it meant that

Jackie would settle down near him in New York City. But Jackie's friends were alarmed by the quickie engagement and appalled by the lack of joy and love exhibited by the new couple at their engagement party at Merrywood.

"They hardly spoke to each other," said one of the guests, "and when they did, Jackie would merely nod her head and smile."

Charlie Bartlett felt that Husted wasn't good enough for Jackie, and he did everything in his power to break up the engagement. So did Janet Auchincloss.

"Jackie's mother deemed me no great catch," Husted said. "Janet asked me how much money I was making and I told her $17,000 [about $120,000 in today's money]. My prospects for making more money were reasonable but not assured. . . . Consequently, she was vehemently opposed to the match and did not approve of me at all."

But as far as Jackie was concerned, the decision to marry John Husted was a fait accompli. She did not care what people thought. She was not going to back down now. Even Janet, with her awesome temper, was powerless to change Jackie's mind.

One day, when Janet and her stepson Yusha found themselves alone at Merrywood, they discussed the puzzling betrothal.

"Do you have any idea why Jackie's doing this — planning to marry Johnny Husted, of all people?" Janet asked.

"It beats me," Yusha said.

"I think," Janet concluded, "that Jackie must have fallen off Sagebrush and hit her head."

A Very Different Destiny

That winter, John Auchincloss, who was in the diplomatic service, gave a cocktail party at his house in Georgetown to which he invited Janet and his uncle Hughdie Auchincloss, John Husted, and Jackie. He also asked his brother Louis to stop by for a drink.

Louis Auchincloss practiced law by day and wrote fiction by night. He had just published his third novel, *Sybil*, and had acquired a growing literary reputation. He was curious to meet his young stepcousin Jackie, whose beauty and charms were often described in Tolstoyan superlatives.

The guests assembled in a small, elegant living room that had been decorated by John Auchincloss's well-to-do wife Audrey with her family's Louis XV furniture, little French master drawings, and Aubusson carpets.

"We have some important news," Janet said. "Jackie and John are engaged to be married."

"That calls for champagne," John

Auchincloss said.

He broke out a bottle and made a toast.

"But I noticed that Janet was in a bad mood," Louis Auchincloss remembered. "She obviously didn't like or believe in the engagement. It wasn't at all what she had in mind for her beautiful Jackie."

By that time, Jackie herself had developed second thoughts, and her long-distance relationship with the New York-based Husted had begun to cool. Johnny, as he was known, wasn't at all like the unconventional men Jackie was normally attracted to. Nor was there anything to the tantalizing rumor about Johnny's connections to the Harkness fortune. It turned out that he was not — and never would be — the beneficiary of great inherited wealth.

Jackie began to be seen around Washington in the company of other men. Her most frequent dates were John White, a former *Times-Herald* writer who had recently joined the State Department; William Walton, another journalist who had decided to become an artist; and Godfrey McHugh, an air force major and popular man-about-town.

"One night," recalled Jackie's stepsister Nini, "John Husted came down to spend the night at Merrywood, and Jackie wasn't there. Eventually, she came home. It was very late. They went upstairs to Jackie's bedroom and had a loud fight about where she had been. It was the first time John Husted realized that Jackie was not deeply certain about him."

"At my brother's party, Jackie and I got into a conversation about books," Louis Auchincloss said. "Jackie had read my novel *Sybil*, which was about a girl who marries a rich but dull man and leads a life drained of all energy. Jackie was eager to discuss it with me."

There was one particular passage in *Sybil* that reminded Jackie of herself.

The very sharpness of her reaction against her mother's concept of domesticity, her disgust at her father's jokes and pretenses, was evidence of a faith . . . that life did not have to be that way, that life itself could be tremendous. She did not know if anything tremendous would ever happen to her; she rather doubted if it would, but she could assure herself that she would never, like her mother, make a compromise with life.

"My fate is to become Sybil Bouvier Husted, the dreary little girl in your novel," Jackie told Louis.

"And it suddenly came over me that she would never marry Husted," Louis said. "What no one seemed to have known about Jackie at that time was that she wasn't this soft little passive, girlish person. She was tough. Very tough. The major motivation in Jackie's life was money. She loved money. And I had the curious conviction that this whole evening wasn't real, that her whole destiny would be different. A very different destiny."

The Dancing Class

In the spring, Jackie was invited to attend the last session of the Dancing Class for the 1951–1952 social season. This exclusive subscription dance had been a hallowed institution in Washington since before World War I, when Vernon and Irene Castle made ballroom dancing fashionable and wealthy young couples gathered to learn the turkey trot and other newfangled steps.

That, however, was no longer the purpose of the Dancing Class. It was now an occasion for the small group of WASPs in the nation's capital to get together in a spree of self-congratulation from which they excluded everyone else in Washington.

"What am I going to do?" Jackie asked Martha Bartlett, a week before the party. "Johnny can't make it down from New York for the Dancing Class."

"Call Jack Kennedy," Martha said.

"That's a good idea," Jackie said. "I will."

Dozens of predance dinners were held all over town on May 17, the night of the Dancing Class, and Jackie and Lee hosted their own small fête at Merrywood for a handful of friends. Then Jack Kennedy and Jackie, Lee and her new beau, the publishing scion Michael Canfield; and Langdon Marvin and Gloria Emerson swept across the Chain Bridge into Washington. There was a light mist in the air when they arrived in front of the Sulgrave Club on Dupont Circle at a little after 11:00.

As Jackie made her way up the paneled staircase, she could hear the familiar strains of Meyer Davis's orchestra, which had played at her debut. She was greeted by a quartet of Washington dowagers — Ethel Garrett, Minna Laagare, Kitty Newbold, and Violet Thoron — who sat side by side in a sofa occupying the strategic heights at the top of the stairs. These formidable ladies were the nominating committee of the Dancing Class. They also passed judgment on the dress and manners of everyone who attended.

A couple of hundred people were jammed into the ballroom. They danced under large bronze chandeliers whose lights were reflected in a dozen gilt mirrors. The men were dashing in their white ties and tails. The young women were dewy beauties in their strapless gowns with tight waists and full skirts.

But as always, it was Jackie, with her long neck and wonderful shoulders, who attracted the most attention.

A short, stocky figure emerged from the crowd and approached Jackie. It was Arthur Krock, his ever-present cigar stuck in his mouth.

"Jack doesn't like parties," Jackie told Krock. "He thinks they're a great waste of time."

"I tend to agree," said Krock, who took Jack aside and began talking foreign policy.

Later in the evening, Jackie and Lee went to the powder room accompanied by the towering Gloria Emerson, who stood six feet in her dancing slippers. Lee's date, the blond and devastatingly handsome Michael Canfield, was already drunk; he grabbed Langdon Marvin and headed for the bar. Left by himself for the moment, Jack looked around and spotted a young woman by the name of Wendy Burden Morgan.

Tall and slim, with a dark page-boy haircut, Wendy bore a striking resemblance to Jackie. She was wearing an off-the-shoulder emerald-green taffeta gown with a tight bodice. She had on an heirloom pin with a large hanging pearl. The pearl swung back and forth over her bosom as she danced with her husband.

Jack cut in.

Before she knew it, Wendy had been maneuvered by Jack into one of the dim alcoves off the dance floor.

"We should have lunch," he said, wasting no time.

"I'm a married woman, Jack," Wendy said. "What on earth can you possibly be thinking of?"

Suddenly, Jack felt a tap on his shoulder. It was Jackie.

"Come on, Jack," she said, pulling him away.

In the powder room, Jackie had put on eye shadow with tiny starlike sparkles. Her eyelids glittered under the lights of the chandeliers.

The Meyer Davis orchestra began to play "From This Moment On," and

Jackie led Jack back onto the dance floor.

Jack had two left feet and had never learned how to dance properly. He held Jackie against his stiff piqué dress shirt and shuffled his feet to the music.

Gloria watched them dance. Jackie's lips moved; she was murmuring the words of the Cole Porter song into Jack's ear. "From this moment on," she cooed, "you for me, dear, only two for tea, dear, from this moment on . . ."

Jackie brought her cheek closer. Her lips brushed against Jack's face.

"From this moment on . . ."

As Gloria continued to watch, Jackie looked up into Jack's eyes, and the sparkles fell off her eyelids onto his padded black shoulders.

Heavy Weather

Word about Jack and Jackie reached John Husted in New York.

"She had been writing me these letters saying that our relationship would work better if we waited six months before getting married," Husted said. "In one letter, she said, 'Don't pay any attention to any of the drivel you hear about me and Jack Kennedy. It doesn't mean a thing.' But I was quite upset. So I went down to my mother's place in Florida to try to get Jackie out of my mind. On my way back from Florida, I stopped in Washington and went out to Merrywood to see her."

They talked all weekend long.

"You are one of the nicest, kindest people in the world," Jackie told the man to whom she had been engaged for the past four months. "But I may not be the most appropriate person for you. I'm thinking of your future happiness, John, not mine."

Late Sunday morning, Jackie drove Husted to National Airport to catch the

12:30 Eastern Air Lines' Silver Falcon commuter flight back to New York. It was raining heavily, and they got soaked as they sprinted across the parking lot to the revolving doors of the terminal.

The airport had been designed in the late 1930s when aviation was still a spectator sport. It was done in a lavish Art Deco style. The grand staircase to the mezzanine level had burnished aluminum railings and posts resembling shafts of wheat.

They stood near the large inlaid-brass compass that decorated the terrazzo floor. In front of them, a wall of paned windows, 30 feet high and 200 feet wide, overlooked the airfield, but all they could see was a dense, impenetrable grayness.

After a while, Husted kissed Jackie on the cheek.

"When a girl tells you she wants to postpone your marriage, you know she really wants to call it off," Husted said. "As we said good-bye in the waiting room, I did not know whether we would ever see each other again."

After he left, Jackie walked over to the window and looked outside.

Through the sheet of rain, she could just barely make out the silhouette of Husted's waiting plane. The rear of the Martin 404 swung open and a boarding ramp unfolded. One of the propellers coughed, then the other, then they both spun to life.

She saw Husted, his collar pulled up against the rain, walking toward the plane.

Suddenly, she turned and made a dash for the stairs.

Downstairs at the departure gate, she ran onto the tarmac.

Husted heard her call his name just as he reached the foot of the boarding ramp.

She reached him, and for a moment they were caught in the wash of the propellers.

Then Jackie slipped the engagement ring off her wet finger, and without a word, dropped it into his pocket.

SEVEN

Out of the Shadows

July, 1952–June, 1953

The Doll Room

Over the Fourth of July weekend, Jack invited Jackie to Hyannis Port to meet his family. She arrived at the Kennedy compound with her hair feathered and frosted and wearing a pair of Roman toga sandals with straps crisscrossed all the way up her calf.

The Kennedys had never seen anyone like her.

Jack's sisters — Eunice, Jean, and Pat — went around the compound in old tennis shirts and sneakers. They took one look at Jackie in her chic sandals and decided that she was a pretentious snob. They poked fun at her kinky hair, wide-spaced eyes, and size-10 $1/2$ feet and joked that her tiny little voice made her sound like Babykin, a popular talking doll.

In phone calls to her sister Lee, Jackie compared her reception at Hyannis Port to a sorority hazing and referred to the hyperactive Kennedy women as "the rah-rah girls."

"When they have nothing else to do,"

Jackie remarked with biting sarcasm, "they run in place. Other times, they fall over each other like a pack of gorillas."

Jack remained a cool observer of the goings-on. He understood that in the eyes of his sisters, Jackie's unforgivable sin was that she was different. For all their family's millions, the Kennedy siblings had been brought up in a gregarious herd, where there was little tolerance for individuality. Jackie endangered this spirit.

"Ever since Joe Junior's death, Jack had been the focal point of the family's ambition, and . . . they feared that he'd be drawn away from them, taking away the center from their lives," said Lem Billings. "It wasn't true, of course, but they didn't know that at the time, and as a result they perceived Jackie as a threat."

Jack's sisters wanted him to remain in the family fold and marry a proper political wife — a tough, resilient woman like Bobby's wife Ethel Skakel, who would gladly shake hands with voters all day and attend rubber-chicken fundraisers at night.

Jackie was no Ethel.

But what no one in the family seemed to understand was that Jack did not want an Ethel. He had struggled all his life to cut himself loose from the raucous Kennedy herd. He was attracted by Jackie's elegant Old Money manners, savoir faire, and exotic otherness. She embodied many of the dreams and ambitions that he had always found hard to express while he was in the shadow of his father and older brother. Around Jackie, Jack felt liberated.

"He saw her as a kindred spirit," Lem Billings said. "I think he understood that the two of them were alike. They had both taken circumstances that weren't the best in the world when they were younger and learned to make themselves up as they went along."

Against her better judgment, Jackie allowed herself to be lured out onto the lawn the next afternoon to play touch football. The Kennedy women blocked and tackled her until she was black and blue. After a while, she had enough and retreated to the main house, where she lit a cigarette and watched the game from the large wrap-around porch.

Growing thirsty, she went inside for a

drink of water. At the end of a hallway, she came to a small office and found Rose Kennedy sitting at a desk.

"Hello, dear," Rose said. "Can I help you find what you're looking for?"

The two women had hardly exchanged a word since Jackie arrived.

"I'd adore a glass of water," Jackie said.

"The kitchen's over there," Rose said. "Would you like me to show you around the house?"

"That would be wonderful," Jackie said.

After she got Jackie the water, Rose led her into the dining room, which was dominated by a heavy mahogany table and wooden chairs, whose cushions were upholstered in a striped pattern. A large bay window looked out on the ocean.

On the other side of the foyer was a large living room filled with comfortable stuffed furniture. A forest of framed photographs covered the piano near the doorway. Rose pointed out the pictures of Jack as a young boy.

Jack had been one of those children who never seemed to get enough attention, and as a result, he had not gotten along well with his mother. Starting in 1929 — when Jack was 12 years old — Rose periodically fled from her unhappy marriage. She went abroad 17 times in seven years and was a regular customer at the haute couture collections in Paris. Although she was gone for only short stretches — two or three weeks at a time — Jack could never find it in his heart to forgive her for those absences.

"My mother was either at some Paris fashion house or else on her knees in some church," he told the artist William Walton. "She was never there when we really needed her. . . . My mother never really held me and hugged me. Never! Never!"

He told Lem Billings much the same thing, adding that every time his mother packed her bags to go on another trip, he would cry — until he realized that his crying irritated her and only made her withdraw from him even more.

"Better to take it in stride," he said.

"His mother was a tough, constant, minute disciplinarian with a fetish for neatness and order and decorum," Lem Billings recalled. "This went against

Jack's natural temperament — informal, tardy, forgetful, and often downright sloppy — so there was friction and, on his part, resentment."

In the large Kennedy household, order was essential. Rose accomplished this by maintaining a file with index cards on each of her children, including their birthdays, vital statistics, and inoculations. She weighed them every Saturday night, and the cook was instructed to give those who had lost weight more food the following week. She encouraged culture in the form of music and art appreciation. She played French records to stimulate their linguistic ability. She poured her prudish ideas and Victorian notions into the ears of her children.

"You stand straight," she told them, "and keep your right hand away from your body — it makes you look thinner — and keep your feet close together, so that your clothes hang right — put your shoulders back, just slightly. . . . Remember how it was with the Greek statues? You see how they stand? See how the clothes flow, just correctly?"

Rose understood that Jack had a natural streak of independence that was largely missing in most of his siblings.

"He had a rather narrow face and his ears stuck out a little bit and his hair wouldn't stay put," she recalled, "and all that added, I suppose, to an elfin quality in his appearance. But he was a very active, very lively elf, full of energy, when he wasn't ill, and full of charm and imagination. And surprises — for he thought his own thoughts, did things his own way, and somehow just didn't fit any pattern."

Searching for the source of Jack's individuality, Rose concluded that she might have been an unwitting contributor, because she neglected him in favor of the retarded sister Rosemary (who was eventually given a prefrontal lobotomy and shipped off to a nursing convent), and Joe Junior, the model child, who was all the things Rose loved — neat, punctual, and obedient.

"In the process," Rose admitted, "I'm afraid that poor little sickly Jack was left on his own too much of the time. . . . The thought still bothers me a bit that he may have [felt neglected] when he was a little boy, and only realized later on why I spent so much time with Rosemary."

Jack struggled to put space between

himself and his mother, but he was never truly successful in freeing himself from her. His struggle indicated just how irretrievably caught he was in her net. His most noticeable character traits — his sense of calm and his distance from others — were acquired from his mother. So was his distinctive accent. Everyone recognized the dominant influence of Joseph Kennedy in shaping Jack's life, but in her own way, Rose left a mark on Jack's soul that was just as indelible.

Although he did not like to admit it, Jack's happiest memories were of the times when his mother came into his sickroom, sat on the side of his bed, ran her hand through his thick hair, and read out loud to him. Then, his mother's voice — a voice he had incorporated and made his own — transported him into a fantasy world inhabited by kings and queens, heroes and adventurers. And in the glow of his mother's voice, the frail little boy felt that he could accomplish anything.

There were 16 for dinner that night — Joe and Rose, who presided at either end of the long mahogany table; the popular Irish tenor Morton Downey, who was Joe's favorite crony; Downey's son, Morton Junior; Bobby and Ethel; Eunice and her new boyfriend Sargent Shriver; Pat, Jean, Teddy, and their orphaned cousins Joey, Ann, and Mary Jo Gargan, who had been raised to young adulthood by the Kennedys; and Jack and Jackie.

"Where do you think *you're* going?" Jack teased Jackie as she entered the dining room, dressed to the nines.

"Oh, don't be mean to her, dear," Rose said. "She looks lovely."

Like all Kennedy activities, dinner was a tournament. Brothers and sisters hurled scorching insults across the table, making fun of each other's tennis serves and golf games. Jackie was quizzed on whether she had read Ernest Hemingway's *The Old Man and the Sea* (she had) and *Witness* by Whittaker Chambers (she hadn't); whether she had seen the movie *Singin' in the Rain* (she had) and the Broadway play *The Seven Year Itch* (she hadn't, but she was planning to). The loudest laughter was reserved for stories about people who had to be rushed off to the hospital with broken arms or legs — or worse.

"The thing that worried [Jackie] the most was handling the family," said Betty Spalding, the wife of one of Jack's closest friends. "And God, they were an overbearing bunch, always charging around, busting into the room constantly, interrupting you, dropping in unannounced, having their own private jokes, ganging up to make fun of someone and then holding the poor fool up to noisy ridicule in front of everyone else. The Kennedys were like the family in Tolstoy's *War and Peace*, but with none of the polish and intellect. All their energies were thrown into sports and politics. It was a culture shock for Jackie, who was absolutely stupefied about how to cope with such an Irish picnic."

At one point, Morton Downey asked Joe about the stock market crash of 1929. The table fell dead silent while for the umpteenth time Joe retold the story of how he had sold all his RKO shares right before the Great Depression. Jackie was not interested, however, and despite dark stares from Joe, she continued to whisper in Jack's ear while his father was talking.

When dessert came, Joe asked Morton Downey for a song. Downey rose to his feet, which were shod in velvet slip-ons with gold monogrammed initials. He went into the living room and arranged his short, rotund body at the piano. Then, he threw back his head, and broke into a rendition of "That's How I Spell Ireland."

"I" is for the Ir-ish in your ti-ny heart, my dear,
"R" means Right, and when you're right, you have no right to fear . . .
Then comes "A" for An-gels who are watch-ing over you . . .

The evening ended in the basement screening room, where Joe showed a new Doris Day movie called *The Winning Team*, a biography of baseball pitching great Grover Cleveland Alexander, who was played by Ronald Reagan. Joe and Jackie sat in the back in large wicker chairs. Some of the servants came in and sat on the sides. During a scene of Alexander's 1926 World Series heroics, Joe tapped Jackie on the shoulder and motioned for her to follow him.

She ducked out of the dark room and made her way through a hallway to another room, which was lined with glass display cases containing hundreds of dolls dressed in native costumes from all over the world.

"Many of these dolls were given to me when I was ambassador to Great Britain," Joe said. "I used to bring Gloria Swanson to this doll room. She liked to make love here. Let me tell you, that woman was insatiable. . . ."

He did not spare Jackie any of the details of his affair with Gloria Swanson, including a description of her genitals and how many times she could sexually climax in a single night. But as the daughter of Black Jack Bouvier, Jackie had heard worse.

Later, Morton Downey took Joe aside, and asked him about his conversation with Jackie.

Joe was impressed by the way the young woman had stood up to him. She displayed the kind of true grit he admired. And she wasn't afraid to give him the needle.

"You have no nuances," Jackie had teased him. "Everything with you is either black or white, while life is so much more complicated than that."

Joe liked that.

"What did you and Jackie talk about?" Downey asked.

"Money," Joe said. "She talked straight to me. She makes a pathetic fifty-six bucks a week from the camera-girl job she's got on the *Times-Herald.* And her old man gives her a fifty-dollar-a-month allowance — and he can barely afford that. Her stepfather's in bad shape, too. I told her that I'd fixed it so Jack had his own money — he wasn't dependent on me. If she married Jack, she wouldn't have anything to worry about. And if Jack didn't look after her properly, I would."

"And what did she say?"

"Not much," Joe replied. "Just looked at me like one of my porcelain dolls. But you know what the trouble is, Morton?"

"What?"

"I like the girl," Joe said, "but I don't think porcelain can carry babies."

One . . . Two . . . Three . . . Surprise!

After the movie, Jack asked Morton Downey Jr. if he could borrow his car to take Jackie to a party at the Wianno Yacht Club in Osterville, just outside Hyannis Port. The 1950 two-door Plymouth had once belonged to Jack, and Morton's father had bought it from Jack for his son's nineteenth birthday.

"Sure, take the car," the young man said.

Morton Junior and Joey Gargan went to the yacht-club party in another car. Later, on their way home along a roller-coaster road, they spotted Morton's Plymouth up ahead on a ridge. When they got to the top of that ridge, they could see the Plymouth down below. They continued to follow the car up and down the road. When the Plymouth got to the top of the next ridge, they saw it pull off to the side of the road and stop.

"Let's surprise them," Morton said to Joey.

"I don't know about that," said Joey,

a big, blondish young man who was devoted to the Kennedys.

Morton ignored Joey's reservations and cut the car lights. He turned off the engine and let the car coast to the bottom of the hill.

It was a dark, unlit road with towering ficus hedges on one side. They sneaked up the hill, practically on all fours, staying as low as they could so Jack wouldn't see them in his rear-view mirror.

"When I say one, two, three, we'll jump up and scare them," Morton whispered.

"One . . . two . . . three. Surprise!"

Morton jumped up and stuck his head in the open window.

Jackie was lying on her back. Her head was next to the driver's door. Her dress was bunched above her thighs. Her right leg was slung across the seat.

When she saw Morton, she let out a piercing scream.

Jack was down on the floor. He smacked the back of his head on the steering wheel as he came up.

"We — uh — lost the cigarette lighter," he told Morton.

Nimble Fox

Jack's stunning victory over Henry Cabot Lodge earned him his first front-page story in *The New York Times* and the beginnings of a national reputation. When he showed up on opening day at Hialeah Park in Florida two months after the election, spectators in the grandstand rose from their seats to get a look at the golden boy of American politics.

The new senator planned to attend Dwight Eisenhower's inaugural ball in a few days, and he had flown down to his family's oceanside estate in Palm Beach to buff up his tan. His face gleamed like burnished copper in the Florida sunshine. As always, he looked clean and fresh, as though he had just stepped out of a shower.

The seventh race was about to begin, and Joseph Kennedy remained a few paces behind his son as they made their way from the parimutuel betting window to the Kennedy box. Joe loved big crowds. He had spent a lifetime rubbing shoulders with movie stars, nightclub entertainers, sports figures, mobsters, and politicians, and he considered himself an expert on the qualities that made a celebrity. The question foremost in his mind right now was whether his son had the star power to arouse excitement beyond the borders of New England.

As Jack negotiated his way through the swarm of people, there was a nervous flutter in the boxes. Middle-aged women, done up in bouffant hairdos and bright lipstick and matching nail polish, giggled and squealed like schoolgirls as Jack passed by. Their husbands — portly aristocrats with names like Vanderbilt, Payson, and Whitney — tripped over each other for the chance to shake Jack's hand.

Joe watched with fascination.

Jack seemed to be surrounded by a magnetic field. The respect and attention that he commanded was something Joe had always desired for himself but had never been able to achieve. He knew that Jack was shy in crowds and did not like to be touched, and yet his son managed to maintain his dignity and poise as the crowd pressed toward him.

Jack offered his hand but did not use the politician's two-handed shake —

the right hand pumping away, while the left grabbed an elbow. He did not even look like the prevailing political models, Ike and Adlai, who were bald, grandfatherly men in ill-fitting sack suits. With his long hair and two-button suit, Jack looked modern. He was a cool, innately charismatic leader who exuded a carefree nonchalance. He seemed totally natural.

Joe Kennedy's appreciation of Jack's talents represented a turning point in the relationship between father and son. For a long time, Joe had desperately wished that Jack could be more like his dead brother Joe Junior — a big, brawling, back-slapping Irish personality. At one point during the Massachusetts senate race, Henry Cabot Lodge had sent word to Joe, through their mutual friend Arthur Krock of *The New York Times*, that Jack's campaign was a waste of Joe's money, and Joe had half believed him. Even after Jack had won, Joe credited the victory to the inexhaustible supply of Kennedy money and Bobby's brilliant organization and ruthless tactics.

But as Joe began to analyze the campaign more carefully, it dawned on him that he had missed the essential point. Sure, money and organization had played an important role in the race, but in the final analysis, Jack had overcome the Republican landslide and won by a 70,000-vote plurality because of the magic force of his personality.

The election of 1952 was the last hurrah of the WASP establishment. With Ike as its standard-bearer, the old guard of the Republican Party captured control of the White House and both houses of Congress. Yet, in the midst of this sweeping victory, the most notable WASP of them all — Henry Cabot Lodge — had gone down to crushing defeat at the hands of a young Irish-Catholic outsider named Jack Kennedy.

His father's belated acceptance unleashed an energy and drive in Jack that even he had not suspected was there. Jack had actually enjoyed campaigning for the first time. He felt exhilarated by the realization that he and his father were embarking on a long and arduous journey to attain the nearly unattainable — the White House. Just the two of them, side by side, arm in arm, without the ghost of Joe Junior between them.

"This is my father, the ambassador," Jack said, introducing Joe to his well-wishers. "And of course you know Senator Smathers . . . and this is our friend from Boston, Police Commissioner Timilty . . . and this is my mother . . . and her friend Mrs. Arpels."

Opening day at Hialeah was one of the major social events of the winter season in Florida, and Rose Kennedy had taken great pains with her wardrobe. She hired a Palm Beach photographer named Bert Morgan to shoot her in three different sets of clothing, and then spent days poring over Morgan's glossy prints. On the advice of Hélène Arpels, an international fashion plate and the wife of the owner of Van Cleef & Arpels, Rose had finally chosen a soft gray-flannel suit, a small grayish hat, and white accessories.

Joe wore a white Palm Beach suit. Back in the days when he had been a bootlegger with ties to the mob, Joe was the second-largest stockholder of Hialeah, and although he had since sanitized his reputation and sold his shares in the race track, he still owned the best box seats in the house. The track was in spectacular bloom, with pink hibiscus and bougainvillea. Pink pennants and flags flew over the Mediterranean-style roofs. Even the pink flamingos floating on the infield lake looked pinker that day, thanks to their diet of shrimp laced with iodine.

As the Kennedys and their guest reached their seats, a recording of "Flamingo" began to play over the loudspeakers. A groundskeeper trotted out to the small dirt island in the infield, and waved his arms. The flamingos took off in a great clapping flutter and flew in formation over the track. The crowd oohed and ahhed as the birds circled overhead, then swooped back to the island.

"It's now post time," Fred Capossel, the announcer, said over the public address system.

The horses were led into the starting stalls. In the lawn area, the crowd pressed against the rail. The day's seventh race was the twenty-second running of the Hialeah Inaugural. George Smathers, who was a regular at the track and knew many of the jockeys and trainers, had bet on a 5-to-1 long-shot named Sagittarius. Joe Kennedy was acquainted with mob-connected bookies who gave tips on fixed races. Whether he had talked to any of those bookies about that day's seventh race, he did not say. But he had put a considerable sum of money on a horse named Nimble Fox.

Earlier, during the flight from Palm Beach to Miami on the Kennedys' private plane, Joe and George Smathers had engaged in a heated argument over Jack's future. Once again, Joe brought up the subject of a wife and family. Bobby was married. Eunice had just announced her engagement to Sargent Shriver. Pat seemed to be developing an attachment to the British actor Peter Lawford. When the hell was Jack going to take the plunge?

Joe had come to the conclusion that Jackie Bouvier would make Jack a swell wife. She had the three B's — beauty, brains, and breeding — and what was more, she had a lot of pluck. Joe and Jackie spoke the same language. Joe didn't see any reason for Jack to delay.

Sprawled on a seat in the plane, Jack turned to Smathers and asked him what he thought about Jackie.

"I think you can do better," Smathers said, not mincing words. "I like Jackie, but I don't see you marrying her, Jack. I don't think she really loves you as much as I think she should. You know how you get an impression. She's such a strong character herself, and she's a beautiful woman, and a lot of guys are after her. Anyway, I just don't see her as the comfortable, I'm-standing-be-hind-you-no-matter-what type of woman."

"You might have a point there," Jack said.

"I always think that the man should be the dominant character in a matri-monial relationship," Smathers contin-ued. "And I don't see Jackie subjecting herself to you and your family."

Jack's political operatives in Massa-chusetts — Dave Powers and Kenneth "Kenny" O'Donnell — shared Smath-ers's doubts about Jackie. Voters weren't going to buy Jackie's little-girl voice and hoity-toity manners. For a man with Jack's driving ambition, Jackie was a definite political liability.

Joe Kennedy's face was glued to his

binoculars. The horses were in the backstretch. His horse, Nimble Fox, was trailing behind Sagittarius. The roar of the crowd was growing louder and louder as the field of horses thundered past the furlong pole.

Jack wasn't paying much attention.

Since his Senate victory, Jack had given a lot of thought to the idea of marriage. He liked to be petted and looked after by a woman just as much as the next man. He felt envious when his old Harvard classmates and PT boat buddies sent him invitations to their weddings. He asked so many friends for advice about marriage that they joked he should put the matter before the Senate for a vote. And yet, like all his brothers and sisters, with the exception of Bobby, he had trouble making a personal commitment. Something held him back.

Most people assumed that Jack was having too much fun as a bachelor to give up his independence.

"The women chased him," said Evelyn Lincoln, the young woman Jack had recently hired to be his personal secretary in the Senate. "I had seen nothing like it in my whole life. Half of my telephone calls were women."

One of his steady girlfriends, a stunning, dark-haired beauty named Noel Noel, tried to bully him into marrying Jackie.

"I told him I was going to send him home to propose to the girl he should marry," Noel explained to one of Jackie's biographers. "I told him Jackie was young and pretty and social and, by a wonderful coincidence, Catholic, which would be ideal for him. He had to marry someone like that if he was going to be president, and we both knew he was going to be president one day."

Even his old flame Flo Pritchett was pushing him hard to marry Jackie.

"How long do you think that girl is going to wait for you to make up your mind?" asked Flo.

Jack complained to his old navy pal, Paul "Red" Fay, that he was "both too young and too old for all this." "Marriage," he said, "means the end of a promising political career, as it has been based up to now almost completely on the old sex appeal."

He was only half kidding. The combination of power and sex was a potent fantasy for many voters, male and female alike. Jack wasn't sure that he wanted to marry a beautiful young creature like Jackie, who might steal the limelight.

He did not object to marrying Jackie because it would put a crimp in his sex life; having a wife wouldn't stop him from chasing women. But he knew that marriage would bring certain wrenching changes. For one thing, he would have to trust Jackie with his deepest secrets. And considering how he had grown up distrusting his own mother, it was hardly surprising that Jack hesitated to trust any woman.

He could not hide from a wife the facts about his health — facts that, if made public, were enough to sink his chances for the presidency. No one would vote for a man with a congenital spinal deformation — a cripple who had to wear a corset and use crutches. He would not last a minute in public life if people found out about his chronic venereal disease. And, of course, there was his Addison's. In 1953, Addison's disease was still considered to be a fatal affliction, generally caused by infectious tuberculosis. It was like having incurable cancer. Just think of what his enemies would make of that!

If all that wasn't bad enough, his future was held hostage by J. Edgar Hoover, the director of the FBI, who had knowledge of a compromising affair that Jack had carried on when he was a 24-year-old naval ensign. The woman in question, a blond, blue-eyed former Miss Denmark named Inga Arvad, had been a correspondent for a Danish newspaper in Berlin, where she had interviewed Adolf Hitler and other top Nazi leaders. After the United States entered World War II, the FBI suspected Inga of being a Nazi spy, and on Hoover's orders, the bureau tapped her phone. The FBI never proved that Inga was a spy, but the tape recordings of her conversations with Ensign John Kennedy remained in Hoover's personal safe, a potentially lethal weapon of blackmail against candidate John Kennedy.

And then there were Joseph Kennedy's old connections with underworld figures like Frank Costello and Sam Giancana. Joe had made a killing in Hollywood in the 1920s with the help of New York and Chicago muscle. During Prohibition, he made millions more in the bootlegging business with the connivance of Chicago mobsters. In the 1930s, Detroit's Jewish Mafia put out a contract on Joe, and the Chicago mob intervened and saved his life. Sam Giancana boasted he had a "marker" from Joe Kennedy, and someday he would call in the favor.

The earth shook as the horses rumbled down the final stretch. Their thundering hooves could be heard above the din of the crowd. Joe Kennedy and George Smathers were on their feet, yelling themselves hoarse.

Nimble Fox was neck and neck with Sagittarius.

Jack remained in his seat, a detached observer.

He had always wondered about his inability to step out of his own skin and feel love and compassion for another person. When he discussed the subject of love with friends, he confessed his total ignorance. He had never been in love, never lost himself with a woman.

Was it different with Jackie?

Did he love her?

He *appreciated* her. She had poise

and refinement. She was just what the Kennedys had in mind when they talked about self-improvement. She was eager to be useful. She translated French articles and books on Indochina for him. She accompanied him to political dinners. She shopped with him for clothes, helping him pick out expensive made-to-order suits that flattered his thin physique. She brought picnic lunches to his office, ladling out bowls of homemade clam chowder to Jack and friends like Abe Ribicoff. . . . She was everything that his rational mind told him he should want.

Jack would have been shocked to learn that his intellectual faculties had little to do with his attraction to Jackie. Her upbringing, her outlook on life, her voice, her manner, her body, her vocabulary, her intellect, her height, her coloring, her smell, her footfall on a hardwood floor, her gestures while smoking, her literary references, her tolerance of extramarital affairs, her tomboyishness, her throaty laugh, her wicked sense of humor — all this and more, worked on Jack's emotions. His future with Jackie was as inescapable as the outcome of the Hialeah Inaugural.

Jack stood up.

Nimble Fox flashed across the finish line, a length and a half ahead of Sagittarius.

"Gypsy Rose Lee's Mother"

"Jack's got to ask me to marry him," Jackie told her mother. "I'm going to call him."

"A girl doesn't call a gentleman, dear," Janet Auchincloss said.

"But I want to tell him," Jackie insisted.

"That's not smart," Janet said. "You are *not* to go after him. You must *not* look too anxious or too eager. You must keep yourself scarce."

It was a gray, drizzly Saturday afternoon in April, and several members of the Auchincloss clan were squeezed into Hughdie's Cadillac. They were on their way to the Holy Trinity Church in Georgetown, where Lee, who was traveling separately in her own limousine, was to marry Michael Temple Canfield.

Jackie was her sister's maid of honor, and she looked festive in a ballerina-length yellow chiffon dress. Her feelings, however, were anything but bright and gay.

Not only was her younger sister beating her to the altar; Lee was marrying a man with socially impeccable credentials — the adopted son of Harper and Brothers publisher Cass Canfield and his Social Register wife Katsy. Rumor had it that Michael, who had been adopted in England, was the illegitimate son of the Duke of Kent, the younger brother of the king. If true, this meant that Lee had snagged a husband with royal blood.

Tall, blond, and elegant, Michael appeared to be the perfect catch. Jackie had heard from Lee about Michael's problems — how he drank too much and suffered from periodic sexual impotency — but that did not alleviate Jackie's public embarrassment over her kid sister's nuptials. People were constantly asking about the published reports of a romance between her and Jack Kennedy. When were *they* going to get married? To which, Jackie's answer was always the same curious non sequitur: "He wants to be president."

The fact was, Jackie did not know where she stood with Jack. She was totally confused.

First, he had deserted her for a period of many months while he campaigned for a seat in the Senate. Then, he had invited her to Hyannis Port to meet his family and taken her to the Eisenhower inauguration, only to drop her once again. And then, he had phoned her out of the blue, without any explanation or apology . . .

What sort of man treated a woman this way?

And why was she taking his punishment?

"By this time, Jackie was very deeply in love with Jack," her stepsister Nina explained. "She was besotted by Jack, entirely devoted to him."

"I came back to Washington from Europe at about this time, and Jackie told me about Jack," said Letitia Baldridge, another of Jackie's friends from Miss Porter's School. "We used to meet on Saturdays at La Salle du Bois, a Washington watering hole. I told her, 'Every woman in Washington is after him. He's numero uno.' And she said, 'He's the most attractive man I've ever met in my life.' "

"She wasn't sexually attracted to men unless they were dangerous like old Black Jack," Jack Kennedy's friend Chuck Spalding observed. "It was one of those terribly obvious Freudian situations. We all talked about it — even Jack, who didn't particularly go for Freud but said that Jackie had a 'father crush.' What was surprising was that Jackie, who was so intelligent in other things, didn't seem to have a clue about this one."

The Cadillac pulled up in front of Holy Trinity Church. It was a simple white stone building, set on four slender Ionic columns, and it did not look at all like a typical Catholic church. Through the rain-streaked window, Jackie could see Lee slowly emerge from her limo in a beautiful ivory Chinese organza bridal gown and a rose-point lace veil that had had been worn by generations of Lee brides.

Throughout their childhood, Jackie had been the dominant sister, bossing around Lee, who was like a chubby, bumbling puppy. Jackie was stronger than Lee — emotionally as well as physically — and always seemed to win their contests, especially for the affection of their father.

In recent years, their relationship had become more complex, as sisterly competition gradually mixed with mutual admiration, emulation, and camaraderie.

Now suddenly, Lee had blossomed into a slim, feminine, seductive beauty. In just a few minutes, she would marry Michael Canfield and fly off to London, where Michael had a diplomatic job with the American embassy.

Everyone was abandoning Jackie — first Jack, now Lee.

In the back seat, Jackie turned to her mother and said, "I know that Jack wants Newport."

"You are that girl," Janet said. "You have *everything* he wants."

All of Jackie's insecurities were coming to the surface, and in this vulnerable state of mind, she found herself more dependent than ever on her mother. The older children in the Auchincloss household — Yusha, Lee, and Nina — dubbed Janet "Gypsy Rose Lee's mother" because of the way she had taken complete charge of Jackie's life.

Janet instructed Jackie where to shop for her clothes, how to do her hair, how often to see Jack, and what to say to him when he called. Janet had even arranged for Jackie to go to England for *The Washington Times-Herald* to cover the forthcoming coronation of Queen Elizabeth.

"Should I see Jack before I leave for the coronation?" Jackie asked.

"No," said Janet. "Tell him you're too busy and that you'll see him when you get back."

Jackie looked at her mother for a long moment, as though she was weighing Janet's words. Then she turned her face to the spattered window just in time to see Lee dash under a canopy of black umbrellas to the church door.

Transatlantic Dispatches

Before setting sail for the coronation of Queen Elizabeth, Jackie went to see her boss at *The Times-Herald*.

"I want little feature stories, nothing hard," said Sidney Epstein, the crusty old city editor. "Send them airmail."

And so, at the end of each day of her trip, Jackie sat down and wrote a letter in her looping, schoolgirl longhand and mailed it to the newspaper.

"We didn't have to edit her much," Epstein recalled more than 40 years later. "Jackie's copy was pretty clean for what it was."

CROWDS OF AMERICANS FILL
"BRIGHT AND PRETTY" LONDON

'Jacqueline Bouvier, of The Times-Herald *editorial staff, is in London to attend the coronation of Queen Elizabeth. The following story was written by Miss Bouvier and air-mailed from London):*

LONDON (via airmail) — "Oh, to be in England now that the coronation's here" — Robert Browning would have forgotten all about April were he to land in Britain now.

The whole country is concerned with the coronation, the whole coronation and nothing but the coronation.

Every home one could see thru the windows of the boat train between Southampton and London bore a picture of Queen Elizabeth — pasted on the outside of the house or in a window.

"Wait till you see the old place — everything's so bright and pretty," said the porter, who handled our luggage when we arrived in London's Waterloo station. "We haven't had it like this for years" . . .

After the theater we went dancing at the 400, a tiny private night club in Mayfair. Lined with accordion-pleated red velvet, it looked like the inside of a jewel box. Among those attempting to dance on the postage-stamp size dance floor were the Marquess of Milford-Haven . . .

NOBILITY AND FILM FOLK STRUT
AT PERLE MESTA'S CLAMBAKE

BY JACQUELINE BOUVIER

LONDON, June 3 (Special) — The Mesta fiesta — second only to the coronation — was the show to see in London last week . . .

Lauren Bacall was the belle of the ball. She had a swooping waltz with General [Omar] Bradley, then a series of romantic foxtrots with the Marquess of Milford-Haven. She wore a tight white lace dress and her long scarlet fingernails rested lightly on his highly burnished epaulet. Bogie, wearing a plain old white-tie-and-tails outfit, cut in on her.

All around the great gold and white ballroom, huge portraits stared down from the walls. George III, Alexander I and Alexander II, czars of Russia, Lord Castlereagh . . . they were all there.

Maybe it was the flickering candlelight, but they appeared to me to want to slip down from their lofty perches and twirl to the strains of "The Hostess with the Mostess on the Ball."

There was a knock on the door.

"Cable for Miss Bouvier," said Mr. Woodham, the night watchman at the South Audley Street flat in Mayfair, where Jackie was staying with her traveling companion and close family friend, Aileen Bowdoin.

The apartment was not heated. Aileen sat on the edge of the bathtub, trying to keep warm by soaking her feet in hot water.

"Just a minute," she called out.

She dried her feet with a towel and padded through the apartment, which was decorated with valuable Edwardian antiques. The occupants, Sir Alexander Abel-Smith and his wife, Henrietta — a lady-in-waiting to Princess Elizabeth — had moved into Buckingham Palace to assist with the coronation.

In the public imagination, the new queen towered above all the personalities of the age. For this brief, shining moment, Elizabeth was thought to be more glamorous than Marilyn Monroe, more charismatic than Dwight Eisenhower, and more inspiring than Winston Churchill himself. Her coronation was being celebrated by nearly a quarter of the human beings on the globe.

Jackie was gripped by royal fever and consumed every word in the British press. The designer Norman Hartnell had submitted nine different proposals for the coronation costume. In the days leading up to the ceremony, Elizabeth played records of her father's coronation, pinned a sheet to her shoulders to simulate her long coronation train, and rehearsed in the White Drawing Room at the palace. For Jackie, the queen-to-be was an object lesson of a woman who left nothing to chance.

Aileen opened the front door, signed for the cablegram, and went to the bedroom. Jackie was lying on the bed reading *The Raven*, a book that Jack had given her.

"For you," Aileen said.

Jackie tore open the yellow envelope. "Oh, this is from Jack," she said.

"What does he say?" Aileen asked.

"He wants to know if I'll marry him."

All Men Are Like That

Jackie's old beau, John "Demi" Gates, was in London for the coronation, and they bumped into each other in the middle of a crowded reception at the American embassy.

Jackie was the first woman Demi had ever loved, and he was still obsessed by her. But they had not been in touch for more than a year — ever since Demi had stopped taking Jackie's desperate phone calls about her mother's objections to Jack Marquand. To Demi's surprise, Jackie greeted him with a big hug.

"Let's have lunch," he said.

The next day, she met him at a small Italian restaurant around the corner from the embassy. She looked smart in a French-cut dark-blue dress with a white collar. Demi, who was 25 years old, tall, and well built, wore a cheap imitation of an English suit that had been made for him in Spain, where he was living.

"Tell me all about your new life,"

Jackie said in her whispery voice, which oddly enough had a commanding quality. "What are you doing in Spain?"

She did not know that Demi was operating under cover for the CIA in Madrid.

"I've started a publishing company called Estudios Histograph," he said. "It produces comic strips. I'm a little embarrassed about that. But it does more. It's also a PR and advertising company."

"Golly, that's just great, Demi," Jackie gushed.

"What about you?" Demi asked. "I'm glad that you broke off your engagement to Johnny Husted. I was jealous as hell of that little toad. He didn't deserve you. He had no right to be involved with the most glorious girl who's ever lived."

"Oh, Demi . . ."

"I've read that you've been dating Jack Kennedy."

"I have been seeing Jack."

"Is it serious?"

She looked at him with an innocent, wide-eyed stare but did not say anything.

"Surely you're not *interested* in Jack Kennedy," Demi said.

"We're seeing each other."

Demi felt that he understood Jackie's predicament better than most. He, too, was a product of a broken home. After his parents divorced, his mother had married Arthur Houghton, the chairman of Corning Glass and one of the richest men in America. Like Jackie, Demi had been brought up surrounded by luxury but had not inherited a penny and was forced to make his own way in the world.

He knew that Jackie could not support herself in the manner to which she had grown accustomed and that her only hope was to find a rich husband. But Demi was snob enough to believe that the Irish-Catholic Jack Kennedy was far beneath Jackie's standards.

"I really think you ought not to marry Jack Kennedy," Demi said.

"Why not?"

"Jack's hard," Demi said. "He may appear charming, but no one ever accused Jack Kennedy of being a gentleman."

Jackie harbored her own serious reservations about marrying Jack, but she was not prepared to discuss them with Demi Gates. She loved Jack — there was no doubt in her mind about that

— but she worried about losing her identity in the big, raucous Kennedy family. She was also concerned that she and Jack would have trouble accommodating to each other's violently independent natures.

"Look," Demi said, "I am quite adamant about Jack not being right for you. You're a lady. You have elegance and style. You're a class act. You have intellectual depth. In my view, Jack is a gutter fighter. He doesn't have class."

Demi's feelings of jealousy were getting the better of him.

"Jack's a womanizer," he blurted out. "When he comes to New York City, he calls up the guys and asks them to line up the girls — bimbos of every shape, color, and creed."

"Oh, well . . ." Jackie said.

"Jackie, don't kid yourself. Jack's reputation is incredible."

Nothing that Demi said surprised Jackie. She had read Jack from the start and knew exactly what she was getting herself into. He would be unfaithful to her. But she figured she could handle it.

"All men are like that," she told Demi. "Just look at my father."

The Most Private Person

After London, Jackie and Aileen Bowdoin went to Paris together.

"We shared a room for ten days at the Hotel Meurice," Aileen said. "During all that time, Jackie was thinking about accepting Jack's marriage proposal, but she didn't talk much about it."

As always, Jackie guarded her privacy. Occasionally, during a stroll through the Louvre, or some other museum, she discussed her thoughts about marriage with Aileen, but only in the most abstract terms.

"I wonder," she would say, staring at a painting, "what it would be like being married into a family like the Kennedys?"

The two young women were inseparable companions during the day. But in the evening, they went their own way. Aileen ate dinner alone at the hotel. Jackie got dressed up and went out on the town with her old lover, Jack Marquand.

"He was very debonair, very gentlemanly, a very polished young man of the times," Aileen said. "Just Jackie's type. You could tell there was a real chemistry between them."

For the 10 days she was in Paris, Jackie resumed her old liaison with Jack Marquand. It was as though the clock had been turned back to the days of her junior year abroad. Once again, she and Jack Marquand strolled along the bank of the Seine, past young couples making love in the shadows. They revisited all their favorite haunts — Chez Allard and La Grenouille, and of course L'Elephant Blanc. They drank grasshoppers and danced and smoked and stayed up to all hours of the night. Aileen was usually sound asleep when Jackie tiptoed back into their room at the Hotel Meurice and slipped silently into bed.

"She always came back to the hotel to sleep," Aileen said. "She never talked about where she had gone or what she had done with Jack Marquand. Jackie was the most private person."

On the flight back to America, Jackie sat across the aisle from Zsa Zsa Gabor.

"Twenty-four hours on the plane she

kept asking me — it was no joke — 'What do you do for your skin?' " Zsa Zsa said. "And I never bothered to ask her name. She wasn't the most glamorous nor the most beautiful woman. She had kinky hair and bad skin."

As they neared the coast of the United States, Jackie went to the lavatory to freshen up for Jack Kennedy, who had promised to meet her plane. She found the bathroom occupied by Zsa Zsa.

"Jackie was fit to be tied," recalled Aileen Bowdoin, "because Zsa Zsa was in there, making herself beautiful, and Jackie couldn't get in to powder her nose."

When they landed at Idlewild Airport in New York City, the Hungarian-born actress was allowed to get off the plane and go through customs before anyone else. She found Jack Kennedy inside the waiting room, leaning casually against a counter.

"And Jack says, 'My darling sweetheart, I was always in love with you,' " Zsa Zsa said. "Jack used to take me out quite often . . . and he was a sweetheart. He lifted me up in the air. Jackie came off the plane and saw Jack do that to me. After twenty-four hours of pestering me, asking about this cream and that lotion, she didn't even say hello to me. So Jack Kennedy said to me, 'I want you to meet Miss Bouvier.' He didn't say 'my future wife.' And I said, 'Oh, my God! We spoke twenty-four hours together on the plane. She's a lovely girl.' "

Jackie ignored Zsa Zsa and rushed forward to embrace Jack.

"Don't dare corrupt her, Jack," Zsa Zsa said.

"But he already has," Jackie said, smiling triumphantly at Zsa Zsa over her shoulder.

EIGHT

For Better, for Worse

July, 1953–October, 1953

"Nothing Fantasy"

"Ambassadeur!"

Louis Arpels flung his arms out wide, stretching the buttonholes on his snug double-breasted suit.

"Welcome," he said. "Welcome back to Van Cleef and Arpels."

Joseph Kennedy entered the hushed salesroom of the famous Fifth Avenue jewelry store. He had come alone, without Jack, to pick out Jackie's engagement ring. His son had no interest in such sentimental things.

A few reproduction Louis XV tables were placed at a discreet distance from each other on the pale blue wall-to-wall carpet. The staff — Jacqueline Wallach, a former French tennis star, and Fuocuo and Philibert de Bourbon, twin princes — stood with their backs to the walnut-paneled wall, in which small, glass-sheathed recesses contained priceless tiaras, necklaces, rings, hair clips, and earrings.

Louis led Joe toward the back of the store, past two attractive jewelry models in low-cut dresses, and into his private salon.

"Voilà!" said Louis, pointing to his desk.

Joe looked down at Louis's latest acquisition, the legendary Blue Heart, a perfectly pure aquamarine diamond of 30.82 carats.

"I prefer it to the Hope," said Louis, referring to another famous blue diamond. "Don't you?"

Joe nodded.

"Its origins are shrouded in mystery," said Louis. "But it is known that during the last century it belonged to a nobleman who was obliged to part with it, having wasted his fortune for the love of a woman. *Quelle sentimentalité!*"

"What are you going to do with it?" Joe asked.

"Sell it for a *formidable* profit," said Louis.

The two men burst out laughing.

Louis was a member of a vanishing breed — the private jeweler who functioned as friend and adviser to some of the wealthiest and most famous people in the world.

In his case, that included everyone from Mrs. Merriweather Post and the

Duchess of Windsor to King Farouk of Egypt and Greta Garbo.

Louis and Joe had a number of interests in common, including women and horse racing. Louis's strikingly beautiful wife Hélène, who had made the Best Dressed List 10 years running, took Rose Kennedy to the collections in Paris, where she would select Rose's entire wardrobe.

"Have you brought along a photo?" asked Louis.

"No," said Joe.

"Well, Hélène knows the young lady in question quite well and has guided me in my selection," Louis said. "Very American, like what a schoolgirl from a good family would wear, nothing fantasy."

Louis snapped his fingers, and the two models came into the room. One of them was wearing an engagement ring with a square-cut emerald of 2.84 carats and a matching diamond of 2.88 carats.

The other model had on a ruby and diamond bracelet and a diamond leaf pin.

Louis described the quality and design of each piece of jewelry, and after a while, Joe got up to go.

"Send them to Hyannis Port," he told Louis. "These will be the first serious pieces of jewelry Jackie's ever had."

The two friends walked to the front of the shop, and Louis held open the door to Fifth Avenue. Louis had not uttered a word about price. And Joe left without asking.

Hammersmith

In the middle of July, Rose Kennedy, a woman who never forgot that she had been born in a cold-water tenement, traveled to Newport to make arrangements for her son's wedding.

As her limousine swept along Ocean Drive, Rose noticed the names emblazoned on the stone gates of the great waterfront estates: Contentment, Idle Hour, East Passage, Broadlawns. Her car turned up a long gravel driveway, past a herd of prize Black Angus cattle grazing on a vast lawn, to the porte-cochère of Hammersmith Farm, the Auchinclosses' shingle-style Victorian manor.

The chauffeur came around to open her door and Rose stepped out. She was dressed exactly as her friend Hélène Arpels had advised: in a light-blue silk dress, white gloves, pearls, and an enormous cartwheel hat.

The Auchincloss coat of arms greeted Rose in the foyer: *Spectemur Agenda* — Judge Us by Our Action. A maid escorted her to a rustic sunroom, where a stuffed pelican hanging from the ceiling peered out on the sparkling blue waters of Narragansett Bay.

Janet Auchincloss soon made her entrance, looking casually elegant in a cream-colored dress. The two matriarchs shook hands and engaged in a few minutes of stiff conversation. Then Janet abruptly announced that they would be having lunch, not at Hammersmith Farm, as Rose had expected, but at nearby Bailey's Beach Club. Jack and Jackie — who were visiting for the weekend — would join them.

All four drove to the Spouting Rock Beach Association — the formal name of Bailey's Beach — which was the most exclusive private club in all of America. The two mothers sat in the front seat. Jackie wore the engagement ring Jack had given her (she did not know that it had been picked out by her future father-in-law). Jack had on an old undershirt, shorts, and bedroom slippers — a get-up that mortified his rigidly conventional mother. The 36-year-old U.S. Senator slumped in the back like a bad child.

"It was, I'm sure, one of his least

favorite days," remarked Jackie.

Once they arrived at the club, the newly engaged couple went for a swim.

"I came out of the water earlier," said Jackie. "It was time to go for lunch, but Jack dawdled. And I remember Rose stood on the walk and called to her son in the water. 'Jack! . . . Ja-a-ck!' — and it was just like the little ones who won't come out and pretend not to hear their mothers calling — 'Ja-a-ck!' — but he wouldn't come out of the water. I can't remember whether she started down or I went down to get him, but he started coming up, saying, 'Yes, Mother.' "

At lunch, Rose could not stop talking, and her gauche behavior grated on Janet's nerves. Janet took a snob's delight in treating her inferiors with an air of self-satisfied superiority, and she did not try to disguise her feeling that her daughter was marrying down. She would have preferred to see Jackie marry a Du Pont or a Vanderbilt — a man who carried an eminent pedigree as well as a lofty bank balance.

Rose finally got around to the reason for her visit. She said that Ambassador Kennedy, her husband, wanted to pull out all the stops for the wedding. The kids deserved the best. They should invite a lot of big names, have a band and entertainers, and generate plenty of press coverage.

Janet said that Mr. Auchincloss, *her* husband, saw things in a different light. They should make the wedding a traditional Newport event and confine the guest list to family and a few close friends.

Jackie supported her mother. She certainly did not want to have reporters at her wedding. That would be demeaning and vulgar.

"We want a simple and very small wedding — just family, we think," Jackie said. "Jack and I want it that way."

That, however, was not entirely true. Though Jack did not want a glitzy wedding, he was under pressure from his father to use the event to his political advantage. At his father's urgings, Jack had been feeding Evelyn Lincoln, his personal secretary, long lists of people Joe wanted to invite to the wedding, including practically the entire Senate and every Democratic leader in New England.

"Look, Mrs. Auchincloss," Jack finally

said, when it was clear that his mother and Janet had reached an impasse, "your daughter is marrying a political figure, a senator, a man who may one day be president. There are going to be photographers whether we like it or not. So the idea is to show Jackie to best advantage."

But Janet remained stubbornly opposed to a large public wedding, and Jack realized that his only recourse was to call in his father.

A few days later, the Kennedys' private plane touched down at Newport Airport. Jackie was standing behind her mother at the gate as Joe came toward them, a killer smile plastered on his Irish face.

Oh, Mummy, Jackie remembered thinking, *you don't have a chance.*

During the drive through Newport, Janet seemed to sense that her supercilious airs would not work this time, and she shrank into silence.

Jackie gave Joe a tour of the house — from the family coat of arms in the foyer to the stuffed pelican in the Deck House, the big room facing the entrance to the harbor. Joe kept a silent count of all the servants they met: a cook, who prepared the family meals; a second cook, who prepared the servants' meals, washed the dishes, and helped out with the kitchen chores; a butler; the handyman, who cleaned shoes, kept the porches in order, and kept wood in the fireplace; the parlor maid, who took care of the downstairs and helped at table for large parties; the chambermaid, who took care of the second- and third-floor bedrooms; the laundress; Janet's personal maid; the groundskeeper . . .

Outside, the gardens were in full bloom. There were numerous greenhouses — two for grapes, two for nectarines, one for orchids, the others for various flowers and plants. There was a dairy where cream and butter were made every day . . .

Joe possessed a special radar that detected the weaknesses in other people, and it did not take him long to size up the real situation at Hammersmith Farm.

"They don't even know how to live up there in Newport," he told Red Fay, Jack's wartime chum, when he returned from the visit. "Their wealth is from an era gone by. Most of them are just keeping up a front and owe everybody. If you pulled the carpets up, most likely you'd find all the summer dirt brushed under there, because they don't have enough help to keep those big places running right."

As Joe suspected, Hughdie no longer had a sufficient income to maintain his old life style. The Auchincloss brokerage firm had fallen on hard times. One of its founding partners was near death, and there was not enough money to purchase his shares and pay off his heirs. Now, to make matters worse, Joe Kennedy was proposing a lavish wedding for well over 1,000 guests, a circus that might cost as much as half a million dollars ($5 million in terms of today's money). The stepfather of the bride did not have that kind of money.

However, under Joe's relentless battering, Janet began to crack.

She only wanted what Jackie wanted, Janet stuttered. And she knew that Jackie only wanted what Jack wanted . . . and . . . well, if Joe wanted a wedding of that magnitude, then . . . somehow . . .

Joe relished his moment of triumph.

He had stripped away the Auchincloss veneer and exposed them for what they were — phony stuffed shirts. *Spectemur Agenda* — Judge Us by Our Action — his ass!

He, Joseph Kennedy, would pay for the wedding.

Ha!

On the back of the wedding invitation that she sent to Ellen "Puffin" D'Oench, her Vassar classmate, Jackie wrote: "Ha!"

Someone asked Puffin what she thought Jackie meant by that.

"If you're an old buddy," she said, "and you haven't really been in touch and you know that something's been all over the papers for months and months and you've become a kind of celebrity and you send a wedding invitation to an old school buddy, you might say, 'Ha!' "

Did it mean, Ha, look at me, I finally did it?

"It's so typical of her," Puffin said. "I think she was madly in love with the guy. And I can't see why she wouldn't have been head over heels for the guy. And 'Ha!' meant just that. 'Ha, I got him!' "

Something Else in Mind

She did not have him for long.

"We were all shocked when we heard that he was going over to France with Torby Macdonald and his old man, leaving Jackie here at the beach," said Taylor Chewning, the Auchinclosses' Newport neighbor. "Of course, it was nothing for Joe to leave his wife. He always did that. But here was a young man who was the toast of the town, very handsome, a lot of money, and theoretically very much in love with this dark-haired beauty, and he just split and went to the Riviera. I mean, why do you go away alone with a group of men? You don't go to Europe unless you have something else in mind. I don't think that shows an awful lot of love."

Jack had instructed Evelyn Lincoln to charter a yacht in the south of France. For public consumption, she let it be known that the Senator was in France conferring with French government officials on the situation in Vietnam. But nobody was fooled by that.

"I called Jacqueline about the engagement," said Betty Beale, the society columnist of the Washington *Evening Star*, "and she said Jack was going to Eden Roc in Cap d'Antibes for his vacation, and he wasn't taking her. I had never before — nor have I since — known a man who preferred to take his vacation away from the girl he had just become engaged to. This, coupled with his reported behavior in Cap d'Antibes, was proof to me that he was not really in love with Jacqueline.

"Friends of mine, a very social couple, rented the same yacht, with the same skipper and cook, a couple of years later," Betty Beale continued. "And when they mentioned that they were from Washington, the captain told them that he had once rented the yacht to Jack Kennedy. The captain described the wild behavior. They had orgies on that boat."

At the time, Michael Canfield was in the south of France looking after his fellow alcoholic, Black Jack Bouvier, who was in an expensive clinic drying out for his daughter's wedding. Michael met up with Jack Kennedy and was impressed with the number of women who were throwing themselves at his future brother-in-law.

When the stories reached Janet Auchincloss back in America, she was fit to be tied.

"No man in love does something like that," she told Jackie. "If you're in love with a girl, you want to be with her."

"Jackie was in love with Jack and was bitterly disappointed when she realized his nature," Hélène Arpels said. "She would come over to my apartment at the St. Regis to try on dresses that I had brought back from Paris to get ideas of what to order herself. Once, she tried on some of the dresses and couldn't get them closed. She was plump — not fat, but not very, very thin — and was mortified that she couldn't close the dresses. The next time I saw her, she was much thinner, and she told me she simply shook her head every time a plate was set in front of her. But she was so unhappy, which might also have accounted for her weight loss. Jack was after everything in a skirt. My husband and I would take Jackie out to El Morocco to cheer her up. She never complained."

A Joseph P. Kennedy Production

Around 10:00 on the morning of September 12, 1953, Jack Bouvier telephoned Hammersmith Farm from the Viking Hotel in Newport and demanded to speak to Jackie. The Irish maid who took the call was aware of the bad blood between the mistress of the house and her first husband, and she rushed upstairs to alert Mrs. Auchincloss. She found her in a bedroom, along with Lee, and Ann Lowe, the Negro dressmaker who had designed Jackie's wedding gown. They were fussing over the bride.

"It's Mr. Bouvier on the wire," said the maid.

"I'll take it," Janet said, leaving the room.

The gown was unbuttoned in the back, exposing Jackie down to her hips. It had a portrait neckline and a fitted bodice that was embellished with interwoven bands of tucking. Each panel of the bouffant skirt was swirled into a rosette with an orange-blossom sprig in the center. It was made from fifty yards of taffeta faille, and was a pale ivory color, rather than white, so that it would blend with Jackie's yellowed rose-point lace veil lent by her grandmother, which lay on the bed in a box of tissue paper.

Jackie looked at herself in the full-length mirror. The ornate gown emphasized her flat chest and did not complement her tall, spare figure. She would have preferred something simpler and more modern, but Jack had cast his vote for a traditional wedding dress, and she had yielded to his wishes.

Jack did not normally care about such things. But like everyone else, he was caught up in the public-relations aspects of the wedding. Every detail of the wedding, down to the gown, was part of a Joseph P. Kennedy production aimed at portraying the new couple as exemplars of youthful glamour, family virtue, and upward mobility.

Joe, the old Hollywood impresario, had arranged for photos of the newlyweds to run on the front pages of *The New York Times* and *The Boston Globe*. He was so concerned about projecting the right image that for the first time, he began to worry about Jack's reckless womanizing.

"Joe discussed with me Jack's problem with women," George Smathers said. "He told me, 'George, you'd better try to keep Jack more discreet. He can't do it in the public eye. Jack can't afford to have people talk about his messing around.'"

It was one thing for a Catholic politician who aspired to the White House to fool around while he was single; it was quite another thing for him to flaunt his affairs once he got married. At the age of 36, it was time for Jack to grow up and put aside his adolescent exhibitionism.

As his wedding day approached, Jack seemed willing to turn over a new leaf. He abruptly put a stop to his 20-year-long correspondence with Lem Billings, his homosexual roommate from Choate; from then on, there would be no more lewd letters from Jack about his sexual exploits. And in an effort to make a clean breast of things with Jackie, Jack took his bride aside and told her all about his life as a compulsive womanizer.

"Jack unloaded," George Smathers said. "He confessed everything to Jackie. She handled it pretty well. She was aware that Jack was a Kennedy and that Joe had never been an example of virtue. Jack wasn't a surprise to her. Women of that class and generation were raised to turn a blind eye to sexual peccadilloes. But Jack talked too much, and he lived to regret that conversation. He was just like Jackie's father, Black Jack. Neither of those guys could change."

When Janet returned, she announced to her daughters that Jack Bouvier was drunk in his hotel room.

The news was a heavy blow to Jackie.

"I knew your father would do something like this to ruin the day," Janet said. "I just knew it. Why you insisted he be here to do this to us, I'll never know."

"How drunk is he?" Jackie asked.

"Drunk," said Janet.

Suddenly, Jackie turned on her mother.

"It's all your fault," she shouted. "You humiliated Daddy by excluding him from all the prenuptial dinner parties.

No wonder he got drunk."

Janet tried to interrupt, but Jackie would not let her.

"You couldn't stand it when Daddy attended Lee's wedding and gave her away," Jackie said. "You tried to stop Daddy from coming to Newport. You only care about what people say — how they'll compare Daddy to Uncle Hughdie."

"I will not permit Jack Bouvier to attend the wedding!" Janet screamed.

Jackie glared at her mother.

"She desperately wanted her father to give her away," noted her cousin, John H. Davis, "but with all those reporters, columnists, and photographers Joe Kennedy had invited to the wedding, could she risk a Jack Bouvier unsteady on his feet? Wouldn't it be safer, from a publicity standpoint, to have Uncle Hugh escort her down the aisle?"

Jackie's face reflected her inner conflict.

"Showing up on Hugh Auchincloss's arm — well, that was more prestigious than her father's arm, anyway," said her stepsister Nina. "And Jackie was always very conscious of the impression she was making. You couldn't make a better impression with the rich and socially prominent than with an Auchincloss."

Jackie fled the room in tears.

A few miles away at the Viking Hotel, Michael Canfield, Lee's husband, observed Jack Bouvier as he dressed.

Michael had been secretly assigned by Janet Auchincloss to get her former husband so intoxicated that he could not possibly make it to the wedding. Michael had stocked the room with the best champagne, liquor, ice, and set-ups, and had made sure that Jack Bouvier had round-the-clock room service.

So far, the plot did not appear to be working. No matter how much Michael encouraged him to drink, Black Jack refused to get falling-down drunk.

He was, however, tipsy, and was beginning to slur his words. He referred to Jackie as "all thingsh holy." His feeling for Jackie had always verged on the incestuous, and he hated the idea of giving her away. It galled him that he would have to walk down the aisle under the withering gaze of the dreaded Auchinclosses and their snobby Newport friends. Everyone would know that he was not paying for his own daughter's wedding. But despite all this, he was determined to make Jackie proud of him.

He stood in front of the mirror, wearing a dress shirt, boxer shorts, black silk socks, and garters. He sported a deep tan, which he had acquired over the past few weeks in the south of France and East Hampton. He looked amazingly trim, thanks to a regimen of diet and exercise. A new, made-to-order cutaway, freshly pressed the night before, hung on a hanger. On the dresser were cufflinks, studs, and his dead father's pearl stickpin.

Michael offered him another drink, then went into an adjoining room and called Jack Bouvier's twin sisters, Maude and Michelle, who were staying at the nearby Hotel Munchener King.

Somebody had better get over here right away, Michael said. Jack is drunk.

The sisters dispatched their husbands — John E. Davis and Harrington Putnam.

"How are you coming along, Jack?" Davis asked as soon as he arrived.

"Great," Bouvier said. "Never felt better in my life."

Black Jack drained another highball.

"He had trouble with the tie, and Putnam had to help him," John E. Davis's son, John H., said. "Then he couldn't find his pearl stickpin. Before long, he was going over to the tray and ice bucket to pour himself another drink."

A chain of communications was set up: John E. Davis and Harrington Putnam at the Viking to their wives, Maude and Michelle, at the Munchener King; the Bouvier twins to Janet Auchincloss at Hammersmith Farm. Was Jack Bouvier fit to perform?

"He was by no means drunk, but he had had a few drinks, and the big question was whether he could walk a straight line and hold himself steady throughout the ceremony," John H. Davis said. "What was to be avoided, at all costs, was to have the father of the bride stumble or fall flat on his face in front of six hundred people, who included members of the nation's press. . . .

"Now things were down to the wire, and the responsibility hung heavy on all concerned," Davis continued. "Jack had begun to rail at the Auchinclosses and how they had excluded him from all the prenuptial events, an ominous sign. However, [John E. Davis] and Mr. Putnam took this in stride — my father had spent half his life listening to Jack Bouvier rail against the Auchinclosses — and ultimately came to the decision that Jack could function adequately. . . . True, his tongue was a little thick, and there was a slight unsteadiness to his gait, but he was coherent and physically fit. There was no doubt about it in my father or in Harrington Putnam's minds: Jack Bouvier could take Jacqueline down the aisle at St. Mary's and do himself and her proud.

"This was communicated to the twins at the Munchener King, who, in turn, communicated it to Hammersmith Farm. But the twins were wasting their breath. Janet Auchincloss would not hear of it. Hugh was now ready to give Jackie away. Time was running out. Soon they would all have to leave for St. Mary's. If the twins brought Jack Bouvier with them, Janet would not let him in the door, and there would be an ugly scene."

"Keep him there," Janet said. "Don't let him out of his room . . . even for *one second.*"

A crowd of more than 3,000 people pressed against the police barricades along Spring Street as Jackie stepped out of her limousine in front of St. Mary's Church. Inside, sunlight streamed through the old stained-glass windows. Ann Lowe, the dressmaker, held the bride's train high so that it would not be trampled. With the first chords of the traditional wedding march, Ann Lowe let go, and Jackie floated down the aisle on the arm of Hugh Auchincloss.

"Newport had filed in on the bride's side, and the Kennedys were on the groom's side," said Marion "Oatsie" Leiter, an old Newport resident. "Newport was dressed only a little bit better than if they'd been to the beach for lunch — neat linen dresses. The Kennedys were dressed to the nines, like chic new money."

"I think Janet Auchincloss was appalled at these blue-suited, baby-faced friends of the Kennedys, these Irish politicians who were swarming all over the place," said Philip Geyelin, the former editorial page editor of *The Washington Post.* "It was not your gracious Newport happening. I remember the Newport gentry looked down at the beefy, vulgar men in their bright-blue suits."

John Kennedy, who moved with ease between these two worlds, was waiting for Jackie at the altar. There were red scratch marks on his face, the result of having fallen into a briar patch the day before during a touch football game. He was flanked by 10 bridesmaids in pale pink taffeta set off by claret sashes. His brother Bobby was the best man.

The couple knelt before the Most Reverend Richard J. Cushing, Archbishop of Boston. Jack's back was acting up, and he was in pain during most of the 40-minute-long nuptial mass.

Finally, Archbishop Cushing pronounced them husband and wife, and they exchanged a chaste kiss. Then they walked slowly toward the door, smiling and nodding to well-wishers on both sides of the aisle. Suddenly, Jackie spotted a familiar face off in a corner, almost hidden in the shadows.

It was her father.

What was he doing sitting there among the spectators? Was he drunk? If he was sober, why hadn't he come to the church in time to walk her down the aisle? What had happened?

There were tears in Black Jack's eyes as he watched his daughter walk by. He was slumped in a pew next to Jack Kennedy's friend Charles Spalding, who was one of the ushers.

"Jack had called me and said, 'Do me a favor,'" said Spalding. "'Would you take Black Jack into the church?' He showed up at the church, a little unsteady on his feet. He understood that he would not be permitted to participate in the ceremony. He had to stay in the background. I sat next to him through the whole ceremony. There was no difficulty. He just sat there and handled himself perfectly okay."

Jackie was blinded by the sunlight at the door. She could hear a tremendous roar from the crowd and the familiar clack-clack-clack of the cameramen's Speed Graphics. Gradually, her eyes adjusted to the light and she saw hundreds of people breaking through the police lines. The cops struggled to catch them and push them back, but they eluded the police and rushed forward, trying to get closer to the senator and his new bride.

Jack flashed a toothy smile and waved to the crowd. He basked in their adulation.

But Jackie recoiled at the frenzied scene of ungoverned public emotion.

The cameramen pressed closer, popping on and on with their Speed Graphics.

Jackie was blinded again, completely unnerved, and terrified.

Off Center

They spent a week in Acapulco in a pink villa overlooking the ocean.

Jackie wrote her father a long letter of forgiveness, which Black Jack's partner, who saw it, described as "one of the most touching, compassionate letters" he had ever read, one that "only a rare and noble spirit could have written."

Jack caught a nine-foot sailfish, played tennis, studied a Berlitz guide to Spanish, and flirted at a party with some local senoritas.

Then they flew to Los Angeles, drove up the old Pacific Coast Road to Santa Barbara, and checked into the San Ysidro Ranch. During his heyday in the movie capital, Joe Kennedy had shacked up with Gloria Swanson at San Ysidro, a luxurious retreat in the foothills of the Santa Ynez Mountains, and he had recommended the place to his son as the perfect honeymoon hideaway.

But by the time the newlyweds arrived there in late September, Jack was bored.

"Boredom was something he fought all the time," said Charlie Bartlett. "I think this was a real sort of goad — he could not stand to be bored, and he would not be bored. It made him rather exhausting to be around for a long period of time."

Jack and Jackie settled into Hillside Cottage, a two-bedroom suite decorated in English country style with lots of organdies, chintz, and bright hunting prints. Jack put in a call to Evelyn Lincoln, and while he waited for the long-distance connection to go through to Washington, he looked out the window. Over the tops of eucalyptus trees, he could see the shimmering Pacific Ocean.

"What's going on back there?" he inquired.

"He asked me to set up certain appointments for him when he got back," Evelyn Lincoln said. "He carried on business: 'Get me this and get me that.' He missed being at the center of things. His mind wasn't on any honeymoon."

As Jack had once told a friend, "It's the chase I like — not the kill. Once I get a woman, I'm not interested in carrying on."

Now that he and Jackie were married,

the chase was over, and so apparently was the thrill. Jackie was not like the ripe, voluptuous women Jack was sexually attracted to. His satisfaction depended on sensuous women who were willing to do anything in bed. Jackie knew how to be coquettish. She could make playful romantic gestures. But she was far too ladylike to be really sluttish.

Jackie knew all about the dangers that lurked in a husband's boredom, and she teased Jack about doing to her on their honeymoon what her father had done to her mother on the *Aquitania*, when Black Jack had slipped away from his bride and slept with tobacco heiress Doris Duke.

"Don't let your better part get the best of you," she said.

She also knew that the way to capture Jack's attention was to appeal to his vanity, and she had written a poem about him in the style of Stephen Vincent Benét.

He would find love
He would never find peace
For he must go seeking
The Golden Fleece

But Jack became increasingly restless and fidgety. When they discussed where Jackie should live after they got back home, Jack suggested that she move in with his parents in Hyannis Port. In fact, he said, maybe she wanted to return by herself *now* — while he went on to San Francisco alone to visit his old Navy chum Red Fay?

Jackie declined his offer.

A couple of days after they arrived, the manager of the San Ysidro Ranch asked Hal Boucher, a photographer for the *Santa Barbara News Press*, to take some publicity stills of the famous couple.

"I had Jack and Jackie walk toward the camera," said Boucher, "and I snapped a few shots. Kennedy said to me something like, 'I hope you're not sending these pictures anywhere, especially not to *The Boston Globe.* My constituents would not be very happy if they saw me in this sunny, beautiful place having a good time.' "

Boucher wielded the same heavy Speed Graphic that Jackie had used at *The Washington Times-Herald*, but she did not show the slightest interest.

"She was very quiet," Boucher said. "Didn't even say two words. I had the impression that she was being made to do this by her husband under protest."

After the photo session, Jack and Jackie walked down East Valley Road to the San Ysidro Pharmacy, a large, rustic establishment with a gift shop and a coffee shop. He bought an armload of magazines — among them, *Time*, *Harper's*, and *Atlantic Monthly* — and the daily papers.

He scanned the headlines. While he had been on his honeymoon, Senator Joseph McCarthy had gotten married, the United States and France had announced a new plan to destroy the Communists in Vietnam, and President Eisenhower had appointed as chief justice of the United States the governor of California, Earl Warren.

"It was a very warm time of the year," said Carol Crowely, then a salesgirl at the pharmacy. "Jackie had on a printed floral dress with a scoop neck and short sleeves. Her hair was chopped short, and she wore very little makeup. Kennedy wore shorts. His hair was a mess. That boy needed Vitalis. They sat down and ordered sodas. And then the strangest thing happened. He sat there and read the newspapers and magazines. He ignored her. And for thirty minutes, she just sat there and looked around with nobody to talk to."

NINE

What Jackie Knew

October, 1953–December, 1955

Scenes from a New Marriage

The volume on the record player was turned up so high that at first Jackie could not hear the telephone ringing. It was late in the afternoon, and she was still dressed in her pajamas and robe. She was wandering around her modest row house in the Georgetown section of Washington, smoking cigarettes, biting her nails, and singing along with the record.

". . . Hurry home, come home to me, set me free, free from doubt and free from long—ing . . ."

At last she became aware of the insistent ringing and picked up the phone. It was Jack's secretary, Evelyn Lincoln.

"The senator is leaving the office now," Evelyn said.

Jackie went into the kitchen to start dinner. Like most young wives of the early 1950s, she was interested in the popular new art of gourmet cooking. But she did not have much talent in this particular domestic area.

She was much better at interior deco-rating. She had done her living room in eighteenth-century French antiques, framed drawings, and tailored uphol-stered furniture. She had a passion for taffeta draperies, and although the house was rented, she had spent a great deal of money on the striped fabric and customized valances.

Once the house had been finished, however, she was at a loss what to do. She was only 24 years old, and despite a certain flair and sophistication, she was ill-equipped for the responsibilities of married life and the rough-and-tum-ble world of politics. She wanted to make Jack happy but did not know how.

She continued cooking dinner.

"I'd heard those silly stories about the bride burning things," she said, "and I just knew everything was going right when suddenly — I don't know what went wrong — you couldn't see the place for smoke. And when I tried to pull the chops out of the oven, the door seemed to collapse. The pan slid out and the fat splattered. One of the chops fell on the floor, but I put it on the plate anyway. The chocolate sauce was burning and exploding. What a smell! I couldn't get the spoon out of the chocolate. It was like a rock. And the coffee had all boiled away."

In New York City for a day of shopping and personal care, Jackie entered the Helena Rubenstein salon at Fifth Avenue and 52nd Street, and asked for Lawrence, her regular hairdresser.

"Lawrence is out sick today," the receptionist told her. "We can give you somebody else."

The receptionist put her lips close to the microphone on her desk, and announced over the public-address system, "Kenneth, Kenneth . . . come to the reception."

In a few moments, a tall, thin man in his late twenties appeared at the desk. He introduced himself to Mrs. Kennedy by his full name — Kenneth Battelle.

A poor boy from upstate New York, Kenneth had risen in the ranks of his craft to the point where he did the hair of Gillis McGill and Melissa Weston — two of the top fashion models of the day — as well as practically every magazine beauty editor in New York City. He escorted Jackie back to his booth and

ALAMEDA FREE LIBRARY

studied her thick, strong hair in the reflection of the mirror.

"Mm-hmm," he said at last. "I think your hair is too short."

"Why?" asked Jackie.

"Well," said Kenneth, "you're very tall, and you have big bones, and I think it makes your head look too small, and I think it's too curly."

"Do you really think so?" Jackie said. No hairdresser had ever spoken to her this way before.

"Yes," said Kenneth. "And we can use rollers to smooth the front, to stretch it, make it look longer."

"All right," Jackie said. "Go ahead."

"You have to remember," Kenneth said of his first meeting with Jackie, "in those days women were running around with their hair sprayed to a fare-thee-well. I used to go out on the road with the magazines, and we'd do makeovers, and I'd say, "What's your hair problem?' And they'd say,'Oh, my hair blows in the wind.' You can laugh at that, but in those days, it wasn't supposed to blow in the wind. But certain people simply develop their own kind of look. Mrs. Paley was like that. And so was Mrs. Kennedy. She paid no attention to the latest style. She was who she was. Her style was *her* style."

One day, Jackie joined a group of other Senate wives in the Caucus Room of the Senate Russell Office Building for a bandage-rolling charity event on behalf of the Red Cross.

These were the same women whose husbands came to her Georgetown house, sprawled all over her furniture, broke her Sèvres ashtrays, and dropped cigarette butts in her vases. Nonetheless, Jackie was making an effort to be a political wife, which meant consorting with people who bored her, charming men and women she did not like, and ignoring those who did not figure into Jack's timetable.

In an earlier era, a 36-year-old senator would have had to wait at least a couple of decades before he could run for president. But television had changed all that, transforming American politics into an exercise in public relations.

Cool and laid back, with a self-deprecating sense of humor, Jack proved to be the most telegenic politician in America. In the first few months of his marriage, he appeared on Edward R. Murrow's *Person to Person*, *Time's Man of the Year Review*, *Meet the Press*, and a host of other TV programs.

"It was the goddamndest thing," Lyndon Johnson said later. "Here was a young whippersnapper, malaria-ridden and yellah, sickly, sickly. He never said a word of importance in the Senate and he never did a thing. . . . Now, I will admit that he had a good sense of humor and that he looked awfully good on the goddamn television screen, and through it all he was a pretty decent fellow. But his growing hold on the American people was simply a mystery to me."

The Kennedy publicity machine started grinding out newspaper and magazine articles. Some of them, like "A City Senator Looks at the Farm Problem," were submitted under Jack's byline by his brilliant new ghost writer, Theodore Sorensen. Other times, selected journalists were offered access to the perfect young couple, who were portrayed enjoying glamorous upscale pursuits — sailing, oil painting, and reading poetry to each other.

What these personality pieces failed

to reveal, however, was that Jack was rarely at home with his wife.

"During our first year of marriage," Jackie said, "we were like gypsies living in and out of a suitcase. It was turbulent. Jack made speeches all over the country, and was never home more than two nights at a time. . . . I was alone almost every weekend. It was all wrong. Politics was sort of my enemy."

But she made the effort for Jack, and that was how she happened to find herself in the vast Senate Caucus Room, with its marbled columns, chandeliers, and thick burgundy carpet, chattering with the wives of other senators. Before lunch at the bandage-rolling event, the women went to a locker room, took off their clothes, and put on Red Cross uniforms. Jackie was wearing the finest silk undergarments, and some of the wives came over and asked if they could touch them. Their behavior filled her with revulsion.

Gradually, however, she began to adapt.

She went to Capitol Hill and sat with the other Senate wives in the Gallery, watching her husband perform his legislative duties and deliver his speeches. She changed her newspaper reading habits; for the first time, she glanced over the hard news on the front page as well as the style and culture sections in the back. When she realized that she was totally ignorant about politics and foreign affairs — the two fields that interested Jack the most — she attempted to rectify the situation by enrolling in a course in American history at the Georgetown University Foreign Service School.

Still, she and Jack had a hard time.

Jack's back was acting up again. The pain made him irritable and short-tempered. He was in a quandary over what to do. He did not want the voters in Massachusetts to think that he was a cripple, and so he hid his crutches when visitors came to his office.

For her part, Jackie could not get pregnant no matter how she tried. This was exactly what Joe Kennedy had predicted when he told Morton Downey, "I don't think porcelain can carry babies." The Kennedys silently blamed her for the barren marriage, even though it was not at all clear that it was Jackie's fault.

In fact, Jack had long been concerned

that his chronic venereal disease — nongonococcal urethritis, or chlamydia — would make him infertile. During the first year of his marriage, he visited Dr. William P. Herbst, an eminent Boston urologist, and had his sperm count tested to see if he was capable of fathering children.

He shared his concerns with Jackie. She knew that he was taking enormous amounts of antibiotics to eradicate the bacteria that caused his sexually transmitted disease, and she lived in dread that he might infect her.

"Where you have a man who carries nongonococcal urethritis," said Dr. Atilla Toth, a specialist in the relationship between infections and infertility, "the woman with whom he has sex can sometimes achieve one pregnancy. However, after the first intercourse, the woman becomes infected, and the bacteria usually stays behind and multiplies, and her subsequent pregnancies can be affected. Her second baby might come to term immature, and subsequent pregnancies can be miscarried.

"Furthermore," said Dr. Toth, "some of these bacteria may infect her ovaries, and after she gives birth, those sluggish ovaries will not produce the normal complement of hormones, and she can go through hormonal withdrawal and severe depression that can last for months."

On Sunday night, May 2, 1954, Jack and Jackie attended a dinner in honor of Langdon Marvin's thirty-fifth birthday. The party was held at the F Street Club, a Victorian residence that had once belonged to Laura Gross, a famous Washington hostess.

Twenty-four prominent Washingtonians assembled in the living room of the club, which had opened in 1933. The members, who included Arthur Krock and Hughdie Auchincloss, had kept the club furnished as a private home, with comfortable upholstered furniture, red carpeting, chandeliers, and an oil portrait of Laura Gross.

Timothy, the butler, served cocktails. Langdon Marvin was drinking more heavily than ever, and he looked terrible. He often ended his nights sprawled in the gutter. His behavior had become erratic. It was whispered that his nose had been bloodied on more than one occasion for making unwelcomed homosexual advances to men in seedy bars.

After drinks, the guests moved to the dining room, and Jack sat next to Priscilla Johnson, a young woman whose prominent cheekbones and little-girl voice gave her an uncanny resemblance to Jackie. Priscilla had once worked in Jack's office as a researcher; she was now employed in New York City as a Russian translator at the *Current Digest of the Soviet Press.*

"I got married so that people wouldn't think I was a queer," Jack said to Priscilla.

"I was sitting on Jack's right, and he was making a play for me but looking across the centerpiece of flowers on the table at Jackie," Priscilla said. "He was eating her up with his eyes. She was like a trophy. He was proud to have her."

Jack played with his food while he toyed with Priscilla.

"He came on strong," Priscilla said. "He made a pitch to me that no self-respecting woman would say yes to. He was propositioning me in front of his wife, and I had the feeling that he wanted to be told no."

Like many Irish-Catholic men of his time, Jack divided the female sex into two categories — wanton women for pleasure, and madonna types for bearing children. Sex was either animalistic (and fun) or pure (and boring). In either case, the man was always supposed to feel that he was superior to the woman and that he was immune to her female powers.

But Jack also had his personal code of honor. He never attempted to bribe or frighten a woman into submitting to him. That was simply not his way. He never pressured a woman or strong-armed her. He never promised a woman a good job or a present or money. His approach was nonchalant. And that was part of the extraordinary power he had over women. He did not really seem to care.

The denizens of Washington were used to politicians with a roving eye. What made Jack different was that he flaunted his flirtations in his wife's presence. People expected some reaction from Jackie; they would stare at her, wondering when she would erupt in rage and indignation. But Jackie always acted as though she did not notice what Jack was up to, even though only a blind person could have missed his flagrant behavior.

But friends noticed a change in Jackie.

"She wasn't the same carefree, happy Jackie Bouvier any more," Charlie Bartlett said. "She was much more solemn."

Jack could not understand why Jackie was so unhappy.

"Jack appreciated her," said Chuck Spalding. "He really brightened when she appeared. You could see it in his eyes; he'd follow her around the room watching to see what she'd do next. Jackie *interested* him, which was not true of many women. Unfortunately, however, this wasn't enough. There were many ways to treat a woman, but as he saw it, only one way to treat a wife — and that was the way his father had treated his mother."

"Jack kept assuring us that Jackie didn't suspect," said Jim Reed, "when it was obvious that she knew exactly what was happening. He was so disciplined in so many ways. Discipline was, after all, the secret of his success. But when it came to women, he was a different person. It was Jekyll and Hyde."

"While on one level Jackie must have known what she was getting into by marrying a thirty-six-year-old playboy," said Lem Billings, "she never suspected the depth of Jack's need for other women. Nor was she prepared for the humiliation she would suffer when she found herself stranded at parties while Jack would suddenly disappear with some pretty young girl. Before the marriage, I think she found Jack's appeal to other women tantalizing — I suspect it reminded her of the magic appeal her handsome, rakish father had had with women all his life — but once she was married, and once it was happening to her, it was much harder to accept."

Collapse and Calamity

Shortly after Congress adjourned in August, 1954, Jack flew up to Hyannis Port. His father was shocked by his appearance. His son's weight had dropped from 175 to 140 pounds, and he had developed an unwholesome pallor.

"My back is getting worse," Jack explained. "I can't make it from my office to the Senate chamber for a quorum call, even with my crutches. If I drop a paper clip or a pencil, I've got to ask Evelyn Lincoln to come pick it up for me. The pain has gotten so bad, I can't sleep at night."

Joe listened, but he was already a step ahead of Jack. He was concerned about the political fallout from Jack's failing health. He had heard from Ted Reardon, one of Jack's aides, that newspaper reporters were starting to snoop around. *Was it true that Senator Kennedy had cancer? Was he going to drop out of politics?* Finally, Ernest Warden, a Boston reporter, asked Ted Reardon to clear up the medical mystery by releasing the senator's health records.

"No," said Reardon, "Old Joe doesn't want that to be done."

Jack told his father that he had consulted the best specialists in the country — Dr. Philip D. Wilson at the New York Hospital for Special Surgery, and a team of orthopedic surgeons at the Lahey Clinic in Boston. They all agreed that he would become a cripple unless he underwent a complicated surgical procedure known as a double spinal fusion.

"I'm going under the knife," Jack told his father.

The doctors had recommended that the operation be performed in two stages — a lumbosacral fusion and a sacroiliac fusion. Jack was determined to have both done in one go-for-broke procedure.

There was a catch, however. Because of Jack's Addison's disease, which significantly lowered his resistance to infection, Dr. Ephraim Shorr, chief of the endocrinology service at the New York Hospital–Cornell Medical Center, was not sure that the senator could survive the severe degree of trauma involved in such an operation.

"What do the doctors say about your chances of coming through such an operation alive?" Joe asked.

"No better than fifty-fifty," Jack replied. "But I'd rather be dead than spend the rest of my life on these goddamned crutches."

Since the death of Joe Junior, the whole family had come to count on Jack. He embodied all their hopes and dreams for the future. But he was prepared to subject himself to an operation that carried a greater risk than Russian roulette. For the Kennedys, it was a calamity.

Joe argued passionately with his son that he could lead a full, rich life even if he was confined to a wheelchair. After all, look at the incredible life FDR had managed to lead despite his physical incapacity.

But he was wasting his breath. For the first time, Joe had no control over Jack. His son had made up his own mind.

"Don't worry, Dad," Jack said. "I'll make it through."

That night, Joe went to bed around midnight but was unable to sleep. He got up at 1:00 and sat for hours in the small library off the living room in Hyannis Port. His mind kept wandering back to the last letter he had received from Joe Junior, in which his beloved eldest son had assured his father that there was no danger involved in his bombing mission.

In anguish, Joe cried out. The sound was so loud that it reached all the way to the second floor and awakened Rose from sleep.

Jackie spent the night before the operation in Jack's room at the New York Hospital for Special Surgery. Early on the morning of October 21, a nurse gave Jack a shot of an opium solution. An hour later, an orderly came in and lifted his emaciated body onto a gurney.

Jackie grasped Jack's hand as he was wheeled out of the room and down the long corridor. At the elevator, she bent down, whispered something in his ear, then kissed him on the lips. A moment later, the door of the elevator opened and closed, and she was left standing alone under the harsh fluorescent light.

"It was the first time in my life I really prayed," said Jackie.

As Jack slipped into unconsciousness in the operating room, he was aware he might never wake again. A breathing tube was inserted in his trachea, and he was turned face down. Drs. Wilson and Shorr went to work on his back. He was given four pints of blood during the three-hour operation.

At first, the hospital put out a press release saying that the operation on Jack had been "successful and his condition is good." But on his third day of recovery, his doctors' worst fears came true: Jack was struck with a staph infection in his urinary tract, and it spread quickly to the rest of his body. Antibiotics did not work, and Jack's immune system was too weak to fight back. He was placed on the critical list.

Then he lapsed into a coma.

That night, Dr. Wilson summoned Jack's parents and Jackie to the hospital and told them that he did not expect his patient to live until morning. Still a newlywed, Jackie was on the verge of becoming a widow.

In tears, Joe called his old friend, Francis Cardinal Spellman, Archbishop of New York, and asked him to come to the hospital to perform the rite of extreme unction on his son.

The cardinal, a figure of immense power in the American Catholic Church, arrived within the hour. He was a diminutive man, with little hands and an innocent, chubby face. He draped a purple stole around his neck and closeted himself alone with Jack to hear his confession. Then he opened the door and motioned Joe and Rose and Jackie back into the room to assist him in the Holy Communion.

"Indulgentiam, absolutionem, et remissionem peccatorum tuorum tribuat tibi omnipotens et misericors Dominus . . ."

"Amen," said Joe and Rose.

"Ecce Agnus Dei, ecce qui tollit peccata mundi . . ."

"Amen," sobbed Jackie.

Then the cardinal began anointing Jack's eyes, ears, nose, mouth, hands, and feet.

A devastated Joe Kennedy visited Arthur Krock in his office at *The New York Times*. Krock had seen Joe like this only once before — after the news of the death of Joe Junior.

"Jack is dying," Joe said.

"Then he wept, for the first and last time, in my presence," Krock said.

Profile in Expediency

Jack rallied during the night.

Over the following two weeks, he fought for his life, and by the beginning of November, he was no longer on the critical list. But he was still ill, and Joe and Jackie never left his bedside.

"Jackie brought him magazines and newspapers by the armload," said Evelyn Lincoln, "but his reading speed — once his friend — now became an enemy. He was able to get through the material so swiftly it was impossible to keep him supplied."

Jack telephoned friends and urged them to send books.

"For God's sweet sake, Oatsie, have you got anything to read?" he asked his favorite Washington socialite, Marion Leiter.

"Do you like spy stories?" Oatsie asked.

"Sure."

"Well, I have an Englishman who's just written a book that I think might amuse you. It's called *Casino Royale* and it's by Ian Fleming."

Oatsie wasn't the only one who tried to buck up the young senator. One evening, Jackie arrived all dressed up in an elegant black suit.

"Where are you going?" Jack asked.

"I'm going to meet another man," she said, eating the mashed potatoes off his tray. "You know, Jack, there are plenty of men around who want to take me out."

Jack smiled; he enjoyed her teasing.

Lee flew in from London and decorated his hospital room with balloons, which she tied with strings to the foot of his bed. Jackie bought a popgun to shoot at the balloons. Hélène Arpels brought him a pair of kissing fish in a plastic bag from Macy's. Langdon Marvin smuggled in some sleeping pills. And Jack's old flame, Flo Pritchett Smith, arranged for Grace Kelly to dress up as a night nurse, and pay Jack a surprise visit.

"Jack, Jack, wake up," whispered Grace, who had just won the Best Actress Oscar for her performance in *The Country Girl.*

Jack opened his eyes and looked into the face of the cool, blonde beauty. He broke into a smile.

"Grace?" he mumbled. "Is that really you?"

"Yes," she said. "Jack, you're going to be fine."

Jack's arms, legs, and neck were immobilized by traction. But he managed to hoist himself up a few inches with the aid of a metal bar.

"When I get out of here," he said, "you're going to be my first dancing partner."

"The marvel was that he could make jokes about his own pain," Chuck Spalding said. "He'd turn everything into a funny remark, sometimes at the expense of the doctor or the nurse or himself or the hospital or science or anything.

"He laughed without much noise, but he really laughed," Spalding continued. "It was not a guffaw; it was more of a chuckle, but it was a full laugh. . . . He always went on to add something to whatever started the laugh in the first place. That's how he got out of it. Until the pain tired him, and he'd go to sleep."

Jack tried to keep up with the news

in the newspapers and on television. But after years of being at the center of action, he suddenly felt like a passive spectator to the most dramatic events of the time.

While he was recuperating, the Supreme Court ruled that the doctrine of separate-but-equal in public education was unconstitutional. The Communist Vietminh overran the French Garrison at Dien Bien Phu in Vietnam. And the Senate finally got around to voting on a censure motion against Senator Joseph McCarthy, a close friend of the Kennedys' and a man who was hugely popular among Irish-Catholic voters in Massachusetts.

Jack did not cast an absentee ballot either for or against McCarthy — an act of political expediency that was deeply resented by liberal Democrats for years to come.

Two months after the operation, with Jack still in poor condition, his father decided to fly him down to Palm Beach for the Christmas holidays. On the way to the airport, the invalid was accompanied in the back of the ambulance by Jackie, who was dressed in a black mohair overcoat and a white beret. It was a cold blustery day, and snow was moving in serpentine drifts around the airplane on the tarmac. Jackie got out and watched as a pair of ambulance drivers in leather jackets pulled out the stretcher.

Jack's bare head lay on a white pillow. He was wrapped in a checkered blanket and strapped down with a belt. When a cold gust of wind blew the blanket off, exposing his chest, a nurse quickly tucked the blanket under his chin with her white-gloved hands. The stretcher was carried up the stairs into the plane.

Several hours later, they arrived at the Kennedys' Palm Beach villa, which was set behind a high stucco wall at 1095 Ocean Boulevard. There was a large main house with two wings, one of which had been converted into a makeshift hospital for Jack. It was a cheerful house, bustling with young Kennedys and their guests, and the rattling of palm fronds and the roar of the surf could be heard through the open shutters of Jack's room.

Jack spent the mornings in bed, waited on hand and foot by Jackie, who dressed the ugly, suppurating wound in his back.

One morning, to cheer him up, she put on a skinny, one-piece bathing suit with polka dots.

"Gosh," she said, "I look like some cheap little secretary."

But despite her efforts, Jack showed no signs of improvement. His spirits, once so lighthearted and gay, began to sink.

"It was a terrible time," Lem Billings said. "He was bitter and low. We came close to losing him. I don't just mean losing his life; I mean losing him as a person."

Jackie grew depressed. When no one was looking, she sneaked into the kitchen and gobbled spoonfuls of caviar and drank vodka. As the child of an alcoholic father, she had always been wary of the effects of alcohol. Now, suddenly, she was hitting the bottle and did not seem to care.

Days passed, and the wound in Jack's back continued to ooze pus and pieces of bone.

"Is it still open?" he asked Lem. "Is stuff still running out of it? Does it smell bad?"

Jack sat by the swimming pool, playing Monopoly with Lem and exposing the gaping hole in his back to the sun. He reread his favorite book, *Melbourne*, by David Cecil, and made handwritten notes.

1. European History
   2. More interesting because of leisure class . . .
   3. American *not* interesting because no leisure class
      Struggle to survive
      Except on Western frontier not glamorous
         Women either prostitutes or housewives
         Do not play much of a role in cultural or intellectual life of country

During these difficult days, Jackie's houseguest was her best French friend, Solange de La Bruyère, the wife of a wealthy count.

"Solange," Jack said, "you have a d.d.s."

"What is a d.d.s.?" Solange asked.

"A deep, dark secret," Jack said.

"I was married at the time," Solange

said, "but Jack thought that I was planning a trip to meet an amour."

Solange and Jackie shared a room near the pool. The room next door was Jack's.

"Jackie!" Jack cried out one morning. Jackie went to help.

As soon as she was gone, Joe Kennedy came into Solange's room and tried to get into bed with her. A week before, he had tried the same thing with Lee. Solange kicked him out of her bed. Later, she told Jackie about the sordid experience.

"Oh, don't worry, Solange," said Jackie. "He's had all the showgirls in the world. Now he wants nice girls."

"By February," Rose said, "Joe came to the conclusion that something had to be done, so he flew to New York to see the doctors and came back with the recommendation for a second operation. He recognized the high risk involved, but now he understood what Jack had meant in the beginning about not wanting to live unless he could really live."

On February 15, 1955, Jack went back into the hospital to have the silver plate in his back removed and a bone graft put in its place. This time, the operation proved more successful. Back in Palm Beach, he was joined by his cronies — Red Fay, Lem Billings, and Dave Powers — and his old zest for life began to return. For the first time in months, the pain receded enough for him to think about work.

Ten years before, during his recovery from a prior back operation, Jack had received word that his brother Joe had been killed in action; he had responded to the news by putting together a book of tributes called *As We Remember Joe.* This time, he began to work on a far more ambitious endeavor — a book about a group of senators who had taken principled positions on controversial issues. It was to be called *Profiles in Courage.*

"In choosing to write about the moral courage of others," said historian Doris Kearns Goodwin, "Jack Kennedy may well have been trying to sort out his thoughts about his own courage. Of all the virtues, Robert Kennedy later wrote, Jack Kennedy admired courage the most. Yet, while his physical courage was undeniable — courage under fire, to endure illness and pain with silence and good humor — it is less clear that he possessed the kind of moral courage he enshrined in his book, the willingness to risk position, power, career for the sake of some abiding conviction."

Jack asked Evelyn Lincoln to send him dozens of books from the Library of Congress. He also solicited ideas from historians and friends.

"We used to discuss chapters," said Charlie Bartlett. "I mean, we'd talk about it, and I read some of it and gave him ideas. I think he was really into it."

Propped up by pillows under his knees and behind his shoulders, Jack dictated his ideas to Jackie. He worked on the outline and came up with many of the organizing principles for the book. Jackie took it all down and shipped off memos to Evelyn Lincoln.

Politics is a jungle [Jack wrote] . . . torn between the local interest and the national interest — between the private good and the politician and the general good.

But the bulk of the research and much of the writing were the work of others, including Professor Jules Davids of Georgetown University, who had been a teacher of Jackie's. Jack also received help from Arthur Schlesinger Jr., James MacGregor Burns, Allan Nevins, and Arthur Holcombe. Theodore Sorensen, Jack's thorough, precise young aide, unified all the drafts into a complete manuscript, for which he was paid $6,000 in royalties by Harper and Brothers, the publisher.

"Jack wrote me about individual questions in the book," said Evan Thomas, his editor at Harper and Brothers. "But the significance of Sorensen's role was that he provided the more intelligent voice."

"I think Jack supervised all of it," said George Smathers, "but how much of it he actually wrote, I would say probably very little. He was physically not able to do much writing."

Torment

In the spring of 1955, Jackie left Palm Beach and flew back to Washington to go house-hunting. Not far from Merrywood, on the Virginia side of the Potomac River, she found a white brick Georgian mansion called Hickory Hill. Stately yet humane in its proportions, Hickory Hill reminded her of her beloved Merrywood. There were stables for her horses, six acres of pasture land for riding, a swimming pool, and an orchard. It was a real home, a sanctuary from the hurly-burly of politics.

Her enthusiasm for Hickory Hill was infectious, and Jack quickly agreed to purchase the $125,000 house. Jackie called Janet Auchincloss's decorator, Elisabeth Draper, and the three women — mother, daughter, and decorator — set about designing a nursery for Jack and Jackie's first child. At last, Jackie was pregnant.

Meanwhile, Joe Kennedy made sure that banks of TV and newsreel cameras and a mob of reporters were on hand to record Jack's triumphant return to the Capitol.

Jack climbed the marble steps without crutches and, with a great effort of will, stood there at the top, posing for pictures. Though he still had shooting pains in his back and could not turn his head without also turning his entire body, he somehow managed to convey the impression of health and vigor. Tourists stopped and cheered. His Senate colleagues came up and shook his hand.

"God," said Jackie, "it was like recording the crown prince taking his first baby steps."

"There wasn't so much talk about death anymore," Lem Billings said. "Jack had grown up thinking he was doomed. Now he had a different view. Instead of thinking he was doomed, he thought he was lucky."

But as always, Jack pushed his luck to the point of recklessness.

He took a suite on the eighth floor of the Mayflower Hotel, which one FBI informant referred to as "Kennedy's personal playpen." This FBI source attended one of Jack's parties, at which Jack and Senator Estes Kefauver and "their respective dates made love in plain view of other partygoers. When they were done, the two senators simply exchanged mates and began anew."

Such exhibitionism thrilled Jack. Overindulgence had left him dulled and jaded. When he had sex in private with a lone woman, he often found it difficult to sustain his state of excitation. According to the testimony of many of his female partners, the sex act with Jack was over almost as soon as it began. It may have been for this reason that Jack preferred groups to one-on-one encounters. Watching two women make love or indulging in sex in the presence of another couple kept him stimulated for a longer period of time.

His group-sex fantasies were common enough among men, but not many had the audacity to carry them out in real life the way Jack did. He found a kindred spirit in the person of William Thompson Jr., a lobbyist for the railroads.

Bill Thompson was a large man, 6'2" or 6'3", slender, and pleasant looking, though not exactly handsome. He had such an uncanny power over women that friends said he could actually fondle strange women on the street and get away with it. Among fellow senators and reporters, much of Jack's reputation as a womanizer came from his close association with the notorious Bill Thompson.

"I had attended the University of Florida with Bill, and I introduced him to Jack," George Smathers said. "The two of them became intimate buddies right away. They liked women, and they liked to do the same kind of thing."

Sometime during Jack's courtship of Jackie, he took a train trip to Miami with George Smathers and Bill Thompson, who, in characteristic fashion, arrived for the journey with three attractive women in tow. After they pulled into the station in Miami, Jack and George got off the train and were greeted on the platform by Rose and the Kennedys' chauffeur. But Bill was nowhere in sight.

Suddenly, a Negro porter came running down the platform, terribly agitated.

"Senator Smathers, Senator Smathers," he yelled, "you gotta do something.

Mr. Thompson says he ain't comin' out till he's finished."

Jack and George walked over to the window of Bill's compartment and George tapped on the glass. Bill pulled up the shade.

"I'm not ready to come out yet," he yelled through the window. "I still have one more girl to go."

There were certain advantages to being Bill's friend. He kept an apartment at the Carroll Arms, a stout, red-brick building that faced the Capitol Plaza diagonally across the street from the Senate Russell Office Building. At lunchtime, senators, members of their staffs, lobbyists, and big contributors flocked to the Carroll Arms. Nearly 200 men congregated in the dark, wood-paneled restaurant (women did not hold jobs of any consequence in the Senate), and the drinking would commence. In the 1950s, Washington's dry laws prohibited the sale or consumption of alcoholic beverages at bars, but the Carroll Arms had its own full-time bartender and the liquor flowed freely.

"A lot of womanizing went on with the drinking, and drinking was a central part of getting business done," said

J. Paul Molloy, who later served as minority counsel on the Senate Commerce Committee. "You'd stay through the afternoon, and then for dinner, and you'd keep on drinking until the place closed at two A.M. The way to get a deal made was to outdrink your adversaries. Railroad lobbyists walked around literally carrying bags of cash. For the squeamish, one way things were done was to have card games, and the winner of the card game would always be the senator."

"I remember once I went down [there] with this pretty little thing, and Jack was already there with someone," George Smathers said. "He went into another room to make a phone call, and a few minutes later Evelyn Lincoln called and said I was wanted back on the Hill. So I left . . . when it dawned on me that I couldn't be wanted back there because the Senate was in recess. I knew then that ole Jack had pulled a fast one on me.

"So I turned around and drove back and entered the place just like I'd left it," George continued. "What do you suppose I found when I walked in? There was the old rascal chasing both of the girls around, having himself a fine old time. He liked that sort of thing, you know. He was something, let me tell you."

In late May, Jackie suffered a miscarriage. Langdon Marvin wondered whether the loss of the baby was somehow related to Jackie's torment and anguish over Jack's philandering.

"I can only guess that [Jack's philandering] caused a great deal of tension," he said. "I have no idea if there's any medical evidence for it, but I sometimes wondered if it wasn't the reason for all those miscarriages and other related problems that Jackie had . . . Her doctor told her that if she remained so high-strung she might have trouble bearing children. That made Jack nervous and probably induced him to have more affairs. He wanted a large family, no fewer than five children, but realized very early in the marriage that this just wasn't going to happen."

After her miscarriage, Jackie sank into a severe depression. At the beginning of July, she sailed alone for England, where she stayed with her sister and Michael Canfield at their mews house in the Belgravia section of London. Lee looked wonderful. She was a big hit on the London social scene, and her house, which was decorated with splendid pieces of early eighteenth-century Regency furniture, was far grander than anything Jackie and her WASPy decorator, Elisabeth Draper, were planning for Hickory Hill. The visit reignited all of Jackie's old feelings of jealousy and sisterly competition.

As always, Lee, not Jackie, was the one with the looks and style. Michael Canfield's new position — special assistant to the American ambassador to the Court of Saint James's — put Lee on the social map. Jackie was dazzled by Lee's glamorous friends: the Marchioness of Blandford; Jayne Wrightsman, the wife of the oil and gas millionaire Charles Wrightsman; Stavros Niarchos, the Greek shipping tycoon; Michael Astor, Lady Astor's third son; William Douglas-Home; Douglas Fairbanks Jr., and on and on.

However, Lee's life was not as romantic as it appeared. Michael was now a full-blown alcoholic. At dinner, Lee treated him with gratuitous cruelty, as though he were no more important than another piece of china on the table. After dinner, Lee and Jackie went out nightclubbing, and Michael collapsed into bed.

The sisters took off for a few days in Paris, where they attended fashion shows and went shopping. By that point, Jackie had unburdened herself to Lee. After all that she had done for Jack, he still treated her with contempt and callous indifference. Her loyalty and devotion obviously meant nothing to him. He gave no thought to how *he* could fulfill their marriage needs. Jackie's anger and frustration had brought her to the point of despair.

"Their lives were oddly parallel," said Diana Dubois, Lee's biographer. "Jack's never-ending infidelities humiliated Jacqueline, so they were both, albeit for different reasons, unhappily married and childless."

Jackie was looking for something — a new start in life, a makeover, a way to change her image. She found all that with Lee in Paris. Every chic woman now wanted to look like Audrey Hepburn in *Roman Holiday* and *Sabrina*. Suddenly, curves were out; a slim-hipped, slightly boyish silhouette was in. Givenchy and Balenciaga were creating a new look for the modern, well-bred woman. With her flat chest, long waist, and wonderful shoulders and arms, Jackie fit the new look to a T. She immediately adopted it as her personal style.

Next, Jackie and Lee traveled to the south of France, where the Canfields had rented a villa for the month of August. At Cap d'Antibes, the Canfields were joined by an English friend, Peter Ward, and his future wife, Claire Baring. The five young people visited Eden Roc, the famous hotel near Cap d'Antibes. After lunch, they rented a cabana and changed into bathing suits. On the crowded beach, they lay side by side on foam-rubber mats that were wrapped in terry-cloth towels, sunning themselves and talking.

Jackie was remarkably candid about her feelings toward Jack. She had left him, she said. She felt bad about leaving him while he was having trouble with his back, but she couldn't help that. She and Jack were split.

To Peter Ward, she did not seem the least bit upset. "She seemed to be having a very good time," he said.

"I'm never going back," Jackie said. "I'm never going back."

However, Jack showed up at the hotel in late August. For the past five years, his father had rented the same villa, Vista Bella, at the Hôtel du Cap during the height of the season. Jack moved into the villa and began working on Jackie with all his powers of charm and persuasion. Soon, Jack and Jackie appeared to have reached a reconciliation.

But some of the romance seemed to have gone out of the relationship.

"Jack and Jackie didn't seem close at all," said J. C. Irondelle, then the hotel's reception manager, who observed them together. "She was always sitting around with her sister, while Jack was moving in a large group of people. . . . There were certainly many beautiful women in the area, but very few actually stayed at the hotel, as it was very expensive, and so they would come to spend the day around the pool."

Jack and Jackie went to Monte Carlo, then took off for a 10-day tour of Poland and an audience with the pope in Rome. They ended their European sojourn with a party on board the yacht of

Aristotle Onassis. The Greek shipping tycoon was entertaining Sir Winston Churchill, one of Jack's heroes. Hoping to make an impression, Jack got dressed up in a white dinner jacket, but Churchill ignored him.

"I think he thought you were the waiter, Jack," Jackie said in one of her more devastating put-downs.

Not long after they returned to the States, Jackie broke her ankle playing touch football at the Kennedys' estate in Hyannis Port. She ended up in a cast at the New England Baptist Hospital in Roxbury, Massachusetts. On November 18, Ted Sorensen wrote her:

Dear Jackie,

Your football antics made the *Washington Post* sports page this morning. As far as I know, this is the first time a Senator's wife has made that section of the newspaper since Mrs. Lucius Lamar deserted bandage-rolling for riding bareback on the Mall. I have already approached several magazines to see if they are interested in an exclusive article by you entitled "Amateur Football is Dirty, Too" — or

"Profiles in Athletic Courage."

After leaving the hospital, Jackie told everyone that her touch football days were over. But she did not tell them the real reason why.

Once again, she was pregnant.

Jacqueline, age 6, and her father, "Black Jack" Bouvier. Jackie never felt pushed aside by her father's many paramours. She was the constant in his life. (Copyright © Molly Thayer Collection/ Magnum Photos.)

Jack Kennedy, LeMoyne Billings, and Jack's dachshund, Office, during their 1937 trip to Europe. Labeled a womanizer, Jack's real intimacy was saved for male friendships. (Courtesy of John F. Kennedy Library, Boston.)

Jackie at her 1947 coming-out party at Hammersmith Farm. "She has poise, is soft-spoken and intelligent," Cholly Knickerbocker wrote of the Queen Deb of the Year. (Copyright © Robert Meservey/Magnum Photos.)

Jack plays catcher while Jackie bats at Hyannis Port. Jack's sisters poked fun at her tiny little voice that made her sound like Babykin, a popular talking doll. (Hy Peskin, *Life* magazine. Copyright © Time Inc.)

The newlyweds cut their wedding cake at Hammersmith Farm. It was Joe Kennedy, not Jackie's stepfather, who ended up paying for the lavish public wedding. (Lisa Larsen, *Life* magazine. Copyright © Time Inc.)

Jackie helps Jack with some research in his senate office, 1958. He tried out his speeches on her first, and she gave him tips on how to improve his oratorical skills. (Copyright © 1996 Jacques Lowe.)

Frank Sinatra and Jack in Las Vegas. Frank rounded up support from all his old friends in Hollywood and generated huge campaign contributions. (Courtesy of Collection Ginies/Sipa Press.)

An intimate moment at a White House reception. Jack and Jackie fused like two nuclei, releasing an enormous amount of energy. (Courtesy of Photoreporters, Inc.)

Jackie and Caroline in Italy, 1962. "A little more Caroline and less Agnelli," Jack cabled Jackie from the White House. (Courtesy of Photoreporters, Inc.)

Hand in hand, Jack and Jackie leave Otis Air Force Base Hospital after the 1963 death of their son Patrick. Jack just "cried and cried and cried," one friend said. (Courtesy of UPI/Corbis-Bettmann.)

John Jr. cavorts under Daddy's desk while Jack confers with aides in the Oval Office. Getting ready to run again, Jack knew the value of a picture spread in *Look*. (Courtesy of John F. Kennedy Library, Boston.)

Jackie and her children leave the White House. "They're never going to drag me out like a little old widow," she said. "I am not going to play that role." (Courtesy of Everett Collection.)

TEN

Hitting Bottom

August, 1956–December, 1956

Breaking the Political Sound Barrier

On the afternoon of Friday, August 17 — the final day of the 1956 Democratic convention — Jackie settled into her seat in a front-row mezzanine box at the Chicago Amphitheater. She was nearly eight months pregnant, and as the call of the states reached the T's, she was hit by a wave of nausea and dizziness.

"*Tech*-suss," boomed the clerk.

"*Tech*-suss . . ." came the voice of Lyndon Johnson, the chairman of his state's delegation. ". . . *Tech*-suss proudly casts its votes for the fighting sailor who wears the scars of battle, and the next vice president of the United States — Senator Kennedy of Massachusetts!"

The cavernous hall exploded in a pandemonium of marching and whooping and placard-waving. After a few minutes, the organist struck up the tune "Linger Awhile," but the delegates ignored the signal and refused to return to their seats.

Up on the rostrum, Sam Rayburn, the powerful Speaker of the House of Representatives and the chairman of the convention, was banging his gavel for order. Directly beneath him on the convention floor, several delegations were vying to be recognized.

Rayburn had his hands full: the party's presidential nominee, Adlai Stevenson, had thrown open the convention, letting the delegates choose his vice presidential running mate. And after an indecisive first ballot, Jack Kennedy had surprised everybody by pulling ahead of Estes Kefauver in the second round of voting.

Jackie stood and cheered.

She was instantly spotted by the delegates — a pregnant young woman in a pearl necklace and earrings — and they descended on the Kennedy box. They made a grab for Jackie's hand and threw their arms around her shoulders.

"Jackie! Jackie!" they screamed hysterically, covering her in sweat and spittle.

She had never witnessed anything like it. In a strange way, her dream of becoming the queen of the circus was coming true. But now that she was the center of attention — an object of raw public emotion — she found that she did not like it. As she later admitted, she felt "unsure and too shy."

Her feelings were reflected on her face. Observing her from a few feet away, a reporter scribbled in her notebook that Jackie looked wide-eyed, like a little girl at a party for grownups.

"How do you feel about it?" the reporter asked.

"It's all too confusing," Jackie said, reverting to her tiny, girl-like voice. "I'm very proud of him, no matter what."

"Jacqueline was standing by herself," the reporter wrote. "She was a very pretty girl; she didn't seem ill at ease, exactly. But she was out of things, not really a part of what was going on."

The reporter noticed that Jackie was not wearing any stockings. Chicago was in the grip of a heat wave, and there was no air conditioning in the amphitheater. Everybody was sweating, and the musky body odor of 9,000 delegates, alternates, and onlookers blended with the stench of slaughtered flesh coming from the nearby stockyards. Jackie's eyes smarted from the smog of cigar and cigarette smoke.

She knew that she should not have come here. Her doctors had made their warnings clear: if she wanted to avoid another miscarriage, she must forgo the physical and emotional demands of the convention.

But she had felt that it was her duty to be by her husband's side in Chicago. The divorced Adlai Stevenson needed a married man as his vice presidential running mate. And who would make a better choice than Jack Kennedy, a man with a visibly pregnant wife?

"What do you think of your husband being the vice presidential nominee?" another reporter asked.

"I don't know whether I'll like it or not," she said with more honesty than was perhaps called for.

She looked up at the electric tote board above the podium. It was broken. She could not tell who was ahead in the balloting. A few yards away, Kefauver's wife, Nancy, sat alone and ignored — no TV or still cameras, no reporters, no hysterical politicians shouting into her face.

Jackie guessed that meant Jack was still ahead.

Torby Macdonald, Jack's Harvard roommate and one of his key lieutenants at the convention, burst into his hotel room in the nearby Stockyards Inn.

"Sam Rayburn's just swung Texas!" he yelled.

Jack was dressed in his undershorts and an open shirt. He knew all about Texas. He was following the roll call on the TV set with Ted Sorensen and a few reporters, who sat around the room kibitzing and analyzing the vote.

Jack was only 38 $\frac{1}{2}$ votes shy of an absolute majority when the convention started the third ballot, and by that point, a cordon of Chicago police was waiting outside his door, ready to escort him to the amphitheater. But he did not feel like a winner. He was physically drained from a lack of sleep and was running out of steam. As a precaution, he had increased his daily dosage of oral cortisone for his Addison's disease.

He went into the bathroom and began drawing a hot bath. The window was wide open, letting in the humid August heat and the sound of other TV sets playing in nearby hotel rooms. Over the noise of the running water, he could hear the voice of Lyndon Johnson.

He rushed back to the bedroom to catch Johnson being interviewed. The Texan did not sound optimistic about Jack's prospects. Something was going wrong.

Maybe Jack should have listened to his father. Old Joe had warned Jack not to run with Stevenson. His father had said 1956 was going to be Eisenhower's year, and many Democrats would blame Stevenson's loss on Jack's Catholicism, rekindling all the bitterness and bigotry of the past.

Joe kept in constant touch by telephone with Jack and Bobby from Vista Bella, his rented villa on the French Riviera. He was in a foul mood due to a painfully enlarged prostate, which kept him up at night. During one phone call, he exploded in an outburst of blue language against his two sons for joining forces against him. For good measure, he denounced Jack as an idiot for ruining his political career.

A photographer stuck his head into Jack's room

"It's Jackie on the phone for you — in the next room," he said.

Jack buttoned his shirt but did not put on his trousers.

"Now don't you fellows take this picture," he said as he dashed across the hall.

A few minutes later, he returned to his room.

"She's not feeling too well," he told Sorensen. "The excitement is too much for her."

In his absence, the tide had begun to turn against him. He stood in front of the television set and watched as one state after another went over to Kefauver. In a matter of a few minutes, it was all over. Jack had gone down in defeat.

Sorensen and the reporters watched in silence as Jack put on a blue suit, white shirt, and red-dotted light-gray tie.

"Let's go," Jack told Sorensen.

He opened the door.

The police escort had been withdrawn.

Jack reached the amphitheater a little after 4:00. He found Jackie, and together, they made their way to the rostrum, where Jack asked Sam Rayburn for permission to speak.

With his pregnant wife beside him, Jack stood before the packed hall. He brushed an invisible speck of dust off his handsome face and waited for the roar to subside. He looked confident, appealing, gallant in defeat. Though he had a smile on his face, his eyes glistened with emotion.

"Ladies and gentlemen of this convention," he began, "I want to take this opportunity to express my appreciation to the Democrats from all parts of the country. . . . I hope you'll make it unanimous."

Then he and Jackie backed away from the microphone.

"Go back and make a motion," Rayburn whispered furiously. "Make a motion."

He handed Jack the gavel.

"I move we suspend the rules," said Jack, "and nominate Estes Kefauver by acclamation."

Then he joined Jackie in the long, dark corridor leading from the rostrum, unaware that defeat had transformed him into a national hero.

"This was his great moment," the historian James MacGregor Burns wrote of Jack's role at the 1956 convention, "the moment when he passed through the political sound barrier to register on the nation's memory. The dramatic race had glued millions to their television sets. Kennedy's near victory and sudden loss — the impression of a clean-cut boy who had done his best and who was accepting defeat with a smile — all this struck at people's hearts in living rooms across the nation. In this moment of triumphant defeat, his campaign for the presidency was born."

Pleasure First

Early the next day, Jack and Jackie boarded a plane at Chicago's O'Hare Airport. They were accompanied on the way home by George Smathers and young Teddy Kennedy, a recent Harvard graduate and the blithe spirit of the family. After the takeoff, Teddy endeavored to banish the gloom of Jack's defeat with some jokes and playful conversation. But he found it hard going.

Soon, the ritual Kennedy banter petered out. As they passed over the vast green carpet of the Allegheny National Forest in northern Pennsylvania, Jack stared out the window in silence.

"We did our best, Dad," he had told his father in a final phone call before leaving Chicago.

His father had tried to sound forgiving, but Jack knew that he had let the old man down. Things would have turned out differently in Chicago, Jack later remembered thinking, if the Kennedy in contention for the nomination had not been him, but his brother Joe.

* * *

When they arrived at New York's Idle-wild Airport, they were greeted by a pack of reporters and cameramen in the one-story cinder-block building that served as the passenger terminal. Construction was under way on a massive new Terminal City on the shores of Jamaica Bay, and dust motes hung in the slanting summer light that came through the windows.

"I've been in the news enough," Jack said, brushing off the press for the first time in his political life.

The reporters let him go. They assumed that the senator wanted to be left alone with his wife. She was obviously with child, as the saying went, though the hard-bitten newsmen would never have written about something so personal and intimate.

Jackie looked exhausted after the hectic week at the convention. But now, politics could be put aside for the moment, and Jack could care for his wife the way she had looked after him during his near-fatal back operation and long convalescence.

However, Jack had different ideas. Weeks before the convention — on Au-

357

gust 5, to be exact — he had applied for a new passport, listing France and Italy as the countries he intended to visit, and the purpose of his trip as "Pleasure."

He had asked Evelyn Lincoln to charter a yacht and crew in the south of France. He planned to take a Mediterranean cruise around Capri and Elba with Teddy, George Smathers, and Torby Macdonald.

Jackie was being packed off to Hughdie Auchincloss's estate in Newport to spend the remaining weeks of her confinement without her husband.

Jackie kissed Jack good-bye amid the dust and debris of the airport construction. Then she walked out onto the tarmac toward the aircraft that would fly her to Newport. The salty breeze off the bay messed up her hair. Before she boarded, she looked back over her shoulder at Jack. It was hard to tell from her expression how she felt about being left behind in America.

Of course, Jack had taken off and disappeared with his friends many times before. Among women of Jackie's class, this was not looked upon as abnormal behavior. The wandering husband was a time-honored figure, and upper-class wives encouraged their husbands to get out of the house and out of their hair. They did not look for a lovey-dovey bourgeois relationship in which their husband would sit by their bed, hold their hand, and call them "honey."

Jack's friend Torby Macdonald was an example of this kind of husband. Torby had been at the convention in Chicago while his wife was in the throes of childbirth back in Boston. It was her sixth pregnancy and fourth live birth — she had suffered two miscarriages — and there had been serious complications with this latest Caesarean section. The infant had required a total blood transfusion. Despite that, Torby had waited until after the convention to fly back to Boston. And then he had stayed only a few hours — just long enough to bring his wife and newborn home from the hospital and celebrate his daughter Laurie's ninth birthday — before getting on another plane to fly down to New York for the trip to France with Jack.

Torby's wife never uttered a word of complaint about her husband's behavior, at least not in public. Nor did Jackie ever complain to others about Jack. Quite the contrary: she encouraged Jack to have his fun.

"Jack's worked so hard and he's nervous about this thing," she told George Smathers, "and I think you all ought to go off and have a good time."

But did she really mean what she said?

When she was alone with Jack, Jackie expressed herself quite differently. She had contempt for George Smathers and everything he stood for. She believed he was a bad influence on Jack. Of all the womanizers in the Senate, including her own husband, George was the most notorious. He had latched onto a number of the young senators and congressmen, many of them war heroes like Jack and Torby, and had led them astray.

So astray, in fact, that her marriage was now foundering. The very traits that had attracted her to Jack in the beginning — his nonchalance, detachment, and indifference — had become obstacles to an intimate relationship. He was totally absorbed by his politicking and womanizing and was not paying any attention to her. He treated her the way he treated all women — as a tool to carry out his designs and purposes. He made her feel almost inhuman.

"I'm having a tough time," she told Chuck Spalding, one of the few friends of Jack's whom Jackie adopted as her own. "But what am I going to do?"

In private, she told Jack that it would be a mistake for them to be separated now. Don't go, she said. Spend the time with me instead.

But he chose to go anyway.

"Jackie was so bitter about him leaving her that she said she didn't care about the baby," a friend said. "She really did [care], of course, but she was so upset by him taking off like that she turned herself inside out, letting it eat away at her. . . ."

A little after 5:00, Jack, Torby, George, and Teddy boarded Pan Am Flight 114, "The President Special," a first-class-only Super Stratocruiser equipped with sleeperette chairs. The plane had two levels, with the main passenger compartment and control cabin on top and a circular stairway leading down to a passenger lounge below.

After they had stowed their belongings, the four men assembled in the lounge. Though they were labeled as "womanizers," they were, in truth, men's men, not women's men. They did not enjoy women's company and in fact did not like women all that much. Their real intimacy was saved for male friendships. And those friendships were based on competition.

Over drinks, they talked about children. It was the hot topic. Everyone was having children. Jack's sister Pat and her husband Peter Lawford were expecting their second child. Torby's wife had just gone through a harrowing experience to give birth to their fourth child. Bobby's wife, Ethel, was expecting their fifth child, putting her in serious contention to match or beat Rose Kennedy's record of nine.

Jack was the only married man in his circle of friends and family who was without a child. But that situation was soon going to be rectified. When he returned from this trip, Jackie was going to make him a father.

Disappearing Act

The pain woke Jackie from an afternoon nap.

Throwing off the covers, she sat on the edge of the bed, hugging her enormous belly. Abdominal cramps tore at her in long, lacerating strokes of pain, taking away her breath. She felt a rush of heat between her thighs and looked down. She was bleeding.

"I came in and found her that way," said her stepsister Nina. "She was in terrible pain. I called our family physician, Dr. Burns."

Dr. Burns told Nina that they had to get Jackie to the hospital right away. He didn't want to alarm the family, he said, but when a woman who was not even eight months' pregnant hemorrhaged, it meant that her placenta had separated prematurely, causing the uterus to contract and go into spasms. There was a real danger of blood clots, which could kill Jackie. No medicine on earth could stop her bleeding. They had to deliver the baby immediately.

A half-hour later, Jackie was lying on a stretcher in the back of an ambulance as it raced down Spring Street to Broadway, then past City Hall to the Friendship Street entrance of Newport Hospital. There, in the operating room, on Thursday, August 23 — less than a week after Jack had gone off to France without her — Jackie had a Caesarean section.

When she recovered consciousness at 2:00 on Friday morning, the first person she saw was her brother-in-law Bobby. He had flown down from Hyannis Port to be by her side.

She wanted to know, was it a boy or a girl?

Bobby told her that she had given birth to a girl — a beautiful little Kennedy girl. But the baby had been born dead.

For a long moment, Jackie tried to absorb the meaning of his words.

She had picked out a girl's name: Arabella. Did Jack know that she had lost baby Arabella?

Bobby explained that Jack had gone to Paris, then stopped for a couple of days at his parents' villa at Val-sur-Mer on the French Riviera to discuss his political future with his father. However, by the time Bobby had managed to reach his parents on the phone with the news of Jackie's stillbirth, Jack had already left.

Where was he?

On a yacht . . . somewhere off the coast of Elba.

Somewhere? Had no one been able to reach him?

Not yet. But don't worry, Bobby assured her. Eunice was on the case.

That evening, just as Evelyn Lincoln was inserting the key into the door of her apartment, the phone started to ring. She got to it just in time. A reporter from the Associated Press was on the other end of the line.

"Where is the Senator? Do you know?" he asked.

"Why do you want to know?" Evelyn said.

"Jackie's in the hospital."

A spokesman at Newport Hospital had announced that Jackie had suffered internal hemorrhaging and had lost her baby. Bobby Kennedy had also made a statement to the press; he had said that

Jack was sailing in the Mediterranean on a boat that didn't have a ship-to-shore radio.

The news took Evelyn by complete surprise. She did not know how much she should tell the snoopy reporter, so she told him nothing useful. After they hung up, the phone rang again. This time it was Eunice Shriver.

"Yes," Eunice said, "Jackie is in the hospital — she's lost her baby. How can we reach Jack?"

Evelyn offered to call him at once.

Like most politicians, Jack was an inveterate gossip and news junkie who spent hours on the phone every day. He enjoyed being at the center of action. No matter where he traveled — to Palm Beach, Hyannis Port, Santa Barbara, the middle of the Mediterranean Sea — he made sure that Evelyn Lincoln knew how to contact him.

In the late summer of 1956, he had more reasons than usual to want to stay in touch. His father was suffering from an enlarged and cancerous prostate, which might require an operation. His wife was almost eight months' pregnant. His political future hung in the balance following his losing battle at the recent Democratic convention, and he was talking to Adlai Stevenson about playing an active role in the upcoming presidential campaign.

Before he left for France, Jack made certain that Evelyn had set up a fool-proof system of communication. Contrary to Bobby's statement to the press, the yacht Evelyn chartered carried a ship-to-shore radio telephone, a safety measure that was mandated by French maritime law.

Evelyn placed the call to Jack.

"I told him what had happened to his wife," she said.

"I'll be right home," Jack told her.

By then, Jack and his sailing companions had been at sea for three days — time enough to turn their boat into a kind of floating bordello. The women they had brought on board in Nice had been passed around among the four men, and Jack had taken a special fancy to one of them, a statuesque blonde who referred to herself in the third person as Pooh. Pooh was just Jack's type — a curvaceous showgirl who excited his sexual desires. After another bout of love-making with Pooh, he decided that there was no compelling reason to hurry home to Jackie.

His decision to delay his return was a terrible lapse in judgment, and it would haunt him for years to come. It was one thing to be seen as a compulsive womanizer; it was something else for Jack to show — in the words of an indignant writer — "his terrible obtuseness, his awesome, willful insensitivity [that] had defined the emotional parameters of his marriage. He had shown what he truly felt — more accurately, what he did not feel. Even after he heard about the [stillbirth], he had initially wanted to stay on the boat, to enjoy himself, to relax. He had little apparent regard for Jackie and her anguish."

Jack would never completely live down the story that he displayed a callous disregard for his wife in her moment of need. However, his decision was motivated by more than mere selfishness and narcissism. Coming as it did on the heels of his defeat at the Democratic convention, news of Jackie's stillbirth was more than Jack was emotionally able to bear. Children evoked in Jack strong emotions — far stronger than his feelings toward women. Losing his baby daughter was a devastating blow to him as well as to Jackie, and he did not want to go home and face it.

"Jackie losing the baby has affected [Jack] more than his illness did during that bad year . . ." Joe Kennedy confided to a friend.

From the port of Genoa on Sunday, August 26, Jack called Bobby. The two brothers set up a telephone conference with Dr. Burns and Jackie's other doctors. Jack told them that he felt there was nothing he could contribute to what they were already doing. It did not occur to him that his presence would be a compassionate gesture that would help Jackie overcome her grief.

"If I go back there, what the hell am I going to do?" he told George Smathers. "I'm just going to sit there and wring my hands."

There was a hitch, however. The day before, *The Washington Post* had carried a front-page story with the headline SEN. KENNEDY ON MEDITERRANEAN TRIP UNAWARE HIS WIFE HAS LOST BABY. Jack's conspicuous absence was turning into a major political embarrassment. Even

George Smathers understood that.

"If you want to run for president," George told Jack, "you'd better get your ass back to your wife's bedside, or else every wife in the country will be against you."

Joe Kennedy agreed, and the next day, George and Jack flew together back to America.

The Offer

In keeping with tradition in many Irish-Catholic families, Bobby waited a couple of days to give Arabella's spirit time to depart from her body. Then he arranged for the O'Neill Funeral Home to bury the infant in St. Columba's Cemetery overlooking Narragansett Bay.

It was unusually cool on Saturday morning, August 25 — the temperature was only in the high forties — and the earth was still moist from a light rain the day before. Kenny O'Donnell, who was Jack's right-hand man, had rushed to Newport to help out Bobby, and he was not dressed warmly enough. He stood shivering by the muddy graveside as Father Murphy, a priest from St. Augustine's Church, performed the funeral service.

Father Murphy said that since Senator and Mrs. Kennedy had planned to baptize their daughter, the Church considered the baby "baptized by intent." She would go to heaven, where the Church expected that God would embrace and accept her.

He blessed the coffin, which was marked "Baby Girl Kennedy," and it was slowly lowered into its miniature grave.

When Jack arrived at Hammersmith Farm three days later, he found the Auchincloss family dressed in mourning. He murmured some words of consolation to Janet, but that did not prevent his sharp-tongued mother-in-law from letting him know exactly what she thought of him. He should have been at Jackie's side when she had needed him.

Jack asked Yusha to drive him to the hospital. Another of Jackie's step-siblings, Nina, was in her room when Jack walked in.

Jackie had made an effort to look her best for Jack. She had put on makeup and was dressed all in pink. They embraced, and Jackie winced in pain. Her breasts were engorged and tender, and her nipples were taped to stop the production of milk.

"Well, Jackie, how are you feeling?"

"Just fine, Jack."

Jackie was so distraught that, in

truth, she did not know how she felt. One moment, she was angry at Jack; the next, she was overcome by feelings of guilt and self-recrimination. She blamed herself for having gone to the Democratic convention and for not getting enough rest. She blamed herself for having smoked during her pregnancy; she should have listened to Rose and quit. She blamed herself for having let Jack go off with his friends, when she should have insisted that he stay with her. She blamed herself for being physically incapable of bearing children. . . .

The Kennedys did not make it any easier for her.

"Though the Kennedys never mentioned it to her face," said Peter Lawford, "there was always the uncomfortable feeling in the air when she was around that, as far as childbearing went, she had rather let them down. Behind her back, they would say things. They would suggest she was maybe too 'highborn' to have children. I mean babies were literally popping out of these women, while Jackie had her share of problems."

The loss of their child was hard on both Jack and Jackie, and it showed in their strained faces as they sat in the small hospital room. They were bitter, disillusioned, and withdrawn. They did not have much to say to each other. It was as though conversation would only deepen their wounds.

When Jackie lit a cigarette, Jack could see that her fingernails were bitten to the quick. She took a deep drag and commented about the strains of the Democratic convention. It sounded as though she was blaming their misfortune on politics.

Jack got up to leave.

Jackie plunged into one of her depressions.

The doctors tried to explain that her feelings of dejection and despondency were normal. After all, she had been dealt a double blow: the psychological shock of losing a nearly full-term baby and the postpartum effects of hormonal withdrawal.

However, Jackie's severe depression — a feature of all her future pregnancies — suggested that there was some unusual cause. After three years of marriage, it was likely that she had been infected by Jack's venereal disease and that her sluggishly functioning ovaries could not replace her body's normal complement of hormones.

Whatever the reason, her depression lingered on. After she returned to Hammersmith Farm, she and Jack had trouble getting along. One of their friends overheard them arguing.

"You're too old for me," said Jackie.

"You're too young for *me*," replied Jack.

Jackie turned once again to her sister for consolation, and in November she flew to London to stay at the Canfields' elegant new house on Chester Square. She found that Lee's marriage to Michael had completely dissolved. Michael had been told by his doctors that he was sterile and could never have children. And Lee had washed her hands of her husband and no longer even tried to hide her indiscretions.

As the more withdrawn of the Bouvier sisters, Jackie was envious of Lee's ability to thumb her nose at bourgeois convention and carry on extramarital dalliances. It was something that Jackie wished she could learn to do. Lee was conducting simultaneous affairs with a number of prominent men:

Lord Lambton, the husband of one of her best friends; David Somerset, the fabulously wealthy heir of the Duke of Beaufort; and Stanislas Radziwill, the descendent of Polish aristocracy who was 19 years older than Lee and bore a resemblance to her playboy father.

To Jackie, who spent her days back in Washington rubbing shoulders with the dreary wives of senators or with Jack's coarse Irish cronies, Lee's adventures were like something out of a book. As a teenager, Jackie had loved to read about Madame Récamier, an eighteenth-century noblewoman of wit and beauty who established a famous literary and political salon in Paris. Jackie burned with jealousy that it was Lee, not she, who had become like Madame Récamier.

"You see," said Ali Forbes, a well-born American expatriate in London, "both the Bouvier sisters longed to be what the Italians call *prominènte,* people who get talked about."

Michael Canfield was totally bewildered by Lee's behavior. When he got home after work, he said, he never knew whose hat he was going to find hanging on the peg downstairs. He sought Jackie's advice about how to handle his wife.

"Get more money, Michael," Jackie said.

She meant it as a joke aimed at her sister. It was well known among Lee's friends that the only thing that interested her was high society and money.

Michael explained that, compared to most couples their age, he and Lee were living quite comfortably and had a reasonable income. Yet nothing seemed to satisfy Lee — not even the fabulously expensive bed jacket from Elizabeth Arden, which he had recently given her and could hardly afford.

Obviously, Michael did not grasp the depths of Lee's greed.

"No, Michael," Jackie said in her most wicked tone of voice, "I mean *real* money."

Jackie threw herself into a round of glamorous parties and shooting weekends in the English countryside. Word reached America of her extravagant life in England, and stories soon began to appear in the American press that she was behaving like an unattached woman. She and her husband appeared to be estranged. There was talk of divorce. The first journalist to print such a report was Washington columnist Drew Pearson. His item was picked up and expanded on by *Time* magazine.

Alarmed, Joe Kennedy decided to take matters into his own hands. When Jackie returned to the States, he invited her to have lunch with him at Le Pavillon, the famous French restaurant in the Ritz Tower Hotel on East Fifty-seventh Street.

Andre Soulé, the short, puffy-faced owner, had opened the original Le Pavillon back in 1941 with Joe's financial help, and the restaurateur had never forgotten the favor.

"Ah! *Votre excellence!*" Soulé exclaimed as Joe came through the door.

Joe did not look well. At 68 years of age, he had recently undergone a prostatectomy — the removal of his prostate gland. He was still a little shaky on his feet. Soulé showed him to his usual table, number 7, in the most sought-after dining area off to the left of the entrance.

Within a few minutes, Jackie arrived, and Soulé led her to Joe's table. The walls and the carpeting were of soft green and the banquettes of regal red. There were vases with red roses on every table. The room shimmered with the light of crystal chandeliers and sconces and the lighting was flatteringly dim. Jackie sat down; she was in her element.

"I have something very special that my chef has prepared for you today," Soulé said, leaning slightly toward Joe.

He recommended a roast boneless squab for Joe, and a chicken *polonaise* for Jackie. When the entrees arrived, Joe got down to business. Later, he described the conversation to Morton Downey, and Jackie gave her version to Lee.

"Jack doesn't want to lose you," Joe said.

"He has a peculiar way of showing it," Jackie said.

"I know your relationship hasn't been so hot," Joe said. "But you have to stick with Jack. He's going to be president."

Jackie said that she did not care for politics or politicians and did not like being a campaign wife. She had her own interests, which centered around literature and the arts. She wanted more freedom.

What's more, though she had always liked Joe personally, she felt that she was being suffocated by the Kennedy family. When she and Jack were in Hyannis Port or Palm Beach, she did not want to have dinner every night with the family.

"Once a week is fine," she said. "Not every night."

Joe did not have any problem with these demands.

"And I don't want to keep Hickory Hill," Jackie said. "I can't bear the sight of the nursery."

"I understand," Joe said. "We'll find you another place to live. The only thing that concerns me is that you and Jack stay together."

Jackie remained silent. Her mother had warned her on many occasions, "If you leave Jack, what will you become? A divorced Catholic woman!"

How would Jackie cope without a husband? Where would she go? Who would support her?

Divorce was out of the question. Jackie was not seriously planning on leaving Jack. But Joe did not know that. And, of course, Jackie was careful not to tell him.

"It's up to a wife to keep a marriage together," Joe went on. "Speaking from personal experience, I can tell you that children are the secret to any good marriage. I'm going to set up a trust for your children. You will have control of it when you have children."

He was offering her a clear-cut inducement to have children.

"And what if I can't have children?" Jackie asked.

"If you don't have any children within the next ten years," said Joe, "the trust fund will revert to you. The money will be yours to do with as you wish."

Joe never mentioned a particular sum of money, and Jackie never asked.

ELEVEN

Big Casino

April, 1957–November, 1960

A Woman of Substance

One fine April day when the cherry trees were blooming in Washington, Ted Sorensen came upon Jack and Jackie sprawled on a rug in their house, surrounded by piles of books.

"Oh, listen to this, Jack," Jackie said. "This fits right into what you're trying to say."

Sorensen was Jack's chief muse and speech writer, but it was Jackie who often found the perfect quote or apt phrase that made Jack's speeches so memorable.

"Jackie wasn't so much a researcher as she was this remarkable font of knowledge about literary matters," Sorensen said.

As a child, Jack had listened to his mother's lectures on how to stand straight and look smart. Now he turned to Jackie for help in shaping his image. He tried out his speeches on her first, and she gave him tips on when to move his hands to emphasize important points and how to improve his oratorical skills.

"Kennedy had decided privately right after he lost the vice presidency at the 1956 Chicago convention to go for Big Casino next time around," said Ben Bradlee, who was covering Congress for *Newsweek* magazine. "By the time I got to know him, he was writing magazine articles, making political speeches, barnstorming across the country, and spending little time in the Senate . . ."

During this period, when many of their friends thought that their marriage had sunk to a low point, Jack and Jackie spent many nights together at home going through books, preparing Jack for his run for the presidency.

To gear up for that campaign, Jack hired a number of new staffers, including Meyer Feldman, the lanky former counsel to the Senate Banking Committee who came to know Jackie well.

"What she would do," said Feldman, "is make suggestions to Jack — ideas on positions he might take, poetry he might recite, historical references. If he spoke to a French-speaking group in New Hampshire, she came up with a phrase that she felt he could use. And he would always incorporate her ideas into what he would say."

"They were doing a hell of a lot of reading together," Charlie Bartlett said, "and Jackie, who was very, very bright, would pick out quotes. There was a very strong collaborative aspect in this supposedly dark period of their marriage. Jackie helped lay the intellectual groundwork for a lot of the ideas in that presidential race. It was she who dug up a lot of the quotes that Jack started dropping in his speeches in the course of the campaign."

Until then, most references in Jack's speeches had come from figures in the political arena — Lincoln, Jefferson, Madison, Churchill, Clausewitz. But starting in the mid-1950s, he began to sprinkle his speeches with quotes from writers, many of whom Jackie brought to his attention. In a speech that Jack delivered to the Mississippi Valley Historical Association in Minneapolis, Minnesota, Jackie managed to work in a quote from Oscar Wilde, her old literary friend from her *Vogue* Prix de Paris days:

But if American politicians have shown an appreciation for historians and their importance, American historians have not always reciprocated. They have not always regarded either politics as very desirable or politicians as very important aspects of our nation's history. Too many seem to agree modestly with Oscar Wilde that "It is much more difficult to write about a thing than to do it — anybody can make history. Only a great man can write it!"

As he traveled around the country making speeches, Jack became more self-confident. He developed a unique style of expression that created a sense of emotional intimacy between himself and his audience. Women adored him.

He was putting on weight and filling out, thanks to the oral cortisone he was taking for his Addison's disease. Standing on a stage, under the spotlights, he looked handsomer than ever.

"I do not underestimate the number of great men in this audience," he told the Mississippi Valley Historical Association. "But neither would I underestimate the importance of great men whose actions have helped shape our history."

He was no longer the reluctant surrogate of his dead brother. Now, Jack saw himself as one of those great men of history.

Jackie was pregnant again.

Everything had worked out just as she and Joe Kennedy had planned. Hickory Hill was sold — at cost — to Bobby and Ethel, and Jack and Jackie moved into a rented place in Georgetown. When their friend Marion "Oatsie" Leiter moved out of a three-story, red-brick residence at 3307 N Street that she had been renting, Jack jumped at the chance to buy it.

"My sweet little house," as Jackie called it, leaned slightly to one side. It had creaky stairs, no front garden, and was in dire need of renovation. But it was an early nineteenth-century gem that had survived the War of 1812, and its uncluttered Federal architecture appealed to Jackie's sense of orderliness. At Joe Kennedy's insistence, Jack gave Jackie carte blanche to transform it into her dreamhouse.

She asked Elisabeth Draper, her

mother's interior decorator who had helped Jackie do Hickory Hill, to come have a look at the new property.

"Bessie," Jackie told Elisabeth Draper, as they walked through the high-ceilinged, double-fireplaced drawing room, "this is going to be it. No more traveling around."

"Of course, she'd made the same vow on moving into Hickory Hill," Elisabeth Draper said. "I felt bad for Jackie — she and Jack had moved from house to house. It gave their marriage a kind of temporary quality, a sense of 'nothing is permanent.' I don't know how to say it exactly — every home she had ever lived in was like a one-night stand."

But Jackie's life as a gypsy was over. Since her lunch with Joe Kennedy at Le Pavillon, she had changed. She became determined to put down roots and get on with the business of marriage. She seemed less fey — a pejorative that Jack had once employed to describe his wife's ethereal quality.

As she set about the task of decorating the N Street house, she made an important decision: she would not allow her mother to interfere in her new home through the person of Elisabeth Draper. Instead, Jackie called Mrs. Henry Parish II, the well-born New York interior decorator who was known for her plump sofas and her style of homey luxury and whose client list included Mellons, Du Ponts, Rockefellers, and Engelhards.

In the summer of 1957, Sister Parish, as she was known, flew down to Washington to meet with Jackie. A blond woman whose hatchet face gave her a passing resemblance to George Washington, Sister intimidated many of her clients with *ex cathedra* pronouncements on matters of taste and style. She carried a large pad of what she called "foolscap" and a tiny Pekingese named Yummy.

"Oh, Jackie," she said, trying her usual bullying tactics, "this is terrible, just terrible."

But Sister quickly learned what others would soon discover — there was an iron will beneath Jackie's pliant exterior. Like her mother, Jackie had a prodigious talent for discipline and organization. She carried a little notebook wherever she went and jotted down observations on hundreds of shades of paint color, swatches of drapery, and samples of carpeting. She insisted on making a scale drawing of the nursery on the third floor. Nothing escaped her attention, including the selection of pink-gilt porcelain cups and saucers for cigarettes and ashtrays.

Her taste was impeccable, and she expressed her opinions with a conviction that was free of self-doubt. The motif of the house would be pink and green, she decreed. She had the broad-planked old floors painted white with an overlying diamond pattern in pale green. She bought Louis XVI chairs with caned green seats. She chose candle-fitted doré wall fixtures, blond wood marquetry tables, French porcelain, a carpet woven with strips of red roses, and, for the mantel, a small French clock balanced on a complaisant bronze lion.

Jackie's swelling self-assurance began to be felt in other areas of her married life.

She transformed the way Jack dressed. In his early days in the Senate, he came to the office looking as though he had just rolled out of bed. But after Jackie took him in hand, Jack became one of the best-dressed politicians on the Hill. His conservative two-button suits, straight-collared white shirts, and narrow, patterned ties would influence the look of an entire male generation.

Until then, Jack had susbsisted on a diet of hot dogs, candy bars, and Dagwood sandwiches. Jackie changed all that by having Jack's valet George Thomas take lunches to his Senate office on china plates with bottoms of nickel layers filled with hot water. The fare consisted of chops, potatoes, and peas — and, of course, Jack's favorite, New England chowder — all prepared in the Kennedy kitchen.

As the wife of a nationally known figure, Jackie began to receive large amounts of mail, and she learned to use this correspondence to promote Jack's political career.

"The Senator brought huge envelopes of [Jackie's mail] every morning for me to handle," said Evelyn Lincoln. "She had read it through, and often I'd get a note or call telling me her thought on how it should be handled."

Like her husband, Jackie was developing a stronger self-image. For the first time in her life, she saw herself as a woman of substance.

Indiscreet

In May, Jack called Priscilla Johnson, the young Russian translator whose dark Mediterranean looks and whispery voice reminded him so much of Jackie.

"I'm giving a speech to the Overseas Press Club at the Waldorf," he told her. "I want you to come as my guest. But when you pick up your ticket at the door, don't ask for me — ask for Mr. Bouvier's table."

Though Priscilla had refused to sleep with him, Jack enjoyed their playful, teasing relationship. His interest in her seemed to be heightened by her un-availability. As he often said, Jack liked the contest between male and female — the chase more than the kill. As part of the game with Priscilla, he was always trying for more, and she was always setting him straight.

"Jack," Priscilla told him, "if you get divorced, cease being Catholic, and get out of politics, I might think of you seriously."

"You've been stringing me along all

these years because I'm an interesting political figure," Jack said.

" 'Interesting'?" said Priscilla. "Are you kidding?"

For the Overseas Press Club dinner, Priscilla wore a pink brocade gown with a boat neck. When she arrived at the Grand Ballroom of the Waldorf-Astoria Hotel, she asked for Mr. Bouvier's table. A few moments later, she found herself seated next to the legendary Black Jack himself.

Jackie's father was a shadow of his former self. His ebonylike glow had turned to a dull, sickly gray. There were large, puffy bags under his eyes. His tuxedo did not fit him. He seemed to wince in pain every time he moved.

He introduced Priscilla to his current mistress and to another couple at the table — John Daly, the urbane host of the TV show *What's My Line?*, and his wife Virginia, who was the daughter of Chief Justice Earl Warren.

Up on the dais, Jack launched into a speech calling for increased aid to Poland as a way of helping that country become more independent of the Soviet Union.

"Stick around for a while," Black Jack

told Priscilla. "My son-in-law will want to meet you."

"That made me laugh," Priscilla said. "How did he think I was at the table?"

Priscilla had heard about Jack's troubled marriage. Her friend Nancy Roosevelt Jackson, who was married to the son of a Supreme Court Justice, said that Ambassador Kennedy had intervened to save Jack's marriage. Old Joe had extracted a solemn promise from Jack that he would be more discreet about his womanizing in the future — or so, at least, it was said.

In the middle of Jack's speech, Priscilla began to wonder what she was doing at the Waldorf, dating a famous married senator while pretending to be his father-in-law's guest. Suddenly, she got cold feet. She excused herself from the table and fled the ballroom.

When she arrived back at her apartment, her roommate, Molly Burgwin, told her that there had been a call from Mr. Bouvier.

"What did he sound like?" Priscilla asked.

Molly described the voice of the man on the phone.

"It was Jack calling in Mr. Bouvier's name," Priscilla said. "That's what Jack meant about being more discreet."

Farewell, Black Prince

On the last weekend in July, Jack and Jackie drove from Hyannis Port to Newport to celebrate her twenty-eighth birthday with Janet and Hughdie Auchincloss. While at Hammersmith Farm, Jackie received a phone call informing her that her father had been admitted to Lenox Hill Hospital in acute pain.

Although she was six months' pregnant and her doctors had warned her not to fly, she caught the next available airplane to New York City. When she entered her father's hospital room, she was shocked at his appearance.

Black Jack's life of alcoholism and dissipation had taken a horrifying toll. He was 66 years old but looked at least a decade older. His body was swollen and distended. His eyes were bloodshot. Veins had burst in his nose and on the cheeks of his once-handsome face, which had turned a dark-yellow mustard brown.

In recent months, he had become a virtual recluse, venturing out of his apartment only on rare occasions, such as for Jack's recent speech to the Overseas Press Club. He had sold his seat on the New York Stock Exchange and was living in retirement on the interest from his meager capital of less than $200,000. He owed his housekeeper Esther Lindstrom almost $5,000 in back wages. He was too weak and too poor to visit race tracks, nightclubs, and his other old stomping grounds. He felt like a total failure.

Jackie sat by his bedside listening to all this — and to his bitter complaints about how she had been neglecting him. Did she realize, he said, that he had learned about her pregnancy in the newspapers!

Jackie did not know that her father was dying from cancer of the liver, and she decided it was safe to fly back to Newport that same day. Before she left, she promised she would keep in touch. A week later, however, Black Jack fell into a coma. The only people present during his final moments were his nephew Michel Bouvier and Michel's wife, Kathleen.

"Jackie?" Black Jack asked Kathleen, clutching her hand. "Is that you? Is that you, Jackie?"

Before Kathleen could answer, Jack Bouvier let go of her hand, smiled a little, and died.

"Through a blur of tears," Kathleen said, "I looked up and saw Jackie standing there, her face as pale as fine parchment. Behind her stood Jack, his tall frame outlined by the deadly white wall of the room. They had missed being at [Black] Jack's side the moment before he died."

A nurse came in and motioned the two couples out of the room. They got into an elevator, along with the emergency-room doctor who had admitted Black Jack to the hospital.

The doctor asked Jackie if he could whisk her father down to the autopsy room. He wanted to study the dead man's skin because the pigmentation was so fascinating.

Jackie did not dignify his question with a reply.

The funeral service took place three days later in the Bouvier Chapel at St. Patrick's Cathedral. Black Jack had left an estate worth only $171,000. After taxes and various individual bequests,

Jackie and Lee had each been left with the paltry sum of $80,000.

Before the coffin was sealed, Jackie stepped forward to say a final farewell to her first love, her Black Prince. She took off her link bracelet, a graduation present from her father, and placed it in his hand.

Black Jack was laid to rest at St. Philomena's Cemetery in East Hampton. It was a hot August day, but a gentle breeze stirred the bachelor's buttons and bright yellow daisies that Jackie had ordered to be heaped on her father's coffin to give the appearance of a summer garden.

As the sun beat down, the mourners could hear the sharp, hollow clip-clop of horses' hoofs on the dirt road beside the cemetery and the melancholy moan of a distant train whistle.

Kathleen Bouvier looked over at Jackie.

"Jackie," Kathleen said, "had a controlled, almost remote look of tightly restrained emotion. Only her mouth would not be reined in. It was drawn up with a vulnerable, hurt look. Constantly on the verge of crying, she never once did. Not in public."

A Test of Character

Joseph Kennedy kept two apartments at 270 Park Avenue — one for Rose, in case she wanted to drive in from Bronxville and spend the night in the city, and the other for himself, in order to have a convenient place to make love to his secretary and current mistress, Janet Des Rosiers.

In the final weeks of Jackie's pregnancy, Joe turned over the second of these apartments — a string of gloomy, high-ceilinged rooms with wall-to-wall carpeting — to Jack and Jackie. They flew up from Washington so that Jackie, who was worried about another stillbirth, would be close to her doctors at the New York Hospital.

On November 27, 1957, Jackie underwent a Caesarean section. She gave birth to a healthy seven-pound, two-ounce girl, whom she and Jack named Caroline Bouvier.

Jack was ecstatic. At forty, he was about to become the youngest man in history to seek the presidency. Some people dismissed him as the spoiled son of a millionaire — too immature to hold the highest office in the land. But now he was a father — a family man in his own right. To emphasize the point, he agreed to pose with his wife and new child for a cover story in *Life* magazine.

But Jackie's recovery was slow, and she and Caroline did not come home from the hospital for 11 days. While Jackie was recovering from surgery, Lee and Michael Canfield arrived from London and moved into 270 Park Avenue.

"Well, here I am in this apartment with Lee Bouvier," Jack told Charlie Bartlett in a phone call from New York. "If that isn't a test of character — which I have passed — nothing is."

Like many men, Charlie considered Lee to be "a walking sexpot." He was glad to hear that Jack had the good sense to keep his hands off his sister-in-law, although that did not alter Charlie's opinion of his friend's flawed nature.

"Introducing Jackie and Jack wasn't one of the smartest things I've done," Charlie said. "I don't think Jack should have been married. He had this thing about him, which was not under control."

There was more truth to that statement than Charlie suspected, for in the end, Jack failed the test of character.

"Lee told me that she went to bed with Jack," said Nina Auchincloss. "The door to the bedroom was open, and Michael could hear them making love."

On Sunday, December 8, Jack went to the New York Hospital to pick up Caroline and her mother.

"Mrs. Kennedy had asked me to go along to help take the baby home," said Maud Shaw, the Kennedys' new English nanny. "But I was hardly needed. Senator Kennedy took the baby himself and held her throughout the car journey back to the apartment on Park Avenue."

The Making of an Icon

"My phone rang at midnight," said the photojournalist Jacques Lowe, recollecting a call he received on September 6, 1958. "A very happy voice said, 'Mr. Lowe, this is Joe Kennedy.'

"Joe Kennedy was a near-mythical figure in those days, much more so than Jack. I thought someone was pulling my leg.

"So I answered, 'And this is Santa Claus.'

"The voice came back: 'No, no, this is Joe Kennedy. Today is my [seventieth] birthday, and Bobby gave me those wonderful pictures you took of him and his family. They're the most wonderful pictures I ever saw and the greatest present I ever got. Could you come and photograph my other son?'

"I drove up to Hyannis Port," Lowe said. "Jack Kennedy had been campaigning hard for re-election to the Senate. And unbeknownst to me, he was already running for president and needed to win the Senate race by a landslide. He'd gotten in at four in the morning from a ten-day campaign trip and was leaving again the next day for another strenuous haul. The last person he wanted to see was a photographer. But a dutiful son always does what his father asks him to do.

"So when I got there, he was all dressed up in a blue pinstriped suit. Not normal weekend gear on the Cape on a beautiful summer's day.

"He was stiff as a statue, morose and in a sour mood when I started to photograph him. I simply could not reach him. Eventually, Jackie appeared with Caroline. Jack began to relax and play with his young daughter. Later, I took pictures of the three of them, including one of Caroline chewing on Jackie's pearls that has since become an icon.

"A few weeks later, again around midnight, I got another call," Lowe said. "It was Senator Kennedy.

" 'Jacques, I'm in New York, just for the night. Could you come up and see me? I have the pictures with me.'

"So I got into a cab and drove uptown to the Marguery, a huge apartment complex on Park Avenue, then owned by the Kennedy family. Jack answered the door himself. And whereas at our last meeting the atmosphere had been very formal, this meeting was informality incarnate. The senator was wrapped in a towel — he had obviously just stepped out of the shower — and I heard water splashing in the background.

"A voice rang out. 'Is that Jacques?'

" 'Yes.'

" 'These are wonderful pictures. Thank you.'

"Jackie was in the bathtub.

"Jack guided me to a low, glass-topped coffee table on which he had spread the contact sheets. First he told me how astonished he was at the quality of the pictures. He remembered his foul mood and apologized profusely. How did I get pictures this wonderful when he'd been so difficult to get along with?

"I sat down on the floor while he sat on the couch so that we could study the contact sheets together. The problem was that every time I looked up, I had to glance past his masculinity. It was very disconcerting to me, but he didn't seem to notice."

Lowes's photographs of Jackie were

fascinating. She was far from a perfect beauty: her jaw was too strong, her eyes too far apart, her eyebrows too thick, her mouth too large. And yet, she was absolutely stunning. There was something breath-taking about her imperfection.

Lowe continued: "Accompanied by a great deal of splashing water, Jackie kept yelling out questions about which photo would make the best Christmas card, and could we combine some of the shots into one . . .

"I [was] a bit shaken by the experience. But I never saw Jackie that night. I heard her getting out of the tub.

"She yelled out, 'Good night, dear Jacques. And thanks for the wonderful pictures.' "

Enough to Make a Man's Heart Race

Dressed in an overcoat and Homburg, Joe Kennedy slipped through a side entrance of the Ambassador East, a modest hotel near the strip of neon-lit bars on Rush Street in downtown Chicago. He was greeted by the hotel manager, a nervous sort who talked a blue streak while he escorted Joe through a labyrinth of passageways to a service elevator.

They got off on a high floor, and Joe was ushered past a pair of beefy bodyguards into a corner suite. He recognized several of the men who were standing around smoking Cuban cigars — Johnny Matessa, Willie Potatoes, Rocky Potenza, and Joey Pignatello. But Joe walked right past them without a second look and offered his hand to a somber little man with a toupee and a set of dark, menacing eyes.

"Hello, Sam," he said.

Sam Giancana was Al Capone's successor, and, as such, the most powerful gangster in America. As the boss of bosses of the Chicago syndicate, he ruled over a vast domain west of the Mississippi that reached all the way to California. No one knew the exact size of his take from gambling, loan-sharking, prostitution, narcotics, extortion, and other illegal activities, but estimates ran as high as $2 billion a year, of which $40 million to $50 million went directly into Sam's pocket.

He cradled Joe's hand in both of his. The two men went back a long way. They had done business together in the early days of Prohibition, and Sam had saved Joe's life when Detroit's Jewish Mafia put out a contract on Joe. In the past few years, they had met on a number of occasions to discuss Jack's plans to run for the White House.

In the winter of 1959, Jack had just won re-election to the Senate by the largest landslide in Massachusetts' history, and the formal announcement of his candidacy for president was only a few months away. It was time for Joe to talk turkey to Sam. He wanted to gauge the sincerity of Sam's commitment.

Sam offered Joe a cup of coffee, and

the other men left the room, affording them privacy. Later, Sam gave his brother Chuck an account of the conversation with Joe.

Joe spoke first. His son would make a great president, he said, but the boy had a lot of obstacles to overcome. He wasn't as well known across the country as Dick Nixon, who had served seven years as Eisenhower's vice president. Jack was young, inexperienced, Catholic, and he did not have the support of the unions, the farmers, the Southerners, and the liberal wing of the Democratic Party. To win certain key states, such as Illinois and Texas, Jack would need money and influence. Joe had the money. The question was, was Sam still willing to supply the muscle?

"You're going to have entrée, Sam; you're going to have the ear of the president of the United States," Joe said. "But I want to make sure we're both reading from the same page."

Sam twisted the star sapphire ring on his pinky finger and looked over at Joe. Helping put Jack in the White House offered Sam tremendous possibilities. But could he trust Joe? A man's word was only as good as his character, and

Sam did not think much of Joe's character.

"Never be misled by appearances," Sam often told his brother Chuck. "Once a crook, always a crook. The Kennedys may put on airs and pretend to be blue bloods, but they know and I know the real truth."

Sam's doubts about Joe had only deepened in recent weeks, and with good reason. Jack Kennedy was a member of the Senate Rackets Committee, and Bobby was its chief counsel, yet the committee had drawn up a subpoena requiring Sam to show up in Washington to testify before the television cameras.

"That subpoena is still sitting around," Sam said. "What's your thinking on that, Joe?"

"Ah, don't worry about that, Sam," Joe said. "That's all show. Nothing's going to come of it. Bobby has everything under control."

Sam had a saying: "If it makes a man's heart race, it's a weakness." There was no question in Sam's mind that the White House made Joe's heart race. It made Joe weak. And weak people would tell you anything you wanted to hear.

Sam no longer trusted Joe. But he sat there and listened and kept his feelings to himself. Every so often, he gave the ring on his pinky a twist. The ring had been given to him as a token of friendship by Frank Sinatra.

Frank Sinatra was a hero to a generation that was bored with the long sleep of the Eisenhower years. With his snap-brim hat, sharkskin suit, and good-looking chicks, Frank was everybody's idea of "cool." Much of Frank's confidence was derived from his close association with Sam Giancana. Frank could thumb his nose at convention, live life his way, and, thanks to Sam, never pay the consequences. Nobody messed with Frank.

Everybody in America was aware that Frank and the Rat Pack — Dean Martin, Sammy Davis Jr., Joey Bishop, and Peter Lawford — were staying at the Sands Hotel while filming *Oceans 11*, a movie about a group of war veterans who try to rob six Las Vegas casinos on New Year's Eve. In the evening, the Rat Pack performed in the Copa Room, a nightclub that had been built specially for Frank by Jack Entratter, the owner of the Sands.

Frank and his buddies sauntered onto the stage and held what they called a summit meeting: they told jokes, sang and danced, boozed, and ribbed each other for two performances. In homage to Sam Giancana, Frank ended the act by singing "My Kind of Town Chicago Is." Twelve hundred people caught the two shows each night; 800 others had to be turned away.

The Rat Pack hung out in the Copa Room until 4:30 or 5:00 in the morning, having "a little hey-hey." Then Frank got bored, and said, "I think it's going to rain," and they all split. They went to their rooms, caught a few hours' sleep, got up and shot *Oceans 11*, drank dozens of gin fizzes, had a quick bite, and started the shows all over again.

On February 7, Frank interrupted the show, pointed to his table in the front row of the Copa Room, and announced, "Ladies and gentlemen, it gives me great pleasure to introduce my friend Jack Kennedy, who is running for president of the United States."

Dean staggered over to the microphone with a drink in hand, and asked,

"What did you say his name was?"

Jack laughed along with everyone else.

After the show, Frank brought one of his former girlfriends over to his table.

"Jack," he said, "this is Judy Campbell." *

Judy was a tall brunette, with a broad face, full lips, and widely spaced eyes. Like Wendy Morgan years ago at the Dancing Class and Priscilla Johnson more recently at the F Street Club, Judy Campbell of the Copa Room bore a striking resemblance to Jackie Bouvier Kennedy. Judy was a raving beauty, and she made Jack's heart race.

At this time, Jack was battling Hubert Humphrey in several Democratic primaries, and he was flying around the country in the *Caroline*, a twin-engine turboprop Convair 240 that had been converted into his private campaign plane. His stewardess and secretary on the plane was Janet Des Rosiers, Joe Kennedy's former mistress.

*It was a fateful introduction. Judy would soon become the mistress of Jack Kennedy and, a while later, of Sam Giancana. One day, she would write a tell-all book, under the married name of Judith Exner, about her secret role as a Kennedy–Giancana go-between.

"On the plane," said Ronald Kessler, Joe's biographer, "Des Rosiers often massaged Jack's feet and hands behind closed doors. Many reporters thought she must have been having sex with him. In fact, he made a pass at her, giving her a printed napkin that said, 'Don't you think it's about time you found me attractive?' But Des Rosiers was not interested."

"Jack never entertained any women on the plane," Janet said. "No girl-friends, not once."

Yet, Jack found time to call Judy. For him, part of the sexual turn-on was the knowledge that Judy was sleeping with powerful and dangerous men. That appealed to Jack's sense of male competition. He wanted to see what these men had taught her in bed and how he measured up. He was especially interested in comparing himself to his idol, Frank Sinatra.

"Every time we talked on the phone," Judy said, "[Jack] invariably would ask, 'Have you seen Frank lately?' I would answer, 'No,' or 'Yes, I saw him on the set,' or 'He called last night and I wasn't home,' or whatever was the circumstance at the moment. Jack would say,

'Ohhh, you still want to see Frank?' I would say, 'We're just friends, Jack.' Then he'd say, 'Okay, okay,' in almost a little boy's 'see if I care' voice. Then the very next day, 'See Frank? Where did you go last night? I called and you weren't home.' I would tell him I had been out to dinner with . . . whoever, and he would respond, 'Is he a good friend — is he someone you're interested in?' [Jack] wanted to be the star of the show."

Several weeks after Jack and Judy started sleeping together, Sam Giancana showed up at the Fontainbleau Hotel for a party to celebrate the last show of Frank's Miami engagement. Sam wore a black fedora and a pair of black wrap-around sunglasses — a disguise that did not fool anyone who knew him. The place was already packed, but Sam found Frank in the crowd and asked to be introduced to Jack's new plaything, Judy Campbell.

"Come here, Judy," Frank said. "I want you to meet a good friend of mine. Sam Flood."

"It's a pleasure, Judy," said Sam, who used Flood as one of his many aliases.

"Do you mind if I say something, Judy?"

"Not at all — I think."

"You're far too beautiful to be wearing junk — excuse me — I mean costume jewelry. A beautiful girl like you should be wearing real pearls and diamonds and rubies."

"A girl like me does sometimes."

"No offense, please," Sam said. "Real pleasure meeting you. Hope to see you again soon."

When it came time for Judy to check out of the Fontainbleau, she found that Sam had already paid her hotel bill. She tracked him down and handed him a check.

"What's this for?" he asked.

"I don't want you paying my hotel bill," she said.

"Can I see you again?" Sam said.

"I'm sorry," she said, "but I'm seeing someone. And you'd better cash that check."

By April, Jack was confident that he would demolish Hubert Humphrey in the Wisconsin primary and knock him out of the race for the nomination. But when the votes were counted in Wisconsin, it turned out that Jack had barely managed to beat Hubert in six out of 10 districts. That meant the rivals would have to duke it out in the next scheduled primary state, West Virginia, where only three percent of the population was Catholic.

Despite this setback, Jack made time for Judy. He arranged for her to fly to Washington to meet him the day after his disappointing squeaker in Wisconsin.

Judy checked into the Sheraton Park Hotel. She had begun to keep a diary with Jack's private telephone numbers, which were changed frequently for security purposes, but which she always had on hand. Her diary contained entries of the exact times and places of her meetings with Jack. She also saved her airline ticket stubs and insisted on paying her own hotel bills, so that she would have receipts.

She hung her clothes in the hotel closet, stretched out on the bed, and phoned Evelyn Lincoln. Jack was expecting Judy at his N Street house at 7:30 that evening, Evelyn told her.

Later in the afternoon, Jack called.

"I wish I could show you the city," he said, "but . . ."

"Jack, please, you don't have to apologize," Judy said. "You know how I feel about being seen in public with you. All I want is to be with you."

He offered to send a car to pick her up. She told him that she preferred to take a cab. She did not want to be held to his timetable, because it often took her three hours or more to get ready to go out.

"Putting on my face takes no time at all," she explained. "The only makeup I use is mascara and powder. What takes time is my bath, my hair, my nails, and selecting the proper attire for each occasion. Everything from top to bottom must be coordinated."

A little after 7:30, Judy showed up at Jack and Jackie's three-story brick house in Georgetown wearing a new black diamond mink coat with horizontal fur.

"You look fantastic," Jack said, helping her off with her coat.

She had on a black knit suit. Jack leaned over and gave her a kiss on the cheek.

She stepped into the living room, which was decorated in muted tones of beige and off-white. There were paintings on the walls, including some that Jack had painted himself while recuperating from his back operation. A fur rug was draped over the back of one of Sister Parish's overstuffed sofas. There was no sign of Jackie, who was one month pregnant and had gone off to Palm Beach with Caroline and her nanny, Maud Shaw.

A large man, at least 6′2″ or 6′3″, stood up as Judy entered the room. He was introduced by Jack as Bill Thompson, a railroad lobbyist. Though not particularly handsome or well dressed, he exerted a strange sort of magnetism.

"I was almost relieved to see him," Judy recalled. "It is hard to describe the feeling, but . . . I was sensitive about seeing Jack in his wife's home. I couldn't even think of it as being his home. I had come to Jackie's house to see her husband."

During dinner, Jack asked Judy to tell him everything about her trip to Florida, especially any gossip she might have picked up about Frank Sinatra.

"I had dinner with a guy named Sam Flood," Judy said.

"Oh, yeah," said Jack, "that's Sam

Giancana, the big mob guy. Listen, Judy, you can help me with the campaign. I want you to take something to Sam when you go back to Chicago."

"What?" Judy said.

"Money," Jack said. "And I also want you to arrange a meeting between me and Giancana in Florida."

"The whole conversation — about the money and the meeting with Sam — was handled very casually by Jack," Judy said. "And it was discussed right in front of Bill Thompson. So I didn't think very much about it or give it a second thought."

Jack and Bill talked about the coming primary battle in West Virginia. Then they had after-dinner drinks in the living room, and Thompson left.

"This has been a long evening," Jack said when he came back into the room. "It was very hard sitting away from you when all I wanted to do was to come over and put my arms around you like this."

They kissed. Then Jack led Judy upstairs to the master bedroom. They sat on one of the twin beds, which was covered in a delicate pale-green spread.

"I hated being in his bedroom, having

that close a contact with his wife," Judy recalled later. "And I worried about the servants, of what they thought of my being there, and I couldn't quite understand how he could do that with the servants in the house."

After they had made love, they lay in bed and talked.

"If I don't get the nomination," Jack told Judy, "Jackie and I have arranged that we will separate. We will part. I want you to know that this has nothing to do with you."

Sam Giancana showered Judy with flowers and presents, and they were soon seen together parading through nightclubs in Las Vegas and New York.

"Judy was a party girl," said Joseph Shimon, a Washington, D.C., police inspector who later became an associate of Sam Giancana's. "She got to go around with Sam, but she wasn't really his mistress. Sam was madly in love with Phyllis McGuire of the singing McGuire Sisters."

Mistress or not, Judy was now seeing both Sam and Jack. For a woman like Judy — a failed actress and a Las Vegas party girl who had been passed around from man to man — the twin involvement represented the opportunity of a lifetime.

"Wake up," Frank told her, "and realize what you've got in the palm of your hand."

Frank Sinatra turned the West Virginia primary into a great piece of theater. He rounded up support from all his old friends in Hollywood and generated huge campaign contributions. Joe Kennedy kicked in hundreds of thousands of dollars more. One of Sam Giancana's top lieutenants, Paul "Skinny" D'Amato, a casino operator, used the money to distribute bribes to key political figures and polling officials throughout the dirt-poor state. The rate of exchange, said Charles D. Hylton Jr., editor of the *Logan Banner*, was "anywhere from two dollars and a drink of whisky to six dollars and two pints of beer for a single vote."

Loudspeaker trucks rolled past the tarpaper shacks of poor mining families, blaring out a song that Frank had recorded to the tune of "High Hopes." Frank's personal composer, Sammy Cahn, had reworked the lyrics for Jack:

K-E-double-N-E-D-Y, Jack's the
   nation's favorite guy . . .
And he's got High Hopes, high
   apple-pie-in-the-sky hopes.

Jack and Ben

On the evening of May 10, Jack and Jackie invited their Georgetown neighbors, *Newsweek* correspondent Ben Bradlee and his wife Tony, to join them in sweating out the results of the West Virginia primary. To pass the time, the two couples went to a pornographic movie called *Private Property*. When they got back to the Kennedys' house on N Street, the phone was ringing.

"It was Bobby Kennedy, the campaign manager," Ben recalled, "and it was a win. Big. After modest war whoops and a glass of champagne, Jack asked if we would like to fly with them to Charleston on the *Caroline* for the victory photo op. I knew it was the story of the political week, and I knew that the whole night (minus the porn film) plus the flight down would give me the personal detail and color that news magazine editors crave."

In 1960, many political reporters were less than scrupulous about covering their friends. As one of the savviest

427

reporters in Washington, Ben was nervous about the conflict of interest in his relationship with Jack, but not nervous enough to sacrifice the advantages that came along with the friendship. Consciously or not, he sometimes wrote stories that were little more than mash notes to Jack and Jackie.

"[Jackie] is kind and generous to her friends, often brings them presents for no particular reason, and she's never catty," Ben wrote in a short file he telexed that fall to Jack Iams, the national affairs editor of *Newsweek*. ". . . It occurs just now that one of the most impressive things about her is that she is utterly unaggressive about herself. It is impossible to imagine her pushing for anything for herself."

The friendship between Ben and Jack was complicated by the fact that Jack had developed a crush on Ben's attractive wife, Antoinette Pinchot Bradlee, and on Tony's beautiful sister, Mary Pinchot Meyer, the recently divorced wife of the CIA's chief of covert action. The Pinchot sisters were nieces of Gifford Pinchot, the noted conservationist and two-term governor of Pennsylvania.

Jack put the make on both the Pinchot girls.

"Before he made a play for Mary, Jack made a play for Ben's wife Tony," said Cecilia Parker Geyelin, a friend of both Tony's and Jackie's. "Tony said she was shocked, and I have no reason to doubt it. I think she was stunned that Jack would do this when he was such good friends with Ben. She did not tell Ben because she felt that it would make him very angry, and because it would skew the friendship he had with Jack."

Ben never had any reason to suspect Tony of being unfaithful, but the Kennedy-Bradlee friendship was nonetheless played out in a sexually charged atmosphere.

"I remember Ben making some remark about how Jack had a fancy for the Pinchot girls," said Cecelia Geyelin's husband, Phillip, who later became a colleague of Ben's at the *Washington Post.*

Even if Ben had been aware of Jack's interest in his wife and sister-in-law, he probably would not have seen that as a matter of any grave importance. After all, such feelings were just part of the heady Washington game in which everybody was using everybody else.

"Jack was using Ben because of *Newsweek*," Charlie Bartlett said. "It was a way for Jack to get out stories the way he wanted them."

Ben was not the only journalist courted by Jack. He was merely the most prominent representative of the new breed of well-born, well-educated reporters who had arrived in Washington after the war and who made journalism a stepping stone to fame and power. Hugh Sidey of *Time*, Theodore H. White of *Life*, and a host of others, including, of course, Charlie Bartlett of the *Chattanooga Times*, all hitched their stars to Jack Kennedy.

Most reporters had heard tales of Jack's "girling," as he liked to call it, but none of them bothered to investigate the lurid rumors, not even after he captured the presidential nomination at the Democratic Party convention in Los Angeles that July.

"It is now accepted history that Kennedy jumped casually from bed to bed with a wide variety of women," Ben wrote in his memoir, *A Good Life.* "It was not accepted history then — during the five years that I knew him. I heard stories about how he had slept around in his bachelor days — [like] other red-blooded males. I heard people described as 'one of Jack's girlfriends' from time to time. It was never topic A among my reporter friends, while he was a candidate. Since most of the 125 conversations I had with him took place with Tony and Jackie present, extracurricular screwing was one of the few subjects that never came up, and in those days reporters did not feel compelled to conduct full FBI field investigations about a politician friend."

And so on the night of Jack Kennedy's spectacular victory in West Virginia — the defining moment in the primary campaign — Ben and Tony boarded the *Caroline* and flew to Charleston with their friends, Jack and Jackie.

"I got exactly what I bargained for," Ben recalled, "especially in Hugh Sidey's expression, as my talented opposite number on *Time* watched me get off the plane at the Charleston airport directly behind the candidate."

Jackie and Solange

In September of 1960, two months before the presidential election, Jackie's French friend, Solange de La Bruyère, came to America, and Jackie flew up to New York to join her for a few days of fun and shopping.

"Jackie had very few girlfriends," Solange said, "but even though we'd be out of touch for months at a time, she always called me 'my best friend.' She and I went back to her student days in Paris. In the summer of her junior year in France, we went to a place called Zarauz, on the coast of Spain. I remember I had a wonderful pink linen dress from Molyneux, the famous English couturier. It had stars made of incredible silver embroidery and was very, very short. Jackie was on a tight budget and didn't have many clothes. We shared that dress that summer."

Solange had four children — one of whom she had named after Jackie — and a philandering husband, Count

Jean de La Bruyere, an oil and real-estate magnate.

"I am unhappy with Jean," she told Jackie over lunch at Le Pavillon. "I can no longer stand his infidelities. But many of my French friends say, 'Solange, you are crazy. Stick with it. Look the other way.' "

Jackie stared at Solange across the table but did not say anything.

Out of concern for her friend, Jackie invited Solange to spend some time with her in Washington. At Idlewild Airport, they boarded a plane, and Jackie crossed herself before takeoff.

After they landed in Washington, Jackie went to a pay phone and called her house. She told Jack's valet, George Thomas, that she would be arriving with a friend and to make sure that the third-floor guest room was ready.

"And put out a tray with flowers," she told George Thomas.

She hung up and looked over at Solange.

"It's wonderful to have a valet to take care of everything," she said.

Then they climbed into her dilapidated light-blue Chevrolet and drove to

N Street, where they were greeted by Caroline, who was not quite three years old and was full of mischief.

"Caroline had a passion for opening bathroom cabinets and taking out Jackie's Kotex box," Solange said.

After Solange got settled, she came downstairs and complimented Jackie on the décor of her house. She especially liked the billowing, rust-colored taffeta curtains in the living room.

"We had all these politicians over for dinner," Jackie said. "Their wives touched the taffeta curtains, and said, 'Oh, this is real taffeta.' "

That night, Jack came home for dinner.

"Solange," he said, "why did you put on so much weight?"

"Jack," she replied, "I just had a baby boy five months ago."

Jackie was six months' pregnant but did not look it because she was eating very little.

"Jack," Jackie said, "do you know that Solange's husband went to Tahiti for two months when Solange was six months' pregnant? The bastard! That Jean is a real son of a bitch."

She turned to Solange. "Maybe we can get him extradicted."

After dinner, Jack left the two women alone.

"Gosh, Solange," Jackie said, "you're so distraught about Jean. The best thing is to keep your health. Get massages. And don't get tired. Get a lot of sleep. Walk. I walk every day with my friend Mary Meyer along the old C & O tow path."

They did not talk about Jackie's marriage to Jack.

"But it was understood," Solange said. "In Jackie's case, there she was, with so much to lose. It was hard to duplicate Jack Kennedy. He was going to be president of the United States."

Looking Good

On the eve of the first televised presidential debate, Jack checked into a suite on the top floor of his father's favorite hotel in Chicago, the Ambassador East. The next day, he went up to the hotel's sunroof to work on his tan and submit to one final grilling on the issues by Ted Sorensen and two other staff men, Meyer "Mike" Feldman and Dick Goodwin. Then, he returned to his room, put on a terry-cloth robe, and climbed into bed.

There was a knock on the door.

"Come in," Jack said.

A short, dark-haired man with bright-red cheeks appeared. This was Dr. Max Jacobson, a New York physician who ministered to an amazing roster of famous patients — everyone from Winston Churchill and Greek shipping tycoon Stavros Niarchos to playwright Tennessee Williams and Broadway composer Alan Jay Lerner. Max was known as "Dr. Feelgood," and he was carrying an attaché case with built-in pockets for his secret elixirs.

"How do you feel?" Max asked.

"My back bothers me," Jack said.

"Why suffer if you don't have to?" Max said.

From his attaché case, Max took out an unlabeled bottle. Using a syringe, he carefully extracted a small amount of medication — a mixture of amphetamines, steroids, placenta, calcium, and liver cells. With his wrinkled hands, he plunged the needle into Jack's buttock.

"You feel like Superman," said Truman Capote, the flamboyant writer and one of the patients who experienced instant euphoria from Max's injections of "speed." "You're flying. Ideas come at the speed of light. You go 72 hours straight without so much as a coffee break. You don't need sleep, you don't need nourishment. If it's sex you're after, you go all night. Then you crash — it's like falling down a well, like parachuting without a parachute. You want to hold onto something and there's nothing out there but air."

After Max had gone, there was another knock on the door.

"Come in," Jack said.

Langdon Marvin, Jack's old Harvard

classmate and legislative factotum, entered the bedroom looking disheveled and unsteady on his feet. He had obviously been drinking, but Jack did not seem to notice. He was more interested in the attractive young woman who followed Langdon into the room.

Jack had never laid eyes on her before, but he swept his three-by-five filing cards off the bed, got up, and introduced himself. While he and the woman were getting acquainted, Langdon slipped away, quietly closing the door behind him. As he walked down the hall, he could hear the first strains of a Peggy Lee record coming from Jack's suite.

"One of the reasons Jack was so calm during the first debate with Nixon," Langdon boasted, "was because I arranged for him to get laid beforehand."

Jackie had invited a group of reporters and Democratic Party bigwigs to her house to watch the presidential debate. When Jack appeared on the screen from the CBS studio in Chicago, everybody stood up and applauded, with the exception of Jackie, who remained seated on a bench in front of the fireplace, staring intently at the TV set.

She was in the last trimester of her pregnancy and was worried about another stillbirth. During the hot summer months, she had sat out most of the campaign in Hyannis Port, sunning herself on a chaise and listening to Bobby Darin sing "Mack the Knife." As far as she was concerned, the campaign was about Jack, not her.

"It's so boring when we keep going to places where everybody loves Jack," she said.

Every so often, however, she would venture forth onto the campaign trail. She made radio tapes, wrote a column for the Democratic National Committee, and spoke at rallies, where her fluency in foreign languages sometimes came in handy.

"Jackie flew with Jack on the *Caroline* on maybe three occasions," said Janet Des Rosiers, the plane's stewardess. "She and Jack slept on the two bunks in his private quarters. The beds had plastic covers on the mattresses, and Jack would say, 'For God's sake, Jackie, will you stop tossing and turning? You're making so much noise, I can't sleep.' Another time, he left a sweet little note on her bunk: 'My darling traveling companion . . .'

"Jackie would stay in Jack's private quarters until it came time for her to actually leave the plane," Janet continued. "She didn't like campaigning, didn't like shaking hands with common people, didn't like sitting up on the stage. She was gracious when she had to be, but you could tell she was seething underneath. The photographers would say, 'Hey, watch out! Here comes the Pepsodent smile.'"

Jackie also held several press teas.

"Mrs. Kennedy," a reporter asked one time, "we have all heard about the tremendously enthusiastic response of the women and girls in the crowds to your husband. Does that response make you jealous?"

"Of course not," Jackie said, staring at her unpolished nails, which were bitten to the quick. "Women are very idealistic and they respond to an idealistic person like my husband. I am delighted that they respond to him so enthusiastically."

"As the girl who married Senator Kennedy," the reporter said in a follow-up, "you can understand the attraction he has for women?"

"Well," she answered, "if *you* want to put it that way."

It was at times like this that Jackie hated everything about politics. She considered most reporters and politicians bourgeois bores, devoid of style and manners. They drove her up the wall.

"They're going to begin the debate," someone in the Georgetown living room said. "Jack looks great."

"Every time I see him," Jackie said, "he looks better than before. It's really bad for one's ego."

Jack had arrived at the CBS studio looking tanned and refreshed.

Campaigning agreed with him. He loved the nonstop action — flying from city to city, racing from hotel room to banquet hall, eating meals on the fly, screwing women in closets, changing his shirt four times a day. He was charged up by the bright lights, the loud brassy music, and all those signs dipping and swaying in front of him that said KENNEDY FOR PRESIDENT.

He basked in the adulation of the crowds and was greatly amused by the "leapers" — those hysterical young women and Catholic nuns who lined his motorcade route and jumped up and down. He derived a deep personal pleasure from the male companionship that was at the heart of American politics. He even liked the way he looked in photographs. Thanks to the cortisone therapy, his face had filled out, making him handsomer than ever.

"Do you want some makeup?" Don Hewitt, the producer of the debate, asked.

Jack declined. However, when no one was looking, he received a light application of makeup under his eyes from a makeup artist named Fanny Orvald.

He stepped onto the set, a gleaming Adonis, and the Nixon people panicked.

One of Nixon's aides rushed up to Bobby and asked for his opinion on his boss's makeup.

"Terrific! Terrific!" Bobby said, looking at the pale and wan Nixon. "I wouldn't change a thing!"

"Between the bleak gray walls and the bright floodlights of the television studio," Ted Sorensen recalled, "[Nixon's] gray suit and heavily powdered jowls looked flabby and pallid beside Kennedy's dark suit and healthy tan."

Three minutes before airtime, Jack took his place at the lectern. He and Nixon had been friendly for 14 years — first in the House and then in the Senate — but today he ignored his Republican opponent, who seemed curiously unnerved by Jack's chilly treatment.

Jack spoke first. Seventy million people — nearly two thirds of the nation's adult population — were tuned in as he began his rapid-fire delivery.

"I think the question before the American people is: are we doing as much as we can do . . . ?"

Afterward, Jack called home and asked Jackie for her assessment.

"You looked wonderful, Jack," she said.

Lyndon Johnson had a different impression. He had heard the debate on radio and was sure that Nixon had been the victor.

"Nixon was best on radio," said Earl Mazo of the *New York Herald-Tribune*, "simply because his deep, resonant voice carried more conviction, command, and determination than Kennedy's higher-pitched voice and his

Boston-Harvard accent."

But to the tens of millions of TV viewers across the country and the small group assembled in Jackie's living room, Jack came across as tougher, smarter, sharper, and more in control.

"It stirred up some interesting discussions about how television differed from radio as a political campaign communications medium, making the candidate's visual image and physical appearance as important, if not more important, than his words," said Kenny O'Donnell.

"I was proud of [Jack] for *not wearing any makeup,*" Jackie wrote in her next column for the Democratic Committee, "[and] simply presenting himself as he is."

TWELVE

Queen of the Circus

November, 1960–December, 1961

The Jackie Magic

Jackie gave birth to a son, John Fitzgerald Jr., on November 25, 1960 — less than three weeks after Jack was elected president of the United States. Seventy-two hours later, she was sitting up in bed in her small, pink maternity room at Georgetown University Hospital, chatting with Oleg Cassini, the fashion desinger.

"How was Nassau?" she asked. "Did you have a good time?"

"It was marvelous," replied Oleg, who had been in the sun and looked as sleek and brown as a wet otter.

"You have a great tan," she said.

"How is the president?" asked Oleg.

"He's talking to Mr. Rusk about becoming the Secretary of State," said Jackie, "and I'm talking to you about making my clothes for the White House."

Jackie had just undergone her third Caesarean section in four years, and despite her cheerful outward demeanor, she was physically and emotionally

447

spent. John-John, who had been born three weeks prematurely, lay in an incubator down the hall fighting for his life, and Jackie was despondent over the prospect of losing another baby. In a letter to Eleanor Roosevelt, she poured out her feelings of inadequacy, confessing that she was afraid she would "panic" as First Lady. There was mounting concern among her doctors that Jackie might be on the verge of a nervous breakdown.

When she was depressed, Jackie's thoughts invariably turned to things that gave her the most pleasure — riding, painting, decorating, shopping. She had covered the walls of her hospital room with dozens of sketches by fashion designers. Like millions of women all over the world, she yearned to look like Audrey Hepburn — elegant and dignified — and she adored the classic designs of Hepburn's French couturier, Hubért de Givenchy. Yet, curiously enough, all the sketches posted on the walls were by American designers — Norell, Sarmi, and Andreas of Bergdorf Goodman.

"Would you like to do some designs for me?" she asked Oleg.

"I don't think so," he said.

"Why?"

"Look," he said, "if you're designing your life to be miserable and capricious, all you have to do is let a few designers design things for you. They'll be fighting for recognition. It'll be a constant turmoil. What I suggest for you is that you pick one designer and stick with him. That way you will avoid so many problems."

During the election campaign, Jackie had been severely criticized in the press for wearing expensive Paris creations. In July, *Women's Wear Daily* reported that Jackie spent an estimated $15,000 a year for clothes in Paris — the equivalent of about $100,000 in today's money — and Jack had hit the roof.

"From now on," he said, "no more Paris clothes. Only American fashion."

"I can't have anybody foreign dress me," Jackie told Hélène Arpels. "He must be American."

Behind her whispery voice and shy public mannerisms, Jackie could be as tough as nails, as she proved when she sent a letter to John Fairchild, the editor of *Women's Wear Daily*, complaining about his coverage of her clothes. The

Givenchy dress and coat sketched on page one, she claimed, were ordered by her sister Lee, not by her. Fairchild's small but influential newspaper had "made things very difficult" for her, she said — a reference to Jack's displeasure with her. She demanded that her letter not be published. But *Women's Wear Daily* printed it almost word-for-word for its readers.

When Jacqueline Kennedy moves into the White House, she will wear only American clothes and she is looking forward to it. They will have a Balenciaga and Givenchy look of utmost simplicity.

But what American designer was up to making clothes like that? And how could Jackie exercise control over her fashion publicity, which had gotten so vulgarly out of hand?

It was Joe Kennedy who came up with the solution.

"Joe said only one thing: 'You can trust Oleg Cassini, you can trust this man,' " Oleg recalled. "And if you think in terms of the Kennedys' tribal attitude, to trust was the most important thing."

And so, on the advice of his father, Jack had called Oleg in Nassau and asked him to fly immediately to Washington to discuss becoming Jackie's official designer.

Oleg Cassini's grandfather, Count Arthur Cassini, had been the Russian ambassador to Washington at the turn of the century, and although Oleg had been raised in modest circumstances and was an American citizen, he affected the strut and swagger of a European aristocrat. He had worked for a time as a costume designer in Hollywood, and his conquests of famous movie actresses — he had been married to Gene Tierney and engaged to Grace Kelly — had won him entrée into the Kennedys' macho inner circle. When he and Joe Kennedy dined together on Tuesday nights at their regular table at Le Pavillon, Oleg always brought the girls.

"[Joe and I] shared an intense appreciation of beautiful women," Oleg said. "He used to love to talk about them, about this one and that. . . . Once, he told me, 'I don't think Jack's a great lover; he's just very charming with the girls.' "

Oleg was considered a second-tier designer, and Jackie knew that his selection would shock the arbiters of style in the fashion press. Yet, in many ways, Oleg was an inspired choice.

"Jackie hated any press coverage of her wardrobe," said Letitia Baldrige, her new social secretary. "Pat Nixon had made a point of Jackie's wardrobe. The president hated all that and the fact that she spent so much money on clothes. By using Oleg and saying he made all her clothes, Jackie could be sure no one would ever say how much was actually made by him. He was a great friend of the family and helped her in many ways. Don't forget, she was only 31 years old."

As Jackie talked, Oleg casually cast an eye over the sketches on the wall. Not one of the designers had bothered to think about Jackie's body. Instead, they had sent her the best of their latest collections.

"You have a geometrical body, like an ancient hieroglyph of Egypt," Oleg told her. "You have square shoulders, a longish neck, a long torso, small hips. You have to dress in a special way."

"Then show me some of your

sketches," Jackie said.

He opened his portfolio. The first sketch, for the inaugural ball, was of a full-length evening gown of graphic simplicity, but fashioned of a sumptuous white Swiss double satin.

"Absolutely right," Jackie said.

"I talked to her like a movie star, and told her that she needed a story, a scenario as First Lady," Oleg recalled.

This was exactly what Jackie wanted to hear. But she was not prepared to give up control, not even to Oleg. If Oleg was to function as her couturier and the fabricator of her wardrobe, Jackie intended to be her own art director. She would become Oleg's collaborator, helping him design his "Cassini originals."

They would design clothes that shimmered in the light. Her clothes would make her the focus of everyone's rapt attention. Together, she and Oleg would realize her girlhood dream of becoming a performer in a tableau vivant — a costumed actress who remains silent and motionless, as if in a picture — the queen of the circus.

After Jackie announced the appointment of Oleg Cassini as her official designer, she and Jack flew down to Palm Beach to prepare for the inauguration.

"There was, thank God, this brilliant pediatrician in Palm Beach who really saved [baby] John's life, as he was going downhill," Jackie said. "I was ill and recuperating in the room I shared with dear Jack. The house was so crowded. He was writing his inaugural speech in the room. I remember the yellow pages being strewn around the room. And when he left, I would get up and try to keep them all together under some weight on the desk."

The soaring rhetoric of Jack's inaugural address sounded the twin themes of America's limitless potential and its willingness to "bear any burden, meet any hardship." From that speech would flow many momentous events — the Cuban missile crisis, Vietnam, and mankind on the moon. Implausible as it may sound, Jackie's wardrobe, which was also taking shape in Palm Beach, was fashioned with almost as much care and thought as Jack's inaugural speech.

"Dear Oleg," Jackie wrote on December 13, 1960:

This letter is just a series of incoherent thoughts that I must get settled so I can spend these next weeks truly recuperating & not have to think about details, otherwise I will be a wreck & not strong enough to do everything I have to do.

1) I wired Bergdorf to send you measurements so you can go ahead with clothes . . .

2) For every evening dress I order from you, will you please send a color swatch to a) Mario — at Eugenia of Florence to have evening shoes made — State if shoes should be satin or faille — if necessary send material to make shoes in — & tell him to hurry. b) to KORET — some man there . . . makes me matching evening bags, simple envelopes or squares . . .

PUBLICITY . . . I refuse to have Jack's administration plagued by fashion stories of a sensational nature — & to be the Marie Antoinette or Josephine of the 1960's — So I will have to go over it with you before we release future things — because I don't want to be seen to be buying too much — You can make the stories available — but with my approval first — There just may be a few things we won't tell them about! . . .

COPIES — Just make sure no one has exactly the same dress I do — the same color or material — Imagine you will want to put some of my dresses in your collection — but I want all mine to be original and no fat little women hopping around in the same dress . . .

In Palm Beach, Jack was engaged in the vital business of picking a cabinet, and to the extent that he was even aware of all the fuss being made over Jackie's wardrobe, he found it amusing. It never occurred to him that his wife's appearance could have any bearing on his political fortunes.

"Nobody suspected back then, not even the president, that Jackie was to become his best public-relations tool," said Oleg.

Nobody, that is, but Jack's father.

"Just send me an accounting at the end of the year," Joe told Oleg. "I'll take care of it."

* * *

Snow began falling on Washington late in the day of January 19, the eve of the inauguration.

"It snowed like I have never seen it snow," said Kenneth, Jackie's hairdresser. "It was a true blizzard. I was taken to the Kennedys' house on N Street, and Mrs. Kennedy showed me her dress, what she was going to wear that night to the gala organized by Frank Sinatra and Peter Lawford. I hadn't seen it before. It was a very beautiful white dress with a geometric design at the waist, a shimmering white organza.

"She had on a robe," Kenneth continued, "and I worked on her upstairs in their bedroom. There were lots of interruptions. The phones were ringing. It was a very, very busy house. But we talked about the fact that it was blowing like you cannot believe. We talked about having her hair fixed enough so that it wouldn't be destroyed. She had to walk out of her house to the car, and there was no covering or anything. So I did her hair in a way that was stiffer than usual."

The president-elect and the First Lady

were due at the National Guard Armory at 9:00, but the hour came and went, and Jackie was not ready.

"For Chrissake, Jackie, we're late," Jack called to her from the bottom of the stairs. "Let's go!"

Finally, at 10:00, Jackie descended the stairs dressed in her long white organza gown, sparkling jewels, and bouffant hairdo.

Jack stared up at her. For a moment, he was speechless. Then, he made an okay sign with his thumb and middle finger.

"Let's go," he said.

By this time, huge snowdrifts had brought the city to a virtual standstill. All along the president-elect's route, hundreds of spectators lined the white streets, watching the Kennedys' limousine creep by at 10 miles an hour.

"Turn on the lights in here," Jack said to the driver, "so they can see Jackie."

At the entrance of the armory, Frank Sinatra waded into the swirling drifts in his patent-leather shoes and personally escorted Jackie inside. He was careful not to step on her white skirt.

At 11 o'clock — two hours behind schedule — the lights dimmed in the armory and Frank walked onto the stage. He began to sing a parody of his hit song "That Old Black Magic":

> That old *Jack* magic
> Has me in its spell . . .

In the darkness of the vast armory, a spotlight swept across the audience and fell on the presidential box, framing the handsome couple. There was an audible sound as hundreds of people sucked in their breath and began whispering "Jack and Jackie . . . Jack and Jackie . . . Jack and Jackie . . ."

> That old *Jack* magic
> That you weave so well . . .

But it was Jackie who held everyone in her spell.

One American Touch

"The trip down to Washington was a dreadful ordeal," said Sister Parish, Jackie's interior decorator, recalling the historic blizzard that disrupted the inauguration. "I went down with my secretary in a car piled to the bursting point with labeled samples for Mrs. Kennedy. We were trapped in the middle of the storm and did not arrive until the wee hours in Washington, where our car completely broke down in the middle of a snowdrift."

Jackie had asked Sister to help her with "the house with the columns," as she coyly referred to the White House, and Sister wasted no time complying with the new First Lady's request. On the morning after the inauguration, she showed up at the White House in a bright-purple rented car that was decorated inside with tiny pink slippers and souvenir monkeys.

Upstairs, Sister saw Jack and Jackie emerge from their separate bedrooms — Jack from the Lincoln Room and

Jackie from the Queen's Room — and walk down the long corridor toward her.

"The president went into his office for the very first time," Sister said. "My impression of President Kennedy that morning was that of a young boy. He looked as if he didn't have a care in the world. His presence was so magnetic that it made one's hair vibrate."

The suitcases with Sister's swatches and samples were unpacked, and the two women went to work. Jackie was still suffering from a postpartum depression that left her drained of energy, but she and Sister worked nonstop through the morning, laying plans to obliterate all the "Mamie pink" and Grand Rapids furniture that dominated the upstairs Family Quarters.

Sister took it all down on her big foolscap pad.

"Oh, Jackie," she said every once in a while, "this is terrible, this is terrible!"

By 11:00, they had picked out materials for each room.

"Do you think it's possible to have lunch here, or do we have to go out?" Jackie asked Sister.

"I began ringing bells," Sister said, "and reached Mr. West [the chief usher], who assured us we could indeed lunch right there."

Jackie chose the menu: hamburgers, vegetables, and a bottle of wine. Lunch was brought on trays, with two servants accompanying each tray.

Halfway through lunch, Jack came in, greeted the women with a cheery "Hi!" and continued on his way through a connecting door into the Lincoln Room.

"I'm going to have a new thing — Metrecal," he said as he disappeared behind the door.

He had put on considerable weight as a result of his cortisone treatment and did not like his jowly appearance.

A half-hour later, he was back — and still hungry. He began to nibble at the food on the trays. As he ate, Jackie told him that she and Sister had decided the White House looked as though it had been decorated by a department store. No, worse: it looked like the inside of a Statler Hotel. No, even worse than that: it looked like Moscow's dreaded Lubyanka Prison!

She and Sister had an idea: they would draw up a master plan to redecorate the entire White House. They would put together a fine arts commission, composed of people they knew in the Social Register, who would find furniture, paintings, and other historic objects, and raise funds to buy pieces as gifts to the White House. And they would appoint Henry Francis du Pont, the greatest living expert on American antiques, as chairman of the group.

"I want to make this a grand house," Jackie said.

Jack violently opposed the idea. Every president who had tampered with the White House — from Martin Van Buren to Harry Truman — had wound up alienating Congress and losing votes. He would not permit his wife to redecorate the White House.

"We're not going to *redecorate* it," said Jackie, "we're going to *restore* it!"

Then, ignoring any further objections from Jack, she showed him the materials she had picked out for the Family Quarters. For his room, she had selected a blue Brunschwig toile fabric with little white cherubs.

"I've always loved angels," Jack said.

Jackie had been thinking about the White House for weeks. Shortly after the election, her social secretary, Letitia

"Tish" Baldrige, the daughter of a Republican congressman, had been given a secret tour of the executive mansion by Mary Jayne McCaffree, Mrs. Eisenhower's social secretary.

"I am in seventh heaven," Tish wrote Jackie in a memo marked Confidential. "Imagine being able to seat a whole dinner incorrectly and be able to do it because 'the White House cannot make a mistake.'"

Tish's seven-page memo, which has never been published until now, spelled out the "ghastly" state of affairs she found in the Eisenhower White House:

> The Head Usher runs the house — the butler, cook, waiters, maids, laundresses, etc. However, he has run it like a military camp the last 16 years or so, and the place definitely lacks real female taste. Par example: in the State Dining Room, the only permanent plant or flower container on view for all the public, is a cheap $2.98 heavy white porcelain jardinière with three sick ivy plants in it, on the great marble mantel piece! The kind your cook wouldn't want in her quarters.

As for Jack and Jackie's private quarters on the third floor of the mansion, Tish noted:

You are going to have to do some work here in the non-public rooms, or you won't be able to stand it. I'm referring now, for example, to the Private Dining Room next to the big State Dining Room, which seats 14 or 16. You will probably want to have intimate fun dinners here. The rug is heavy awful dark maroon, and the whole room is so dark, it gives one the shudders. The wrong silver pieces sit on the sideboard . . .

You will probably have to pay for your nurse out of your own salary budget. You MIGHT be able to get your cook on the W.H. payroll . . . The W.H. chef is a Philippino, and the staff is mixed, noir et blanc. The Eisenhowers eat on trays in their sitting room every night. The food must be plenty cold by the time it reaches them, is all I can say, since it's prepared two floors below in another part of the house.

Many things about the White House

horrified Tish, and she noted some of them under "SHOCKING FACTS":

I just couldn't believe this. When the E's have their big musicales, for example, NOTHING is served the guests to drink. Mary Jayne said once in a great while a California or NY State wine grower donates horrible champagne for one specific party. Otherwise the budget won't allow. At large receptions, only punch, coffee and sandwiches are served. Well, that's all right, it's understandable, but not to have something to drink after dinner is practically a disaster.

We must do something about this, somehow, even if it means laying the whole problem before the domestic wine growers' industry . . . Every little hick embassy in the world has all the good things to eat and drink it wants. But not the White House!

Henry Francis du Pont made a careful, room-by-room appraisal of the White House, and, together with Jackie, drew up a master plan of suggested changes. The Chippendale chairs in the Family Dining Room were all wrong. The Red Room had mismatched furniture. The Green Room needed American Sheraton pieces. And an entire renovation was needed in the Oval Room, which was the president's reception room for distinguished visitors.

"All furniture purchased for the use of the president's house," du Pont decreed, "shall be, as far as practical, of domesic manufacture."

But Jackie had other ideas. She preferred French Empire–style furniture, and she encouraged one of her rich friends, Jayne Wrightsman, who was a member of the Fine Arts Committee, to begin combing Paris for antiques.

Jayne wrote a note to Sister Parish suggesting that the committee hire Stephane Boudin, the principal designer of the Parisian firm Jansen, who had directed the restoration of the Grand Trianon at Versailles and had recreated Josephine's château at Malmaison. Though Sister Parish was a respected interior designer, she was not in the same league as Boudin, and when she received Jayne's letter, she flew into a rage and threatened to quit.

In a follow-up letter, Jayne pleaded with Sister:

First things first. You must *never* think of resigning from the Committee! It would break Jackie's heart & mine too, I might add! The White House is so lucky to have you. You must not be confused by Jansen. Boudin is doing nothing at all for the White House.

But that was simply not true. In the spring, Jackie had arranged for Boudin and du Pont to be given a joint tour of the White House.

"From the first day the two men met, it was apparent they'd never see eye to eye on anything," said J. B. West, the chief usher. "Mr. du Pont, a dignified Eastern millionaire, was interested only in authenticity and didn't care about arrangement and proportion or compatibility. Monsieur Boudin, a bubbly, dramatic little Frenchman, cared only about pleasing the eye. . . .

"Mr. du Pont, who was slightly deaf, spoke rapidly, walked slowly, and mumbled," West continued. "Monsieur

Boudin was also hard of hearing, spoke halting English, and bounced energetically around the room. They tried desperately to be polite to each other. There were so many 'beg pardons' and 'so sorrys' and 'I'm afraid I don'ts' and 'but don't you means . . . ,' Mrs. Kennedy and I both had to interpret. We wove in and out of the state rooms, dumbfounded by their total lack of communication."

"This is *not* going to work!" Jackie whispered to West.

"We'll just have to see to it that they aren't here at the same time again," West said.

"Absolutely!" Jackie said, laughing. "Must keep them apart!"

"Jacqueline Kennedy, like H. F. du Pont, grew up in opulent surroundings and was accustomed to fine furniture," said Elaine Rice, an expert on American furniture. "However, her interest in interior decoration was more aesthetic than historical. . . . One exchange between the First Lady and H. F. du Pont highlights their different approaches to restoration. The object in question was a mirror of the Federal period, which featured an eagle. Ambivalent over whether or not this item of French manufacture should be displayed in the White House, du Pont inquired if Mrs. Kennedy felt it should be accepted.

"Mrs. Kennedy replied, 'I think the mirror should be accepted if you like it. As long as it has the eagle, it doesn't matter if it's French.'

"This statement illustrates Jacqueline Kennedy's priorities in selecting period furnishings — appearance over provenance. . . . In reality, the preference of the First Lady, especially for French design, led to a redecoration of the executive mansion that placed fashion above accuracy."

Du Pont was a purist. He had amassed the largest collection of early American decorative arts at his home in Winterthur, Delaware, which he had turned into a museum. During his visits to the White House, du Pont liked to move furniture around the way he saw fit. After he left, however, Jackie would order aides to go through the White House re-placing the items of furniture in the positions they occupied before.

In pursuit of her vision, Jackie refused to be intimidated either by Sister or du Pont. She wanted Boudin's French touch in the White House, and she convinced Sister to use the Frenchman in redecorating the Red and the Blue Rooms, and the Oval Room. But Jackie wanted to keep Boudin's involvement in the project a secret. It would not do for the newspapers to find out that a Frenchman was playing a major role in the White House "restoration."

> I talked to Jayne today [Jackie wrote Sister], and she said Boudin wouldn't mind a bit our using his designs — & he wouldn't say anything — so that is lovely.

Sister objected to the lavish French treatment Jackie wanted for the Oval Room, but in the end, Jackie got her way. She drew sketches with little swatches and paint smears indicating exactly what she wanted. The color scheme of this great space was yellow, brown and green. The walls were covered in pale-yellow silk, and the curtains in matching silk faille were trimmed in contrasting beige and brown. Six shamelessly French Louis XVI chairs covered in mustard velvet were placed around the perimeter of the room. Underneath, there was a smooth yellow rug; above, a bronze doré and rock crystal chandelier. The price of the room was more than $50,000, and the result was nothing short of breathtaking.

In a note to Sister, Jackie remarked that "the one American touch" in the Oval Room was the little stars on the curtains — which she subsequently removed from the design.

Jack was unhappy with the Blue Room, which Boudin had painted white, using blue only as an accent in the curtains and in the antique Savonnerie rug, which had a gold-and-pink scalloped design on a light-blue field.

"It's too French," he grumbled. "Before you open it up [to the public], have the floors darkened and get a great big blue rug on the floor."

J. B. West sent Jackie a memo with the president's instructions.

"Fine — Darken the floors," she scribbled in the margin. "I'll talk to the Pres. about the rug."

She did. And just as she wanted, the antique Savonnerie rug remained on the floor.

The Polite Brush-Off

Less than a month after he became President, Jack summoned Angier Biddle Duke, his chief of protocol, to the Oval Office. Tall, lean, and impeccably tailored, Angie was so naturally limber and light on his feet that he reminded people of Fred Astaire.

"Jackie and I have been talking about what I should expect of her as First Lady," Jack told Angie. "I'd like you to help me straighten her out. Would you talk to her about it?"

"Sure, Mr. President," Angie said.

A career foreign-service officer for his entire adult life, Angie had never heard of a president calling in his chief of protocol and asking him to speak to his wife. But he did not think that Jack's request was unreasonable, and as soon as he left the Oval Office, he went off in search of Jackie. He found her, dressed in jodhpurs and riding boots, in Tish Baldridge's office in the East Wing of the White House.

"The president has asked me to talk

to you about your official obligations and responsibilities as First Lady," Angie said after he and Jackie had settled down over freshly brewed cups of coffee.

"Gosh, Angie, I want to do everything I can," Jackie said. "But I want to be sure I'm not going to be trampled on in the process."

"First tell me, what is the least you will do?" said Angie. "Where is the botton line on this?"

"My family," Jackie said. "They come first. The children come first in my life. I've got a problem: the kids are young and I just want to do as much as I can within the bounds of my responsibility to my children. And however you want to phrase it, that means I want to do as little as I have to."

"All right," said Angie. "That's good to know."

"I mean," Jackie continued, "kings and queens — that's fine. But all those banana-republic presidents — forget it. Can't we work out a way to give them the PBO?"

"The PBO?"

"You know," she said, "the polite brush-off. Can't we give them to Lady Bird to handle?"

"I get it," Angie said. "Now let me see; how does this formula strike you? When chiefs of government, prime ministers, and heads of state come here on working visits *without* their wives, you don't have to appear. However, if they come *with* their wives, you'll take part. You can't make exceptions. You can't pick and choose. You've got to support me on this, because if you play favorites here, it's going to hurt feelings and have political consequences."

Jackie thought for a moment, then said, "I guess I understand."

"I think if we work along those lines, we'll be able to keep your appearances on these occasions to as minimum as possible," Angie said. "I'll work with Tish Baldridge on all these matters. We'll draw up guest lists to include artists, writers, and intellectuals — the kind of people *you're* interested in."

"Fine," Jackie said. "But there's one other thing."

"What's that?"

"The title 'First Lady,' " Jackie said. "I don't like it. It's corny."

"Corny?"

"Yeah, corny."

"Well, Jackie," said Angie, "we just

won't call you that, will we?"

"Good."

"What *should* we call you?"

"Call me Mrs. Kennedy."

A Few Laughs Upstairs

April 6, 1961
Dear Puffin,

I adored your letter and would so love to see you when you are in Washington. I will be away the weekend, including Monday, but it might amuse you to come to the Senate ladies lunch on Tuesday, April 25th. The lunch is at one o'clock, so why don't you come a little early so we can have a few laughs upstairs. Call my social secretary, Tish Baldrige, and tell her if you can fit this in.

Much love,
Jackie

About an hour before the Senate ladies lunch was scheduled to begin, Ellen "Puffin" D'Oench, who was now a housewife living in Middletown, Connecticut, presented herself at the White House. She was shown upstairs to the Family Quarters and greeted by her old

Vassar classmate, Jacqueline Bouvier Kennedy.

"Jackie was wearing a wonderful pink suit," Puffin recalled. "She hadn't changed at all, not remotely. She didn't wear much makeup. She had such vivid coloring and wonderful white teeth, although she smoked. She showed me her closets and around the bedrooms and all that stuff. And all I could hear myself saying was, 'I just don't believe it; I don't believe this.'

"On a table, there was this enormous object," Puffin continued. "Sukarno, the dictator of Indonesia, had just been there, and he'd given her a gift of coral bells. They're silver-handled objects with a long coral piece that babies could suck on. I picked this thing up.

"She said, 'Isn't it the most phallic-looking thing you ever saw? Sukarno gave it to me because he had a thing for me.'

"Then we went in this long limousine to the Senate, and Jackie got out of the car, and I was right behind her when they took pictures. But of course I can never find myself in any of those pictures. The Secret Service wanted me to get out quickly so they could move her very fast up the steps. And it was enormously tense, even though it looked so simple.

"She told me on the way over that she wasn't looking forward to this lunch, where they come into the locker room and take off their clothes and put on these Red Cross uniforms and roll bandages. But now that she was First Lady, the one good thing was she didn't have to change her clothes.

"After it was over, we drove back in the car, and I remember at one point Jackie put the window down and asked the Secret Service man if he would give her her cigarette case. He handed it back to her. And I remember asking her if it wasn't something of a thrill to have this kind of power.

"And she didn't very much like that question. It did not go over well. It was a question about personal power and whether that gave her some kind of pleasure. I asked it because I thought it would give *me* pleasure. *I'd* love to be able to put the window down and ask for my cigarette case and not have to carry money. I could really be quite happy with that.

"But she never answered the question. Jackie didn't like to think that she might enjoy power in that sense."

A Star Is Born

"About a month before we went to Paris," said White House press secretary Pierre Salinger, "the president called me in and said, 'You know what we ought to do? We ought to get French television to do a show with Jackie as the star — have Jackie take French television through the White House and talk to them in French. And I'll do a little interview at the end in French and English.' "

Pierre was a master publicist, and he built an elaborate marketing strategy around Jack's simple suggestion. He traveled to Paris with the president's advance team and wined and dined French journalists, filling their heads (and their notebooks) with charming anecdotes about the handsome American president and his beautiful young wife. He made sure that for every tale about Jack's humble Irish origins, there was a story about Jackie's elevated French forebears.

As a person of French ancestry himself, Pierre understood the average Frenchman's mentality. The French, despite their egalitarian pretensions, were no different than any other people when it came to a fascination with royalty. And so Pierre played up Jackie's regal aspects — her expert horsemanship, her couture clothes, her restoration of the White House, her patronage of the arts, and her widely discussed plan to hold a majestic ball at Mount Vernon, the home of George Washington, for Pakistani President Ayub Khan.

Pierre's campaign reached its climax when France's state-controlled television devoted an entire hour to a program on the Kennedys. Just as Jack had hoped, Jackie came across as a dewy young princess of the television age.

Two days later, Jackie followed Jack down the stairs of Air Force One onto the tarmac of Orly Airport. They were greeted by French President Charles DeGaulle and Madame DeGaulle, who appeared like a pair of grizzled figures from the past next to the trim American president and his wife. As soon as the crowds pressed against the airport fences spotted Jackie in her navy-blue silk suit and black velvet pillbox hat, they broke into a rhythmic chant: *"Vive Jacqui! Vive Jacqui!"*

Hundreds of thousands of people lined the motorcade route into Paris. They waved little French and American flags as the open limousine carrying Jack and DeGaulle passed by. Then, moments later, the second car appeared with Jackie and Madame De-Gaulle, and the crowd broke into an ear-splitting roar.

"Jacquiii!" they screamed. *"Jacquiii! Jacquiii!"*

Jack heard the deep rolling thunder of the crowd behind his car. He was sensitive to every nuance of public emotion, and he understood that Jackie was stirring a kind of visceral reaction among the French throngs. That throaty animal roar was a familiar sound to Jack — it had greeted him in countless cities during the presidential campaign in America. Now, here in Paris, it was Jackie's turn.

"She was the princess and he was the prince — that must be it," said presidential adviser Clark Clifford in an effort to explain Jack and Jackie's impact on the French. "She was the beautiful princess on the balcony and he was the handsome knight in shining armor who comes riding by on a white charger, gathers up the princess in his arms, and off they ride into the sunset. That's why they transcended boundaries, that's why they appealed to the world."

The motorcade stopped at the Place de la Concorde, and Jack and Jackie got out and received a 101-gun salute. The mayor of Paris then presented Jackie with a $4,000 diamond watch, and, like Clark Clifford, he compared her to royalty. Her visit, he said, reminded him of the recent reception given Queen Elizabeth II.

"Queen Elizabeth, hell," said Dave Powers, leaning toward Jack and whispering in his ear. "They couldn't get this kind of turnout with the Second Coming."

Only a few weeks earlier, Jack had thrown out his back while planting a ceremonial tree in Canada, so he arrived in Paris in excruciating pain. During his hectic, three-day visit, he used every free moment to soak his back in a hot tub.

In the King's Chamber, the suite of rooms he occupied in the Palais des Affaires Estrangères, a nineteenth-century palace on the Quai d'Orsay, there was a gold-plated bathtub the size of a table tennis table. Late on the afternoon of his second day in Paris, Jack again slowly and painfully lowered himself into the steaming water. He and Jackie were due in a couple of hours at a candlelit supper in the Hall of Mirrors at the Palais de Versailles. But first, he was in the mood for what his aides had come to refer to as "tub talk," and he called out for Dave Powers and Kenny O'Donnell to join him.

Dave and Kenny entered the cavernous marble bathroom accompanied by a surprise visitor — Janet Des Rosiers, once the stewardess on the *Caroline*, by that point the secretary to the American ambassador in Paris.

"You'll excuse me if I don't get up to shake your hand," Jack said to Janet.

"I understand perfectly, Mr. President," she said.

"God, we ought to have a tub like this in the White House," Jack said.

"If you play your cards right with DeGaulle," Dave Powers shot back, "you might be able to take it home as a souvenir."

"Jackie looked so beautiful today," Jack said.

He spoke with deep satisfaction about Jackie's performance in Paris. He was amused by the jealous reaction of Madame Hérvé Alphand, the chic wife of the French ambassador to the United States who was known to be one of Jack's occasional lovers. At an Elysée luncheon hosted by DeGaulle, Nicole Alphand had tried to win attention, but she had finished a poor second to Jackie, who had proved to be a potent political asset for Jack.

"Kennedy had been warned that DeGaulle would be distant and difficult to reach," Kenny O'Donnell said. "The general's strained wartime relationship with Roosevelt and Eisenhower made him suspicious of American presidents, and, as Kennedy fully appreciated, he regarded the NATO alliance as a plot by the United States and Britain to undermine France's independence.

"But DeGaulle was captivated by Jackie's knowledge and interest in France," Kenny continued, "and by her fluency in the subtleties of his language. Acting as his interpreter, she drew him into long and entertaining conversations with her husband that probably made him more relaxed with Kennedy than he had ever been with another head of a foreign government."

Jackie's coup could not have come at a more opportune moment for Jack. Over the previous month, he had suffered a series of humiliating setbacks — the Russians' first-man-in-space triumph, the Communist takeover of Laos, and, most spectacular of all, the bungled Bay of Pigs invasion of Cuba.

In the weeks before their Paris trip, Jack was frequently close to tears over Cuba. Jackie remarked that she had not seen Jack so depressed since his near-fatal back operation.

"After [Cuba]," said Jack's friend Chuck Spalding, "he was totally different in his attitude toward everything. From then on, it mainly became an arduous, back-breaking job that would kill you, one way or another. Before the Bay of Pigs, everything was a glorious adventure, onward and upward. Afterward, it was a series of ups and down, with terrible pitfalls, suspicion everywhere, [with him] cautious of everything, questioning always."

Jack arrived in Paris feeling like a man who had run out of luck. Fidel Castro had inflicted on him the most shameful defeat of his life, and Jack kept shaking his head, rubbing his hands over his eyes, and mumbling, "How did I ever let it happen? How did I ever let it happen?" America looked like a paper tiger, and Jack's aides warned him that when he left Paris and went on to Vienna, where he was to meet next with Nikita Khrushchev, he should expect a hostile, even bellicose reception from the Soviet party chief.

Beneath his easy charm and boyish manner, Jack could be just as tough as his father — and just as vindictive. He had an iron will and was determined to even the score with Castro. Before he left Washington, he gave orders to set up a covert plan, later to be called Operation Mongoose, to rid the Western Hemisphere of Castro by any means necessary, including assassination. As part of that plan, he reactivated a secret CIA-Mafia effort to kill Castro and he stepped up his correspondence with Sam Giancana through Judy Campbell.

After a half-hour or so of tub talk,

Jack dismissed Dave, Ken, and Janet. He climbed out of the gold-plated bathtub, wrapped a towel around his waist, and padded into his bedroom. He was all alone. Jackie occupied a separate bedroom — the Queen's Chamber — at the other end of the huge hall.

Jack was still in agony from his back. He had brought along his special, extra-firm horsehair mattress, his crutches, and a pair of White House physicians — Admiral George Burkley and Dr. Janet Travell. But when he pressed the buzzer next to his bed to summon help, it was Dr. Max Jacobson — "Dr. Feelgood" — who appeared at the door.

After ministering to Jack, Max walked down the long hallway and entered the Queen's Chamber. Tall French doors opened onto a view of the formal Quai d'Orsay gardens and, beyond, the broad sweep of the Seine River. Max asked to see Jackie, and he was shown into her bedroom, where she was preparing for the night's state dinner at the Palais de Versailles.

She sat in front of a mirror, being fussed over by Alexandre, the famous Parisian hairdresser, and a bevy of his assistants. Weeks earlier, Jackie had sent Alexandre a lock of her hair through the diplomatic pouch, and she had reserved his services for the duration of her Paris visit.

"A beautiful face needs foliage around it," exclaimed Alexandre as he went about experimenting with various hairpieces and wigs. He was creating a sweeping fourteenth-century-style bouffant hairdo around Jackie's prominent cheekbones.

In another part of the room, Jackie's maid was laying out two different gowns for the evening — one an American design by Oleg Cassini, and the other a French creation by Hubért de Givenchy. Earlier, Jackie had planned to wear the Cassini, but then she was not so sure.

As Max paced back and forth across the room, Jackie looked at herself in the mirror. Alexandre's hairdo was something entirely new for her. It made her look more grand and glamorous.

Or was it Paris that was changing her?

For the first time in her eight years of marriage, Jackie was creating a bigger stir than Jack. She was the star in

Paris. Jack had said it all at a press conference: "I do not think it altogether inappropriate to introduce myself to this audience. I am the man who accompanied Jacqueline Kennedy to Paris, and I have enjoyed it."

This was a new role for Jackie, and in some ways it still did not fit her.

"Many times when I watched her play with [her children], exactly as a child plays," said J. B. West, the chief usher at the White House, "I felt, strangely, that *this* was the real Jacqueline Kennedy. She was so happy, so abandoned, so like a little girl who had never grown up. Many times, when she was performing with such grace and authority the role of First Lady, I felt she was just pretending. 'She really longs for a child's world,' I thought, 'where she can run and jump and hide and ride horses.' I thought of her as an actress — constantly playing a role."

But her success in Paris had begun the metamorphosis of Jackie.

"Jackie was very smart," said Oleg Cassini. "Suddenly, this enormous adulation was showered on her, and it changed her. Outwardly, no. The voice was the same, the mannerism the same. But she became different. Because when the entire world constantly lauds you, it would take a tremendously disciplined mind not to fall a little bit in love with yourself. She knew she had a fantastic hook into her husband, who as a good politician realized that she was a huge asset.

"Until Paris," he continued, "Jackie was nothing but a little housewife. But then, she singlehandedly began to create Camelot. The furniture, the ideas, the cooks, the food, the fantastic people she invited to the White House — Casals, Bernstein, Frost. And she did it all herself. While Jack was busy with the presidency, Jackie was creating an American Versailles."

Yet, even while this transformation in Jackie's character was taking place, she felt physically weak. She had never recovered her health after the Caesarean birth of John Jr. She still tired easily.

"I need pep," she said. "That's why I need Max."

When Alexandre had finished with Jackie's hair, he left the room for a moment so that she could get dressed.

Jackie turned to Max and told him that she was ready for her shot. But as the little doctor opened his attaché case and took out a syringe, Letitia Baldrige stepped between him and Jackie. Tish was concerned that Jackie was developing a strong dependence on Max's amphetamines.

"Jackie," Tish said, "you don't know what's in that needle. This could be dangerous. I'm against this. Don't do it."

"Nonsense," said Max. "There's nothing in this needle but vitamins. Here, come with me, and I'll show you."

He led Tish away to her nearby bedroom, where he gave her a shot that sent her into orbit. Then he returned to Jackie and injected his magic elixir into her buttock.

She was ready for Versailles.

She took one last look at the two ball gowns hanging side by side — one American, the other French. They were both so beautiful. But without thinking, she chose the one she knew would attract the more favorable reaction from the French press. She slipped into the Givenchy — a rhinestone-studded white satin gown with a red, white, and blue bodice.

She called Alexandre back into the room and asked him to put the finishing touches on her coiffure. She could not sit down without wrinkling her gown, so he stood on a chair, leaned over, and carefully secured a sparkling diamond tiara into the elaborate topknot on the crown of her head.

"Not the Usual Bullshit"

After Paris, it was on to Vienna — and the summit meeting with Soviet party boss Nikita Khrushchev.

"Khrushchev will be here any minute," Jack told Max Jacobson in the upstairs bedroom of the American ambassador's residence in Vienna. "This could go on for hours. I can't afford any complications with my back."

"You won't have that for an excuse," Max replied.

He snapped open his attaché case and took out a syringe and an unlabeled bottle.

Max was waiting in a vestibule when Jack and Khrushchev emerged several hours later from the embassy's music room.

"Are you all right, Mr. President?" Max asked as Jack walked by.

"I'm fine," Jack snapped, clearly annoyed by the question. "Do you mind if I take time for a piss?"

The president's advisers followed him out of the room. They, too, looked shaken and angry.

Jack went upstairs to the ambassador's living quarters.

"How did it go?" Evelyn Lincoln asked.

"Not too well," Jack said.

Ten minutes after his final session with Khrushchev, Jack met in a room at the U.S. embassy with James Reston, who had replaced Arthur Krock as chief of *The New York Times*' Washington bureau. The blinds had been drawn, casting the room in somber shadows.

"How was it?" asked Reston.

"It was awful," Jack said. "Worst thing in my life. He rolled right over me — he thinks I'm a fool — he thinks I'm weak."

Reston carried a pencil and a notebook, and he jotted down an observation about Jack's unusual dress: he was wearing a hat — indoors.

"[He] pushed it down over his forehead, sat down on a couch beside me, and sighed," Reston said.

"I think I know why he treated me like this," Jack said. "He thinks because of the Bay of Pigs that I'm inexperienced. Probably thinks I'm stupid. Maybe most important, he thinks that I had no guts."

"Reston thought that Kennedy was practically in shock, repeating himself, blurting out things he should never say in other circumstances," Richard Reeves wrote in his account of the Kennedy presidency. "The gentleman from the *Times* was shocked himself, thinking this had nothing to do with him, that he just happened to be the first person the president was talking to after a kind of trauma."

"Not the usual bullshit," Reston jotted in his notebook. "There is a look a man has when he has to tell the truth."

"So we've got a problem," Jack said, regaining some of his composure. "We have to see what we can do that will restore a feeling in Moscow that we will defend our national interest. I'll have to increase the defense budget. And we have to confront them someplace to show them we're tough."

"Where?"

"We're going to confront them in Vietnam," Jack said. "We'll stop them in Vietnam."

"Good Night, Mrs. Kennedy, Wherever You Are"

At the beginning of October, Henry Francis du Pont, the world's foremost expert on American antiques, arrived in Washington to check on the progress of the White House restoration. Du Pont, who was in his eighties, shuffled from room to room, mumbling to himself, until he came to the Family Dining Room, where he stopped dead in his tracks.

Jackie and that French decorator Stephane Boudin had moved another piece of furniture!

"I sincerely hope we can see the room together the way I planned it," du Pont wrote Jackie after he returned to his museum at Winterthur, "and that you put back between the windows the little Baltimore desk with Dr. Franklin's mirror above it."

But Jackie was no longer paying attention to du Pont.

"I remember, on one occasion," said David Stockwell, a Wilmington antiques dealer and a colleague of du Pont, "we got down there at nine, and she called down and said she was at the hairdresser's and would be late. We waited three quarters of an hour, and she again called and said she'd be late. After another three quarters of an hour, she called to say her next appointment had already arrived, and so she wouldn't be able to meet with us. I think this really insulted Mr. du Pont."

Her treatment of du Pont was symptomatic of a new, independent Jackie. She disregarded Angie Duke's pleas to abide by protocol and was photographed water-skiing with astronaut John Glenn when she was supposed to be at the White House greeting a Latin American president and his wife. She ignored the objections of Jack's aides and announced plans to go off on an extended trip to Asia and the Far East with her sister, Lee Radziwill. She spent so much time away from the White House riding at Glen Ora, her new country estate, or sunning herself in Palm Beach that a columnist suggested that a TV newscaster should sign off his program with the words: "Good night, Mrs. Kennedy, wherever you are."

"She had begun to enjoy the title, and the life, more than anyone ever suspected that she would," said J. B. West, the chief usher at the White House. "She guarded her own social life in the White House as jealously as she guarded that of her children and invited 'working' press only to those elaborate . . . parties — such as the one for forty-nine Nobel Prize winners or for André Malraux, France's minister of culture — which she deemed to be in the 'national interest.' The others — the dinner dances until dawn or the intimate little parties on the second floor — were strictly off the record."

It was those intimate little parties that gave Angie Duke the biggest headaches.

"She would have her friends from New York come down — people like Chuck Spalding; my wife-to-be Robin; Flo Smith; Bill Draper; Leland Hayward and his wife Pam [later Pamela Harriman]; Fifi Fell, who was married to John Schiff; and Bill Paley," Angie said. "Jackie would have tables out in the hall, and a band. It was just great. But it caused resentment in some official circles, particularly by the vice president when he read about it the next day in *The Washington Post.* So the president asked me to go and explain the problem to Jackie. I said to her, 'I'm having a hard time with the vice president and Mrs. Johnson because they're not invited to your parties, and their feelings are hurt and it's causing friction.' To which she replied, 'Good God, do I have to have *them?*' "

"It was the best-looking group of people you ever saw," said Robin Chandler Duke. "They were all well-educated people, for the most part, and wore wonderful clothes, and loved to dance and sing and have a good time. You had these two beautiful young people in the White House on the crest of a wave. It was fantasy land. And I remember one time Bill Paley turned to Jayne Wrightsman and asked, 'Now what day-of-the-week diamond necklace is this, Jayne?' It was known that she had seven diamond necklaces. 'Is this the Wednesday necklace or the Friday necklace?' "

"I was at the famous White House private party where Gore Vidal got into trouble," said the writer George Plimpton. "Gore went up to Jackie and put his arm around her in this rather familiar way. She was wearing one of those odd-looking Japanese obis with a satchel in the back. Bobby was standing there and he removed Gore's hand from Jackie and made a rather sharp remark. It made Gore angry.

"Later at the party, Gore began to insult Lem Billings," Plimpton continued. "He went after Billings and called him an idiot and a fool and all sorts of things. That was the end of it for Gore at the White House. Everybody had too much to drink at those things. The drinks came in big tumblers and they tended to be filled as soon as you emptied them. So there tended to be excessive behavior."

Toward the end of Jack's first year in office, Jackie was asked to host a televised tour of the White House, an event that would be seen by nearly 60 million Americans over the CBS and NBC networks and turn her into an instant celebrity. Jackie's power as First Lady seemed to be increasing in inverse proportion to Jack's troubles as president. His administration was caroming from one crisis to another — the Berlin Wall, the price dispute with big steel, the civil rights disturbances in the South. Ted

Sorensen counted 16 crises in Jack's first eight months as president.

A new drama began to unfold in the Kennedy marriage. For the first time, Jackie felt secure enough to challenge Jack's attempts to control her.

"Where is this great Irish wit you're supposed to have — this celebrated wit?" she taunted Jack on one occasion. "You don't show much of it when you're home."

"They played a lot of these psychological marriage games on each other," said Laura Bergquist, a writer for *Look* magazine. "She was always trying to deflate his ego, and he was hitting at her core of self-contained privacy."

Jackie was changing from a shy, insecure young wife and mother into a self-confident woman who asserted herself more and more forcefully. When Arthur Krock's wife, Martha, insisted on treating Jackie like a protégée and launched into an alcoholic tirade about her lack of punctuality, Jackie barred the Krocks from the White House.

Most of all, Jackie began to realize how valuable she had become to Jack.

"It gradually dawned on her that she had all these people fighting for a smile, fighting for a nod of approval," Oleg Cassini said. "Some days, when she was in a good mood, she was the most fantastic, charming person. But I was at parties where she would barely say hello to you — she was mad at you because you didn't do something according to Hoyle. She began to be aware that she might go down in history as one of the great women of the period."

Jackie kept up the pretense that she wore only clothes designed by Oleg Cassini, while in fact she purchased the latest Paris fashions through a secret back channel that she had established between Tish Baldrige, her social secretary, and Janet Des Rosiers, the secretary to the ambassador in Paris.

September 19, 1961

Dear Janet:

Mrs. Kennedy is ordering some Givenchy clothes — discreetly, we might say. When they are ready, which will be some time yet, would you be kind enough to get them at Givenchy's and deliver them into the hands of the Air Attaché for transmittal by air to us . . .

Sincerely yours,
Letitia Baldrige
Social Secretary

"There was a wife of an officer at the embassy in Paris who was close to Jackie," said Janet, "and this woman would pick out the clothes for Jackie. She knew Jackie's taste. The couturiers in Paris would deliver boxes to me — Courrèges, Balmain, Givenchy. The boxes were never sealed. I used to open them up and show the clothes to the girls in the office. Then I'd seal them and give them to a Marine guard to deliver to the airport."

If the role of the First Lady is to help win the public's endorsement of the president and advance his political cause, then Jackie was becoming one of the most effective First Ladies in history. With her magnetic star quality, she drew millions of people to Jack's side. As Christmas, 1961 approached, she had emerged as the most valuable operative in Jack's presidency, his chief ally, the one person in the world he could not do without. Her brilliant success created a kind of chain reaction in the White House. She and Jack fused like two nuclei, releasing an enormous amount of energy.

"Jack began to think, *Hey, wait a minute — I discovered her!*" said Oleg Cassini. "And he, so to say, 'fell in love' with Jackie all over again."

Access

On the morning of December 19, 1961, Joe Kennedy and his favorite niece, Ann Gargan, teed off at the Palm Beach Golf Course. Joe had helped raise Ann and her brother Joey after their parents died, and he had encouraged her to become a nun. But Ann had left the convent when she developed a mild case of multiple sclerosis, and since then, she had become Joe's constant companion. Her devotion to Joe bordered on the religious.

"We finished the sixteenth [hole]," Ann recalled, "and, as Uncle Joe picked up the ball, he said he felt rather faint."

Four hours later, Joe was being rushed by ambulance to St. Mary's Hospital. A blood clot in one of the arteries of his brain had triggered a massive stroke. He could not move the right side of his body or speak. At the hospital, his condition was deemed so serious that a priest was summoned to administer the final rites.

"It was an opportunity to pull the

plug," Lem Billings said. "But Bobby said no, let him fight for his life."

Jackie and the kids were already in Palm Beach for the Christmas holidays, and Jack flew down from Washington on Air Force One. Frank Saunders, Joe's long-time chauffeur, met the president at the airport and took him to St. Mary's. When Jack arrived at the hospital, he found Ann Gargan keeping vigil beside Joe's bed. The old man's face was twisted out of shape, and rivulets of saliva dripped from the corners of his mouth.

"Dad, how are you?" Jack asked, grasping Joe's right hand, which had been badly deformed by his stroke.

"Noooooo!," Joe shrieked, flailing away with his left arm. "Yaaaaa!"

A nurse came in and calmed him down.

"He tried to write with his left hand, to give us instructions, and tell us what he wanted, but it frustrated him," said Frank Saunders. "I would see this look of fear creep into his eyes too — the look you can get from a wild caged animal."

"It was the most frustrating day I ever

spent," Lem Billings recalled of the time he visited Joe shortly after his stroke. "The old man couldn't talk. Instead of making words, he would groan and gurgle. Jack and Jackie were there, and they were very upset. Especially Jackie. The old man was used to giving orders, barking at people, yelling. Now he was reduced to two words. The words were *no* and *shit.*"

Joe was able to understand everything that took place around him, but he was unable to speak. Deeply frustrated, he would thrash people with the cane in his left hand. His face was drawn, and his hair had turned completely white. Behind his glasses, his steely blue eyes were so full of rage that his nurses said he looked like evil incarnate.

"His bodily functions were not under his control," said Janet Jeghelian, who became his physical therapist. "He was totally dependent on a nurse. He would defecate in his pants. They tried very hard to train him and to put him on a potty seat, which was always right beside his bed, although I think quite often, the nurses had to give him enemas and things of that sort, just to keep his system open and functioning."

Joe was not a good patient, and Ann Gargan, in her misguided devotion, did not make things any easier for the doctors and nurses.

"Uncle Joe," she said, "if you don't feel like doing it, you don't have to."

"There were a lot of questions raised about the relationship between Joe and Ann," Janet Jeghelian said.

Ann staunchly denied that Joe had ever made a pass at her, but Janet said: "I heard stories from the nurses that something was going on. Occasionally, the nurses — especially the night nurses — would go into his room and find Ann on the bed with Joe. Whether they were just snuggling or what, I don't know."

In the early spring, Joe was moved to Hyannis Port. His large, airy bedroom overlooked the sea, and it was furnished with a hospital bed, several chairs, and a couple of bureaus, which were covered with photographs of his children and 20 grandchildren.

When Rose returned home after her annual visit to the spring couture collections in Paris, she burst into Joe's room. She was wearing a beautiful new French dress, and she whirled around and around in an imitation of Loretta Young's entrance on her weekly television show.

"What do you think of this one, Joe?" she asked.

"Unnh," Joe said, rolling his eyes in exasperation at Ann Gargan.

Rose danced out of the room, only to reappear a few minutes later in another Paris creation.

Every Friday, three of Joe's cronies — Richard Cardinal Cushing, Francis Xavier Morrissey, and Morton Downey — came to visit. If the weather permitted, they sat outside on the deck. They wore identical velvet slippers with their initials embossed in gold. They laughed a lot and, occasionally, they said something to Joe, who of course could not reply.

Jackie came often. She went out of her way to touch and kiss Joe on his paralyzed right side. She sat in his bedroom, dressed in a pair of white cotton poplin slacks and a T-shirt, chain-smoking and chatting with the nurses and physical therapists.

"How's he doing?" Jackie asked. "Are

the treatments making any difference?"

The answer was always the same. Joe's condition was not improving.

"I called the White House every morning," said Luella Hennessey, the Kennedy family nurse. "When Jack came on the phone and told his father what was going on, Mr. Kennedy would say, 'ahh,' or 'ohhh,' a kind of grunt, acting either pleased or not pleased. And then the next day Jack would tell him how it came out."

Jack tried to keep his feelings to himself. When he was asked by Bobby how he managed to get along without their father, Jack replied, "I'm the president."

Once, however, he described to Ben Bradlee the poignant phone calls he received at the White House from his father. He had to "grit his teeth," Jack told Ben, while his father responded to everything he said with "No, no, no, no, no."

"What nobody should ever forget was that Jack had a tremendous respect for his father, just a *tremendous* respect," George Smathers said. "He was really quite in awe of his father all the time; he had the greatest admiration for him of anyone, and I mean *anyone!*"

Jack had lived his entire life in a tight paternal clasp. His father had loved him and, at the same time, had been his severest critic. It was impossible to ask Bobby, a younger brother who was in awe of Jack, to be like Joe. Instead, Jack turned to Jackie to fill that vital role.

"In those days, nobody wanted to admit just how much power Jackie wielded around the White House," *The New York Times* society columnist, Charlotte Curtis, said. "You get power in several ways, but two of them are access and leverage, and Jackie certainly had access. . . . Unless you understand this concept, you don't understand Washington. It explains how someone like Jackie [got] to play a vital role in political affairs without being very blatant about it."

THIRTEEN

The Abyss

February, 1962–October, 1962

Associate of Hoodlums

In late February, 1962, Courtney Evans, a slight, sandy-haired FBI man, was ushered through the double doors of J. Edgar Hoover's office.

"Good morning, Mr. Evans," Hoover said.

He came around his desk and showed Courtney to a chair.

"How are you today?"

"Fine, Mr. Hoover," said Courtney. "Just fine."

Directly behind Hoover was a tall window with a view of the capitol. A large fish was mounted on the wall. The only picture was of Harlan Fiske Stone, who, as attorney general, had appointed Hoover acting director of the FBI back in 1924, the year Jack Kennedy turned seven.

Hoover returned to his desk, which sat on a small, raised platform that elevated him above the eye level of his guest. To his right was a Bible that had been given to him by his mother. To his left there was a telephone and an intercom that connected him to the FBI's associate director, Clyde Tolson, and the 11 assistant directors, of whom Courtney Evans was one.

Courtney was more important than his title implied. Several years before, when Bobby Kennedy served as chief counsel to the McClellan committee, Courtney had helped him expose corruption in the labor movement. The two men had developed a close bond, and Courtney and his wife, Betty Fern, were frequent guests at Hickory Hill, the home of Bobby and Ethel Kennedy. The day Bobby was named attorney general, Courtney became Hoover's indispensable link to the president's brother.

Over the years, Hoover had been through more than a dozen attorneys general, all stiff and formal men. He bristled when Bobby showed up at the bureau with his family dog, went around the office introducing himself to people, and lectured Hoover on the need to hire more blacks, do something about civil-rights abuses, and investigate organized crime.

"Another thing that irritated Hoover," said Courtney, "was the fact that he was accustomed to seeing presidents —

with the exception of Truman — on a regular basis. When he tried to continue this custom under the Kennedys and was rebuffed, he really got incensed. So I told Bob, 'Look, if you want to preserve the peace around here and not have an all-out war, you'd better get your brother to invite the director over for lunch occasionally.' "

"There wasn't any doubt about it," said George Smathers. "Hoover hated Bobby."

Hoover peered down at Courtney.

"I want you to deliver this memorandum to the attorney general," he said.

He passed the document across his desk.

Before he took it, Courtney looked up at Hoover. He could not read the expression on the director's face.

The memo was addressed to Bobby, with a copy to Kenny O'Donnell, the president's chief political aide. It contained information that had been developed by the FBI on the basis of wiretaps, telephone interceptions, and physical surveillance of Sam Giancana, the chief of the Chicago Mafia, and his handsome West Coast henchman, Johnny Roselli.

"The memo reported what various mobsters had been overheard saying to each other regarding Judith Campbell and the President," Courtney recalled. "They talked about the fact that while Judith Campbell was associated with Giancana and Roselli, she also had entrée to the president. Giancana wasn't jealous that Judith Campbell was seeing the president, because it was a good source for him to develop information. Wasn't Giancana smart! The memo also reported numerous calls to the White House switchboard from Judith Campbell.

"That's as far as the memo went, however," Courtney continued. "It did not draw the broad conclusion that the president was necessarily sleeping with Judith Campbell. There wasn't any hard evidence of that. Nor was there anything to indicate that the president had passed on any compromising information.

"Bureau memos never reached a conclusion as to what the facts meant. So there was nothing in this memorandum about a sexual relationship between Judith Campbell and John Kennedy. It was not expressed, but it was there if you read between the lines."

A few hours later, Courtney entered Bobby's fifth-floor office, which featured a stuffed tiger mounted in a walking pose.

"Hello, Bob," he said.

"What's up?" Bobby said.

Courtney handed him the envelope and watched as the attorney general opened it and read the three-page memo inside.

In many ways, Courtney was a typically straitlaced product of the FBI. He came from a family of teachers, married his high-school sweetheart, and was a man of rock-solid values. Yet, he was not particularly shocked by the sexual revelations in the memo.

"With the exception of Truman, I don't know that Kennedy's moral standards were too different from those of other presidents," he said. "Kennedy may have been more prolific at it. Perhaps he did it more frequently and with a wider variety of women. But going back to Harding, or even all the way back to Washington and Jefferson, it's just human nature. If you compare Kennedy with Lyndon Johnson, you're talking about two peas in a pod."

However, the information in this memo went beyond mere womanizing. As Bobby knew, Sam Giancana was working with the CIA in a plot to assassinate Cuba's Fidel Castro. Jack's sex life was mixed up with national security.

When Bobby was finished reading, he looked up.

"I'll take care of it, Courtney," he said. "I'll take care of it."

Almost a month later, Hoover was invited to one of his infrequent lunches with Jack at the White House. Before Hoover went, Courtney briefed him by memo on the status of the Judith Campbell matter.

Subject: JUDITH E. CAMPBELL
 ASSOCIATE OF HOODLUMS
 CRIMINAL INTELLIGENCE
 MATTER

This is being submitted as the Director may desire to bear this information in mind in connection with his forthcoming appointment with the President.

Information has been developed that Judith E. Campbell, a free-lance artist, has associated with prominent underworld figures Sam Giancana of Chicago and John Roselli of Los Angeles.

A review of telephone toll calls from Campbell's Los Angeles residence discloses that on November 7 and 15, 1961, calls were made to Evelyn Lincoln, the President's secretary at the White House.

Telephone toll calls were charged to the residence Campbell rented in Palm Springs, California, to Evelyn Lincoln at the White House on November 10, 1961, and November 13, 1961. Campbell was also charged with a call to Mrs. Lincoln on February 14, 1962, from Cedars of Lebanon Hospital in Los Angeles, where Campbell was a patient at the time. . . .

[Frank Sinatra] referred to Campbell as the girl who was "shacking up with John Kennedy in the East."

"It was not in Hoover's character to bring up the Campbell episode during lunch with the president," Courtney said. "Hoover wanted these meetings to be pleasant. They were more stroking sessions than anything else. He may have dropped a hint about the Campbell matter, but that would be all he would do."

But a hint was all that was necessary. Just hours after Jack's lunch with Hoover, he placed a call to Judy through the White House switchboard. It was the last call to her that he would ever make — from the White House, at least.

At the Justice Department, Bobby had assembled a group of gung-ho prosecutors and ordered them to stamp out "the conspiracy of evil" that was organized crime. Sam Giancana and his pals were high on Bobby's list.

"Don't let anything get in your way," Bobby told his staff. "If you have problems, come see me. Get the job done, and if you can't get the job done, get out."

"We are out front fighting organized crime on every level," one of Bobby's bright young lawyers told him, "and here the president is associating with Sinatra, who is in bed with all those guys."

"Give me a memorandum and give me the facts," Bobby shot back.

In private, Bobby went to Jack and demanded that he cancel his plans to spend a weekend in late March at Frank Sinatra's house in Palm Springs.

"Johnny," he told his brother, "you just can't associate with this guy."

"Everybody complains about my relationship with Sinatra," Jack told Charlie Bartlett. "Sinatra is the only guy who gives Peter Lawford [Jack's brother-in-law] jobs. And the only way I can keep this marriage [to Pat Lawford] going is to see that Peter gets jobs. So I'm nice to Frank Sinatra."

Nonetheless, Jack called Peter and told him to break the news to Frank.

"I can't stay there . . . while Bobby's handling [the Giancana] investigation," Jack told Peter. "See if you can't find me someplace else."

Something's Got to Give

Someplace else turned out to be Bing Crosby's home in Palm Springs.

Bing was a Republican, but he jumped at the chance to outdo his rival Frank Sinatra and nab the president of the United States as a house guest. His ranch-style house was perched on top of a hill and commanded a spectacular view of the desert. It was located at the end of a mountain road, making it ideal from a security point of view. There was room for Jack's Secret Service detail at songwriter Jimmy Van Heusen's nearby house.

By the time the presidential entourage arrived on Friday night, March 23, Bing had left for the weekend. Jack moved into the crooner's master bedroom. The king-size mattress was hauled away and the president's traveling horsehair mattress was put in its place. The next morning, Jack took a dip in the pool. Afterward, he removed his bathing suit and wrung it out in plain sight of the entire presidential party.

Although the next presidential election was $2\frac{1}{2}$ years away, Jack was already starting to think seriously about running for a second term. He had come west to lay early plans for the 1964 campaign. That evening, he threw a poolside party for a number of big California contributors and show-business personalities. Peter Lawford showed up with Marilyn Monroe.

Jack and Marilyn were old, if only occasional, lovers. They had first met back in 1954 when he was a promising young senator with a new bride and she was Hollywood's reigning sex goddess and Mrs. Joe DiMaggio.

"He couldn't take his eyes off me," Marilyn boasted to a friend about that fateful night.

After Marilyn divorced Joe, she moved to New York City, where she began attending acting classes at the Actors Studio. One day in 1955, Jack phoned her from his duplex apartment at the Carlyle Hotel and asked her to come over. Their affair immediately blossomed into a bicoastal romance. When Jack was in California, he slept with Marilyn at Peter Lawford's beach house in Santa Monica. And when he became president, he called her to his side in Washington.

"Peter Lawford disguised her and took her to Washington on Air Force One as a secretary," said Lawford's wife, Pat. "She hated it. She cursed him the whole way. And he'd make her take letters, to really play it out. And they went to the White House."

It was after 9:00 when Marilyn walked through the double doors of Bing Crosby's house into a hallway filled with flowers. A formal dinner was being served in the dining room, but only three or four people were seated at the large table. Most of the guests were out by the pool, drinking and listening to music.

Marilyn was wearing a black wig. At 35 years of age, she looked more beautiful and alluring than ever. Beneath her glamorous exterior, however, there dwelt a fragile woman who suffered from bouts of suicidal depression.

She had just emerged from a long stay at New York's Payne Whitney Psychiatric Clinic, where she had been treated for a dual addiction to sleeping pills and alcohol. Hollywood producers considered Marilyn unstable and unreliable, far more trouble than she was worth. Frequently sick or late, she was constantly on the verge of being fired from her latest movie, a big-budget CinemaScope production called *Something's Got to Give.*

Marilyn found Jack in the crowd. She seemed to be on something — booze or pills — and it made her slur her words. After most of the guests had left, she followed Jack down a hallway and staggered drunkenly into his bedroom. They made love on his horsehair mattress. When it was over, she massaged his bad back.

"You should get a massage from my masseur," she told him.

"That wouldn't be the same as getting it from you," Jack said.

Suddenly, Marilyn picked up the telephone on the night table and dialed Ralph Roberts, an actor who doubled as her personal masseur. Marilyn shared many intimate details of her life with Ralph, and he knew that she planned to be with the president that weekend.

"She asked me about the soleus muscle," Ralph said, "which she knew something about from the Mabel Ellsworth Todd book [*The Thinking Body*], and she had obviously been talking about this with the president, who was known to have all sorts of ailments, muscle and back trouble."

"I've been arguing with my friend," Marilyn said, "and he thinks I'm wrong about those muscles we discussed. I'm going to put him on the phone."

"A moment later," Roberts said, "I was listening to that familiar Boston accent. I told him about the muscles and he thanked me. Of course, I didn't reveal that I knew who he was, and he didn't say."

By the spring, Jack's political operatives had started to put in place a strategy for the upcoming presidential campaign. Money was their foremost concern. In late May, the Democratic Party threw a fund-raising gala in Madison Square Garden in honor of Jack's forty-fifth birthday. The turnout included the royalty of American show business — Jack Benny, Maria Callas, Henry Fonda, Ella Fitzgerald, Peggy Lee, Peter Lawford and, as the pièce de résistance, Marilyn Monroe herself.

When Jackie heard that Marilyn would be performing at the birthday salute at Madison Square Garden, she decided not to attend. Instead, Jackie went to her weekend house in Glen Ora and participated in the Loudoun Hunt horse show.

And so, as the lights dimmed and the show began at the Garden, Jack sat without Jackie in the presidential box. He slumped in his chair, his feet up on the rail, puffing on a small cigar. His sisters — Pat and Eunice — were his female companions.

"Mr. President," Peter announced, "on this occasion of your birthday, this lovely lady is not only pulchritudinous, but punctual. Mr. President — Marilyn Monroe!"

Fifteen thousand people broke into cheers, but Marilyn did not appear.

She was backstage in her dressing room drowning her stage fright in alcohol.

An hour or so later, after all the other acts, Peter made another introduction:

"Mr. President — the *late* Marilyn Monroe!"

In the wings, Marilyn stood paralyzed in her skin-tight Jean-Louis gown, which had been sewn onto her body. Peter's partner, Milt Ebbins, shoved her onto the stage.

"When she came down in that flesh-colored dress, without any underwear on . . ." said Hugh Sidey of *Time*, "you could just smell lust. I mean, Kennedy went limp or something. We all were just stunned to see this woman."

"What an ass . . . *what* an ass," Jack whispered.

"Happy . . . birthday . . . to you," Marilyn began to sing in a soft, seductive voice. "Happy birthday to you . . ."

After her seven-minute performance, Marilyn returned to her dressing room and collapsed from nervous exhaustion. Her maid, Hazel Washington, cut her out of the gown, bathed her, and helped her into another dress. Then Marilyn joined Jack and a throng of happy Democrats at the Park Avenue apartment of Arthur Krim, the president of United Artists.

During the party, a photographer caught Marilyn, Jack, and Bobby huddling in a corner. It was a totally unguarded moment, and the solemn expressions on their faces indicated that all was not well.

Nonetheless, after the party, Marilyn went back with Jack to his suite at the Carlyle Hotel.

"I learned from an FBI agent that they remained in the suite for several hours," the gossip columnist Earl Wilson said. "It was the last prolonged encounter between them."

From the beginning, the relationship with Marilyn was just another casual diversion for Jack. He never romanced her with sweet words and sentimental gestures, and he always maintained his cool. Months would sometimes go by without a word from him. He needed the time away from Marilyn to recharge his sexual batteries.

"Once I get a woman," Jack had frequently said, "I'm not interested in carrying on, for the most part."

But for Marilyn, the affair with Jack meant a great deal more. There was nothing cool about Marilyn. As the illegitimate child of an unstable mother and the survivor of several orphanages and foster homes, she took all her relationships seriously. More than anyone she had ever met, Jack satisfied her need to live out a life of fantasy.

"I am the little orphan waif indulging in free love with the leader of the free world," she said.

One of her friends, Harry Rosenfield, remembered that Marilyn was proud that she was sleeping with the man she considered the most important person in the world.

"She was so excited," Rosenfield said, "you'd have thought she was a teenager."

But like a teenager, Marilyn could not control herself. She was telling everybody in Hollywood about her affair with the president. And in the summer of 1962, word was getting around. Newspapers and magazines were looking into the rumors.

After Marilyn's unforgettable appearance at the Madison Square Garden party, those rumors took on a life of their own. Jack asked one of his men, William Haddad, a former *New York Post* reporter who was working for the Peace Corps, to squash any stories that might be in the works at *Time* and *Newsweek*.

"See the editors," Jack told Haddad. "Tell them you are speaking for me and that it's just not true."

"He lied to me," Haddad told Jack's biographer Richard Reeves years later. "He used my credibility with people I knew."

"Marilyn realized the affair was over but couldn't accept it," Peter Lawford told author C. David Heymann. "She began writing these rather pathetic letters to Jack and continued calling. She threatened to go to the press. She was bitter enough to tell [a friend] that the president made love like an adolescent. The president finally sent Bobby Kennedy to California to cool her off. She took it pretty hard."

Getting Even

That summer, the Radziwills rented a villa in Ravello, a picturesque town set above the limestone cliffs of Amalfi on the southern coast of Italy. When Jackie arrived there with Caroline in early August, she was greeted by the mayor, Lorenzo Mansi, as though she were royalty.

"Grazie, molto gentile," said Jackie, who actually did look like royalty in her beautiful white fretwork dress and matching black shoes, bag, belt, and gloves.

After the long trip from America, she appeared a bit drawn and tired. But she was happy to be back in Ravello, which she had visited more than 10 years earlier when she was a student in France.

"We were young," she said, "and we traveled with little money in our pockets. We stopped only one night in Ravello, without seeing much, while spending lots of time washing and putting our clothes in order because we didn't have anything else to change into."

Jackie's brother-in-law, Prince Stanislas Radziwill, had rented Villa Episcopio, a sixteenth-century Gothic structure that had been inhabited by the last king of Italy, Vittorio Emmanuel III, and his wife Elena. It had a lovely library and a beautiful, large bedroom, which Jackie turned over to Caroline and the two Radziwill children, Anthony and Christina.

"We visited the kids one night," said Mario d'Urso, a socialite investment banker, "and they were all asleep except for Caroline. She was sitting up in bed with the lights on. She had gathered all the Italian magazines with pictures of her mother and herself."

Two days after Jackie arrived — Friday, August 10, Saint Lorenzo Day — word spread throughout the town that the First Lady was going to play the piano. Within a few minutes, the whole of Ravello — women, children, and tourists — had gathered in the town square near Villa Episcopio. Dozens of radio and television technicians came to record her notes.

At 8:30 that night, the strains of the Neapolitan songs *"O Sole Mio"* and

"*Anema e Core*" could be heard coming from Villa Episcopio. After a while, the music stopped and the people of Ravello, who until then had listened in awed silence, broke into applause.

On Sunday, Jackie put on a burnt-orange-colored dress and took Caroline to mass at the cathedral. Father Francesco Camera had prepared an ornate sixteenth-century prie-dieu with red velvet pillows for Jackie — an honor normally reserved for the visiting Bishop of Amalfi. But Jackie chose to sit on one of the regular wooden benches, next to Mayor Mansi and a toothless old woman. Caroline looked at the woman and laughed.

"Buona Caroline," Jackie said in Italian, "preghiamo per papa" ("Good Caroline, let us pray for Father").

Jackie left the villa at 10:00 every morning.

There were 17 people in her retinue — the three children and their two nurses, Stash and Lee Radziwill, journalist Benno Graziani and his wife, Nicole, photographer Robin Douglas Home, *New York Times* columnist C. L. Sulzberger, three Secret Service agents, and two Italian-speaking T-men on loan from the Treasury Department's anti-narcotics bureau.

Cheering crowds lined the roads to get a glimpse of La Bella Jackie. Her motorcade roared by, accompanied by the wailing sirens of Italian police cars and outriders mounted on motorcycles.

At Amalfi, her party boarded a speedboat and headed for Conca dei Marini, a bay set between the steep cliffs. There, Jackie disappeared into a cabana and emerged a few minutes later in a green one-piece bathing suit and white cap with green flowers on it. As soon as she and Caroline waded into the water, a speedboat full of photographers bore down upon them. Two police speedboats went out to meet the intruders and, as Jackie and Caroline watched in amusement, a battle of the boats ensued.

"Eh, you photographers, watch it!" the police announced through a bullhorn. "If you get any closer, we'll ram your boat."

Jackie sent one of her bodyguards to negotiate with the paparazzi. They struck a deal: the First Lady would agree to pose for photographs for 10 minutes, and they would agree to leave after that.

Once back at Villa Episcopio, Jackie took a nap. Then, in the early evening, George Griffin, an American consular officer stationed in Naples, arrived in his Fiat Spider convertible. He delivered presidential envelopes sealed with wax, and Jackie tore them open and eagerly consumed the gossip from Jack.

As Jackie knew, a story was making the rounds in Washington that Jack had been secretly married as a young man to a woman named Durie Malcolm. This tale, based on a privately printed book called *The Blauvelt Family Genealogy*, was being circulated by right-wing and anti-Catholic circles and, if left unchecked, could hurt Jack's chances for reelection. However, it now appeared that Jack had the situation in hand. His friend, Ben Bradlee, was preparing a piece for *Newsweek* that would unmask the story for what it was — a false rumor.

A candlelight dinner was served at night on the terrace of Villa Episcopio. The Radziwills often invited their friend, Princess Irene Galitzine, the famous

Italian couturier. One time, she brought along Gianni Agnelli, the heir to the Fiat automobile fortune, and his wife, Princess Marella Caracciolo di Castagneto.

Gianni was a ruggedly handsome man with slicked-back hair. He had met Jack and Jackie in 1955 on board the yacht of Aristotle Onassis. A notorious playboy and avowed hedonist, Gianni had been unimpressed by Jackie back then, and he had paid her little attention. But on the terrace of Villa Episcopio, he was amazed to see how much she had changed. Sleek and tanned, she was wearing a thick French braid that reached all the way down her back to her waist. The boring little debutante had become a sophisticated woman of the world.

Soon, Gianni was escorting Jackie around Amalfi and suggesting to Princess Irene that he bring Jackie as a guest to her waterfront house in Capri.

"I said no to Gianni," the princess recalled. "All those Secret Service agents and the confusion. But he insisted, and so they came over — Gianni, Jackie, and young Mario d'Urso." In addition, the princess said, "there were dancing parties at clubs until two or three in the morning. . . . He should not have gone with Jackie and us to those nightclubs, where one can be so easily photographed."

Gianni scandalized Italian society by inviting Jackie on his 82-foot yacht. She was photographed by the paparazzi scuba diving with Gianni and dancing barefoot on the deck of his boat to a five-man mandolin band.

Now when George Griffin, the American consular officer, showed up in the evening in his Fiat Spider convertible at Villa Episcopio, he saw Jackie going off with Gianni.

"I was disillusioned," he said. "She was the president's wife. Even the cynical Secret Service agents felt bad about it."

So did the CIA and the deputy secretary of state, George Ball, who also got into the act.

"An Agency official told me with some amusement that the CIA got a private message from Ravello to get Jackie's — what do you call it? — her diaphragm," said Ball. "They were ordered to fetch her diaphragm and send it over to Italy by the next plane."

Finally, Jack could take no more, and

he sent Jackie a telegram:

A LITTLE MORE CAROLINE
AND LESS AGNELLI.

"There was, I strongly suspect, a hidden drama being played out here, one that future biographers will explore at greater depth," said Margaret Truman. "Jackie was challenging Jack's attempts to control her — perhaps warning him that two could play the extramarital sex game."

Worldly Italian aristocrats speculated that Jackie was carrying on an affair with Gianni as a way of getting back at Jack for all his years of womanizing. It must be true, they said, because Jackie could easily have stopped the gossip but had obviously chosen not to.

Turning Point

"I got a call from the White House saying that President Kennedy would like me to come down to Washington to see him," recalled Clare Booth Luce, the playwright, diplomat, and journalist.

"We chatted a while, and then he turned to me and asked, 'Clare, what's on your mind?'

" 'A great man is one sentence,' I replied, 'and that sentence is characterized by having an active verb in it that describes a unique action. You shouldn't even need to know a man's name, because the action describes him.'

"He listened for a minute, then said, 'I don't follow you, Clare.'

" 'Well,' I said, 'you and I are both Americans and Catholics, so I'll give you a sentence that we both are familiar with: "He died on the cross to save us," or "He set out to discover an old world and discovered a new one," or "He preserved the Union and freed the slaves," or "He lifted us out of the Great Depression and helped to win a world war." I don't have to tell you who any of these men are. So if you ask me again, "What was I thinking?" — it's this: I wonder what sentence will be written after your name when you leave the White House? It certainly won't be "He got the agricultural bill passed." '

"The president suddenly read my thoughts.

" 'Oh,' he said, 'you're talking about Cuba.' "

In the middle of October, Jack was shown aerial photos taken by an American U-2 reconnaissance plane flying over Cuba. The photos confirmed that missiles capable of carrying nuclear warheads were being deployed by the Soviet Union in Cuba, just 90 miles off the southern coast of the United States.

Jack convened an emergency session in the Cabinet Room. As he headed for the meeting, he stopped to have a playful conversation with Caroline, who was almost five years old.

"Have you been eating candy?" he asked his daughter.

She did not reply.

"Caroline, have you been eating candy?"

Still no answer.

"Answer me. Yes, no, or maybe."

Caroline scampered off into the garden, and Jack entered the Cabinet Room for the fateful meeting.

He was under tremendous pressure from his advisers to launch a pre-emptive air strike against Cuba and destroy the Soviet missiles. The Pentagon estimated that the missiles could reach an arc of American cities that included Miami, Atlanta, Houston, New Orleans, and Washington, D.C. Unless he acted, he would go down in the history books as the commander-in-chief who looked the other way while the Soviets won the Cold War.

Ever since his humiliation in the Bay of Pigs, Jack had been searching for an excuse to crush Fidel Castro. Now, the Russians had handed him one. He knew he would be justified if he bombed the Cuban leader into extinction. Yet, to almost everyone's surprise, he exercised enormous restraint and ordered a naval blockade.

Though Bobby was by his side throughout the 13 days of tense deliberations, Jack made the final decision by himself. He carried around a poem, written by Robert Graves, that captured his feelings.

Bullfight critics row on row
Crowd the enormous plaza de toros,
But only one is there who knows,
And he is the one who fights the bull.

"Kennedy," said Vice President Lyndon Johnson, "was the coolest man in the room, and he had his thumb on the nuclear button."

"He did not want anyone to be able to write, at a later date, and say the United States had not done all it could to preserve the peace," Bobby said.

"Part of this attitude may well have reflected a growing sensitivity Kennedy was experiencing toward his own family," said the historian Thomas Reeves. "From all accounts, Jack had reached out to his children and had become emotionally engaged in their lives. He enjoyed them, fretted about their well-being, and worried about their future."

"If it weren't for the children, it would be so easy to press the button!" Jack told Dave Powers while they were paddling around the White House swimming pool. "Not just John and Caroline, and not just the children in America, but children all over the world who will suffer and die for the decision I have to make."

Later that day, Dave went to the Family Quarters to deliver a folder.

"Coming into the dimly lit living room to give the president the papers," said Kenny O'Donnell, "Dave heard [Jack's] voice as he talked quietly, and he assumed that he was alone, speaking to somebody on the telephone. Then he saw the president sitting in a chair with Caroline on his lap, reading to her from a storybook.

" 'I watched him sitting there with Caroline,' Dave said to me later. 'I thought of what he had been saying to me in the pool, about how worried he was about the children everywhere in the world, and, you know, I got the strangest feeling. I handed him the papers and got out of there as fast as I could. I was all choked up.' "

Others noticed a marked change in Jack's treatment of Jackie.

On the eve of his nationally televised speech about the missile crisis, Jack telephoned Jackie in Glen Ora and asked her to come back to Washington.

"We are very, very close to war," he said.

He wanted to spend the next few nights alone with Jackie and their two children.

"I remember there was a little squib on page 38 or something in *The New York Times*," Chuck Spalding said. "It said that 'at four o'clock in the afternoon, the president had called up Mrs. Kennedy and they went and walked out in the Rose Garden.' He was sharing with her the possible horror of what might happen.

"If it was earlier in their marriage, I don't think he would have called her then. But things were beginning to break up in his head."

Jack informed Jackie about the Pentagon's plans to evacuate the White House and send him to an underground shelter outside the District of Columbia. He couldn't wait until the Russians fired their first missile, because once a nuclear war began, the United States would have a warning period of only 18 minutes. He asked Jackie to leave Washington at once, so that she would be closer to their assigned underground shelter. He would follow.

But she refused. She did not want to leave him alone in the White House.

Jackie telephoned Chief Usher J. B. West at his home and asked him to come to the White House right away.

"But come up through the kitchen elevator so nobody will know you're here," she said.

"I'll be there in twenty minutes," West said.

When he arrived, Jackie greeted him dressed in colorful Pucci pants and loafers. She did not have on any makeup.

"Thank you for coming, Mr. West," she said. "There's something brewing that might turn out to be a big catastrophe — which means that we may have to cancel the dinner and dance for the [maharajah and maharani of Jaipur] Tuesday night."

West glanced toward the Oval Drawing Room. He could hear men's voices through the closed door.

"Could you please handle the cancellation for me?" Jackie said. "This is very secret, and I'm afraid Tish would get all upset and rant and rave — *you* know — and I think you could do it more calmly."

"Certainly," West said.

"As I walked down the hall toward the elevator," West recalled, "Robert Kennedy stepped out of the Yellow Oval Room into the hall. Glancing our way without a smile, he closed the door quickly behind him. Something very grave was happening, but I had no idea what it was."

"In the old days," said Secretary of State Dean Rusk, "you could have a confrontation or a showdown, you could go to sleep, and you'd wake up in the morning, and you'd be there, and the city would be there."

Jack was the first president in history to face Armageddon. He and Soviet Premier Nikita Khrushchev had come close to blowing up the world. For the first time in his life, Jack understood the consequences of his behavior. The missile crisis marked a turning point in his life — and in the life of his marriage to Jackie.

"There had been a noticeable closeness between Kennedy and his wife during the crisis," Richard Reeves wrote in *President Kennedy: Profile in Power.* "They had canceled several events, public and private, during those two weeks, spending time alone together and with their children."

When the crisis was over, and Khrushchev had backed down, Jack called Tiffany's and ordered small silver calendars showing the month of October, 1962 with the 13 days of the crisis engraved more deeply than the others. He gave one to each of the men who had helped him through the danger — and one to Jackie.

"In the first year or so in the White House, Jackie and Jack related to each other like professionals," Angie Duke said. "They were co-workers. But then, after the Cuban missile crisis, they became more personal with each other. Jack became more focused. He got the point. He understood what it meant to exercise power. Jackie started to talk about him in a more personal way. Like, 'Angie, the president is tired; lay off him, okay?' She seemed more concerned about him as a person. I could see them working more closely together. And there is one other thing that I might add. Jack had fewer women around."

"Their marriage got better," said George Smathers. "When you're president, you get kicked around a lot. The wife of the president starts feeling very protective. He sees that she's loyal and that they're in this thing together. They have to pull together; they have no choice. That's what happened to Jack and Jackie.

"Jack loved Jackie very much and, in his fashion, he was relatively true to her. He may not have stopped looking at other women, but I know one thing — he didn't like anybody better than her."

On the Sunday after the crisis, Jack was soaking in a bathtub at Glen Ora, talking to Dave Powers about his appointments. Dave was sitting on the toilet seat taking notes, when suddenly Jackie burst into the room.

She had been out riding, and she had a whip in her hand. She was wearing a long white riding shirt — and nothing else.

"Your next appointment —" Dave

said, stopping in midsentence.

"His last appointment has passed," Jackie said. "Just cancel the rest of his appointments."

"I felt so much sexual energy," Dave said later. "Like nothing was going to stop her from having Jack."

FOURTEEN

Love Lies
Bleeding

November, 1962–December, 1973

Let's Twist Again

It was snowing when Mary Pinchot Meyer, Ben Bradlee's blond sister-in-law, pulled her car to a stop in front of the White House. Mary rolled down the window and handed an engraved invitation to the guard. Next to her in the front seat was her escort for the evening, Blair Clark, the number-two man at CBS News.

As they waited to be waved through, Mary noticed a photograph of Langdon Marvin inside the guard shack. Langdon had become a wild and uncontrollable alcoholic, and his photo had been posted along with those of other people who were barred from entering the White House.

The passing from favor of Langdon Marvin, one of the president's most prolific procurers, was symbolic of a fundamental change. In late November, 1962, the Kennedys were gearing up for re-election, and Bobby swept through the White House like an avenging angel, ridding the place of anything that smacked of foulness and corruption. Sam Giancana complained to a fellow mobster that the president was not paying him his due respect: "We broke our balls for him and gave him the election, and he gets his brother to hound us to death."

To be sure, Jack might still indulge himself from time to time, but nude young women were no longer openly cavorting in the White House swimming pool. Movie stars like Marlene Dietrich, who had shuttled in and out of the presidential bedroom, were hard to find. And aides did not have to scour rooms in the Family Quarters for hairpins and other incriminating evidence before Jackie returned from her weekends away.

Mary Meyer, however, remained the president's regular mistress.

In her early forties, Mary was an attractive woman in a fey sort of way. Years before, she had lost a son in an automobile accident, a tragic event that had contributed to the breakup of her marriage to Cord Meyer, a panjandrum of the CIA. She dabbled in art and drugs, adopted the manners of a bohemian, and was a devotée of Timothy

Leary, the LSD guru.

She had known Jack since his student days at Choate. They had flirted at the Bradlees' house when Jack was a senator and had started sleeping together in January, 1962. Like many other women who had slept with Jack, Mary considered her affair with the president a feather in her cap. She boasted that she and Jack had smoked marijuana on more than one occasion in a White House bedroom.

But it was not merely excitement that Jack was looking for in Mary. They were old friends and, as such, they were cozy with each other.

Mary dropped the car off with a valet, and she and Blair entered the White House.

"I found myself sitting at a table with Jack and others, on the edge of this dance floor, not far from where Lester Lanin's jazzy little group was playing," said Blair, who had been at Harvard with Jack. "Jack said, 'Blair, tell Lester to play the twist and get Teddy to do it.' Then Jack laughed like hell at Teddy doing the twist. . . . Jack couldn't do it, with his back."

Mary disappeared in the middle of the party.

"Since I came with her as her escort, I went looking for her," Blair said. "Then, after about an hour, she turned up. It was wintertime, and it was snowing, and her dress was wet and muddy. Her hair was bedraggled and looked wet. And I said, 'Mary! What the hell! Where've you been?' And she said, 'Oh, I just got a little upset and went out and walked around, outside the White House.'

"I later learned that the president had taken her upstairs and talked to her. That was the night Jack broke up with Mary."

It was not as black and white as that, however. After that night, Jack and Mary continued to see each other — but more as friends than as lovers.

Against the Laws of Nature

"All I want for the nursery . . . is a pair of curtains like John's room," Jackie wrote, ungrammatically, in a memo to J. B. West, the chief White House usher.

She and Jack were expecting their third child in August and, in her usual fastidious fashion, Jackie gave West detailed instructions on how to prepare the "high-chair room" between little John's room and the Presidential Dining Room.

> [White] glass curtains you can still see through — like John's — & a white rug not wall to wall — I don't think the one in the children's & my room is too practical — I'd just . . . buy a rather shaggy inexpensive one at Sloane's which we can throw in washing machine — & a rubber pad beneath it . . .

In May, Jackie departed with Caroline and John Jr. for the Cape, where Jack had rented Brambletyde, a shingled house on Squaw Island, not far from the Kennedy family compound. By that point, there were 20 Kennedy grandchildren — eight of them belonging to Bobby and Ethel, who was pregnant with her ninth child — and as far as Jackie was concerned, that was more Kennedys than she could handle.

She persuaded Jack to make 1963 their last summer at Hyannis Port. The following year, they would rent a place in Newport.

But first she had to get through another pregnancy.

At 11:37 A.M. on August 7, Jerry Behn, the Secret Service agent in charge of the White House detail, approached Evelyn Lincoln outside the Oval Office.

"They called me from up at the Cape," he said, leaning over Evelyn's desk and speaking in a low tone so that no one else could hear, "and told me that Mrs. Kennedy was on her way to the Otis Air Force Base Hospital."

"Did she say she wanted the president to know?" Evelyn asked.

"No," Jerry said.

Evelyn realized that something was terribly wrong. Jackie was not supposed to give birth for another five or six weeks, and she had planned to deliver her baby at Walter Reed Hospital in Washington. What was she doing at Otis, which was located on Buzzards Bay near Falmouth, Massachusetts?

The secretary telephoned the Kennedys' house on Squaw Island, and got a member of the kitchen staff on the phone.

"Why did she go to Otis?" she asked.

"To have the baby, I guess," he said.

While she was talking, Jack came into her office. Evelyn stole a look at Jerry, and Jerry looked at Evelyn.

Then Evelyn told the president, "Jerry tells me that Mrs. Kennedy is on her way to Otis."

Jack was alarmed. He called Dr. Janet Travell, his personal physician, who was up on the Cape looking after Jackie. While he was waiting for Dr. Travell to call back with the latest news, he phoned Larry Newman, an old neighbor in Hyannis Port.

"I want you to go over there and just sit in the lobby of the hospital until I get there."

"I'll go right away," Newman said.

Then he called Godfrey McHugh, his Air Force aide.

"How long would it take to fly if I said I wanted to go somewhere?"

"Thirty minutes," McHugh said.

"I want to fly right now," Jack said. "So get ready."

By then, Dr. Travell was back on the phone. She informed Jack that his wife was about to undergo a Caesarean section at Otis.

"That's it," said Jack, "we're going to Otis."

This time, no one had to tell him to "get your ass back to your wife's bedside."

Born 5 $^1/_2$ weeks early, the baby weighed 4 pounds, 1 ounce. He was so sickly that a Catholic chaplain was summoned to come and baptize him while he lay in a pressurized incubator. He was named Patrick Bouvier Kennedy.

Larry Newman was waiting when Jack arrived at Otis Air Force Base Hospital.

"He came over and made a move as if he were going to put his arm around my shoulder," Newman recalled, "then just shook hands and said, 'Thanks for being here. It made me feel so much better knowing you were here.'

"I've never seen him more emotional," Newman went on, "and the way he said it, I was very close to tears. And I don't cry very easily."

Later, Evelyn Lincoln found Jack sitting on a bed in a hospital room. He was staring into space.

"How are things with little Patrick?" Evelyn asked.

"He has a fifty-fifty chance," Jack replied.

"That's all a Kennedy needs," said Evelyn. "He will make it."

But the tiny boy had trouble breathing. He was suffering from hyaline membrane disease, a respiratory disease in prematurely born infants. He was flown to Children's Hospital in Boston.

Jack commuted by helicopter between Otis and Children's Hospital, where he donned a white surgical gown and cap and watched as his son fought for his life.

At 3:00 in the morning on August 9, a Secret Service man came into the room where the president and Dave

Powers were catching some sleep.

"Dave," the Secret Service man said, "the doctor has told me the baby has taken a turn for the worse."

Dave woke Jack, and they went to Patrick's side.

"I was with him at the hospital when he was holding Patrick's hand and the nurse said, 'He's gone,' " Evelyn Lincoln said, "and tears came into his eyes. I had never seen tears in his eyes before."

"He just cried and cried and cried," Dave said.

Patrick had lived less than 39 hours, and all Jack could say when it was over was, "It is against the laws of nature for parents to bury their children."

Jackie was devastated. But she told Jack that they would somehow manage to go on with their lives.

"The one blow I could not bear," she said, "would be to lose you."

"It was a blow," said Jack's old PT-boat buddy, Paul "Red" Fay. "The bride and I were up at Squaw Island, their rented place on the Cape, and we talked with Jack. And he said, 'It would have been so wonderful to have a second son.' And then he stopped, and then said, 'But there's nothing I can do about it now, so we've got to put it behind us.' But it really was a blow to him. I mean, it was a great loss."

Jack invited Bill Walton, the artist, to spend the weekend with them.

"It was just the two of them and the kids and me," Bill told the author Ralph G. Martin. "Probably the most intimate weekend I've ever had with them.

"We were sitting in his office and he was going through the papers on his desk, mostly condolences from the leaders of the world. He'd read them and pass them over to me to look at, and he'd say, 'Look at what the pope said,' or 'How am I going to answer that one?'

"Then we went swimming and he took off this corset brace, a big contraption for his back, which he didn't want even the Secret Service men to see. He really wanted to bathe in the water rather than swim. While we were out there, he unburdened himself of everything that came to his mind, talked about everything from Khrushchev to Berlin.

"The house was full of sadness that weekend and Caroline was being a very bad girl, acting up a lot, and Jack was the only one who could quiet her down by talking to her.

"Jack and Jackie were very close after Patrick's death. She hung onto him and he held her in his arms — something nobody ever saw at any other time because they were very private people."

Tales of Ancient Smyrna

"That was the weekend that Jackie got a cable from Lee, inviting her to Greece to go on Onassis's yacht for a trip," Bill Walton said, "and she and Jack were discussing whether she should go. Jack remembered something hanging over Onassis on some court case, and I was instinctively dead set against it.

"But Jackie didn't want to go back to Washington. The White House was not a real home to her. And, at that time, it would seem more like a prison. Besides, she just wanted to get away. So that weekend it was finally decided that she should go."

Jackie had been on Aristotle Onassis's yacht before. Back in 1955, she and Jack had spent an afternoon on board the *Christina* having cocktails with Winston Churchill. With its crew of 60, including two hairdressers and a Swedish masseuse, there was no other luxury yacht like it in the world. It had marble bathrooms with solid-gold fixtures, barstools upholstered in the skin of whales' testicles, a fireplace made out of carved lapis lazuli, El Greco paintings, a twin-engine seaplane, and a swimming pool whose bottom could be elevated to create a dance floor. Her first time aboard, Jackie found the *Christina* vulgar.

This time, however, she was ready for over-the-top opulence. The cruise would be an antidote for the pain and torment she still suffered over the loss of Patrick. Jackie had never seen the infant during his three days on earth, and she had not been by Jack's side during the funeral. When she stepped aboard the *Christina* and joined her sister, Jackie was still in deep mourning.

The boat had nine double guest cabins, each decorated in a different style and named after a different Greek island. Jackie was given "Ithaca," which had been occupied at various times by Lady Pamela Churchill, Greta Garbo, and Maria Callas. After spending millions of dollars renovating and redecorating the White House, Jackie considered herself to be a connoisseur of luxe. She knew what things cost. She ran her hand over the solid-gold water tap in her cabin. She picked up the phone and asked for a massage. She snacked on caviar, as she had in Palm Beach, and washed it down with shots of vodka.

"Life on board the *Christina* was casual and guests did pretty much what they wanted," Diana Dubois wrote. "The yacht's actual voyages were often accomplished in short hops, with the majority of time devoted to amusements on shore. . . . The [cruise] retraced a path the *Christina* had followed many times: it touched at Lesbos and Istanbul and then navigated along the coast of the Peloponnesus."

Jackie let it be known that she expected Ari himself to escort her when they went ashore. Ari gladly did the honors, showing her the Blue Mosque of Istanbul and his own private island of Skorpios.

Jackie was excited by the superabundance of luxury, and she was fascinated by Ari, who reminded her of her swarthy father. Ari's features were repulsive; his education, rudimentary; his cultivation, practically nil (he thought the Impressionists were artists who wanted to impress people). But Jackie found him to be a fabulous raconteur. He mesmerized her with tales of life in ancient Smyrna, the city of his birth.

As Jackie knew, Lee was in love with Ari and had petitioned the Vatican to annul her marriage to Stash. She wanted to marry the Greek shipowner. Less clear, however, was whether Ari, who was in love with opera singer Maria Callas, wanted to marry Lee.

As the *Christina* made its way across the Mediterranean, it began to dawn on Jackie that her sister might actually win Ari away from Callas and claim all this luxury for herself. As Mrs. Aristotle Onassis, Lee would become a richer and more resplendent queen than Jackie who, after all, would one day have to vacate the White House.

She began giving Ari the full Jackie Treatment.

She gazed at him adoringly with her widely spaced, asymmetrical brown eyes. She punctuated her sentences with girlish words like *gosh* and *golly* and *gee.* She whispered to him at night as they sat on the poop deck under the stars. She accompanied him to tea with Queen Frederika. She danced with him to bouzouki music at nightclubs. She strolled with him through the streets of Smyrna. And she swam with him in warm lagoons when the yacht anchored toward the end of the day.

A paparazzo with a telescope lens caught Jackie in a bikini, and the shocking picture of the president's wife was seen all over the world.

"Touring with her sister, Lee Radziwill, Mrs. Kennedy allows herself to be photographed in positions and poses which she would never permit in the United States," wrote United Press International's respected White House bureau chief Merriman Smith. "The results at times are quite charming, but they serve to point up the fact that she's almost a different person when traveling, as it were, on her own . . ."

The others aboard the *Christina* could not help but notice what was going on between Jackie and Ari. Every morning at breakfast, there were feverish conversations among the passengers — Princess Irene Galitzine; Arkadi Gerney, Jackie's old friend from her student days in Paris; and Franklin D. Roosevelt Jr., who had been sent along by Jack to act as a chaperon.

"Maria Callas wasn't [on board] for the first time in four years," Roosevelt said. "Jackie's sister brought Stash Radziwill along, but Stash left during the trip. We began to look like a boat full of jet-setters, and President Kennedy didn't want that image."

Jackie appeared oblivious to all the gossip. She wrote long, rambling letters to "My dearest Jack." One of them ended with this disingenuous thought: "Wish you could enjoy the Mediterranean calm with me."

Jack put in calls to the yacht late at night. Jackie often wasn't there. He sent her a telegram demanding that she return home. She ignored it.

At the end of the cruise, Ari presented Jackie with a diamond and ruby necklace and so many other gifts that Lee said, "I can't stand it."

"Lee would tell her intimates later that she was only trying to do something nice for her sister when she brought her along on the *Christina*," wrote the author Diana Dubois, "and that Jackie co-opted Onassis on that cruise. . . . Jackie's expropriation of

Onassis drove a deep wedge between the two women. . . ."

Jackie had won the battle with her sister, but her victory was tinged with guilt. She had done everything but sleep with Ari — and a lot of people thought, mistakenly, that she had done that, too.

"I don't think that Jackie had an affair with Onassis on that cruise," said Robin Duke, Angie's wife. "The only way to keep Onassis interested in you was to drive him nearly mad with desire. You would not go to bed with him, because once you did, you would be like everybody else. And believe me, Jackie wasn't like everybody else. She was not about to lose her mystique."

You Can't Lose

While Jackie was cruising aboard the *Christina*, Jack called Stanley Tretick, a *Look* magazine photographer, and asked him to come to the White House and shoot some pictures of John and Caroline.

"I was surprised to get the call," Stanley said. "I knew that Jackie had been against me taking her kids' pictures for *Look*. She didn't view me as somebody artistic like Avedon. She just viewed me as a press photographer. But Jack was getting ready for the presidental campaign, and he felt differently. He knew the value of *Look*."

"Things get kind of sticky around here when Mrs. Kennedy's around," Jack told Stanley. "But Mrs. Kennedy is away. So now's the time to do some of those pictures you've been asking for of John and Caroline."

The photo session lasted five days, and when it was over, Stanley made large, glossy prints and set them up on the table in the Cabinet Room.

"It was just the president and me," Stanley said. "I put the pictures in little categories, and he walked around the Cabinet table and reached over and looked at the pictures. He grabbed the one of John playing under his desk, and he said, 'With this one, you can't lose, Stan.'

"Later, I went over to the White House and gave him an advance copy of the magazine with my picture on the cover and the photo spreads inside. He looked through it, and turned to me and said, 'Well, Stanley, are you coming to Dallas with me?'

"I said, 'No, Mr. President, I have another story to do.' It was on George Romney, the governor of Michigan.

"And the president said, 'Oh, Stanley, you'll have a lot more fun in Dallas.'"

"As Close as I've Ever Seen Them"

If Jack loved the photographs of his children at the White House, he hated the ones of his wife in her bathing suit aboard the *Christina*. Those images of a scantily clad Jackie were a political and personal embarrassment. For once, Jack was getting a taste of his own medicine.

However, when Jackie returned to America, suntanned but exhausted, Jack did not say anything. Instead, he seized the opportunity to play on Jackie's guilt.

"Maybe now you'll come with us to Texas next month."

"Sure I will, Jack," she said. "I'll campaign with you wherever you want."

Her doctors advised against it. They told her that it was still too soon after Patrick's death for the rigors of a campaign trip.

But Jack insisted. The presidential election was only a year away, his popularity ratings were down, and he needed

Texas to win. She had to make an appearance.

"Okay, Jack," she said. "I'll go. What kind of weather is it going to be down there?"

"Cool," he said. "They tell me it's going to be cool."

So she packed heavy clothes.

Jack emerged from his bedroom at 7:30 on the morning of November 21 and found Kenneth, Jackie's hairdresser, waiting in the hall of the Family Quarters.

"John wants to go to the airport and see us off," Jack told Kenneth, "but Miss Shaw [the nurse] doesn't want him to go."

"She probably doesn't want to bother dressing him so early in the morning," Kenneth said.

"You're probably right," Jack said. "*I'll* dress him."

A few minutes later, he returned with a fully dressed son.

"The president had on a light gray-blue suit," Kenneth said. "I had never seen him in anything but a dark suit. And he was tanned and fit and he looked thinner — absolutely marvelous."

Providencia "Provy" Parades, Jackie's maid, came out and told Kenneth that Mrs. Kennedy was ready for him. He was ushered into her bedroom and began doing her hair for the trip to Texas. While he was putting the finishing touches on her hairdo, Jack came in.

"Are you ready?" he asked. "The helicopter is here."

"There was none of the strain that I sometimes had seen between them before important state dinners and things like that. And I remember thinking, *They look marvelously happy together, as happy and close as I've ever seen them.*"

"It's My Husband — His Blood . . ."

"We're really heading into nut country today," Jack said.

It was November 22, and Jack was reading *The Dallas Morning News.* There was a full-page, black-bordered ad denouncing him for signing the nuclear test–ban treaty. He handed the newspaper to Jackie.

"Last night would have been a hell of a night to assassinate a president," he said, pacing back and forth in the hotel room where he was waiting for the motorcade that would take him through the heart of Texas — Dallas. "I mean it. There was the rain, and the night, and we were all getting jostled. Suppose a man had a pistol in a briefcase. Then he could have dropped the gun and the briefcase, and melted away in the crowd. . . . Jackie, if someone wanted to shoot me from a window with a rifle, nobody can stop it. So why worry about it?"

Texas was a political snakepit. Part of

the reason Jack had gone there was to resolve a bitter dispute between the feuding factions of the state's Democratic Party led by Vice President Lyndon Johnson, Governor John Connally and Senator Ralph Yarborough. As a sign of solidarity, the three men had agreed to accompany the president wherever he went in their state.

Jackie peered out the window and examined the sky. It was dark and threatening. It looked like rain. She hoped so. She had spent hours making herself ready, and she did not want to ruin her hairdo in a 45-minute ride in an open car.

"Oh, I want the bubbletop," she said.

But the sky cleared and the sun came out and it started to get hot.

Jack and Jackie climbed into the back seat of the lead limousine, a 1961 Lincoln Continental. The "bubbletop" had been removed so the crowds would feel closer to their president and First Lady. In the front were two Secret Service agents, Roy Kellerman and Bill Greer, the driver. Connally and his wife, Nellie, took the jump seats behind the driver and in front of the Kennedys. Behind the president's Continental was a car of Secret Service agents, followed by the car carrying Vice President and Mrs. Johnson and Senator and Mrs. Yarborough.

The crowds lining the route screamed, "Jack, Jackie, Jack, Jackie!"

"They seemed to want her as much as they wanted him," said Nellie. "As we would drive along, the people were screaming and yelling, and you could hear Jack say, 'Take your glasses off.' And apparently she took them off, but then a little bit later she put them back on, and he said, 'Take your glasses off' . . . When you're riding in a car like this, in a parade, if you have your dark glasses on, you might as well have stayed at home."

"Clint Hill [the First Lady's Secret Service agent] was watching the windows," wrote historian William Manchester. "So was Yarborough, and he didn't like them. The senator was delighted by the throngs on the sidewalks. Next to the president, he was the most exuberant campaigner in the motorcade. . . . Yarborough kept bellowing lustily, 'Howdy thar!' He searched for familiar faces and spotted a surprising number of friends from rural east Texas. But there were no friends in the office windows. The men there, he noticed, weren't cheering at all. He squinted up, trying to read their thoughts. . . . It occurred to Yarborough that anyone could drop a pot of flowers on Kennedy from an upper story. *It will be good to have the president out of this,* he thought."

The motorcade moved slowly toward a triple underpass.

"Then we saw this tunnel ahead," Jackie remembered. "I thought it would be cool in the tunnel, I thought . . . the sun wouldn't get in your eyes."

Jack raised his hand to wave at a boy.

Gunshots shattered the bright, peaceful day.

A 6.5-millimeter bullet struck Jack at the base of the neck, a little to the right of his spine, and exited at his throat, nicking the knot of his tie. It was not fatal.

Another hit Connally in the back.

"No, no, no, no, no!" Connally shrieked. "They're going to kill us all."

Jackie turned toward her husband.

"Then Jack turned back so neatly," Jackie remembered later. "His last expression was so neat . . . you know that wonderful expression he had when they'd ask him a question about one of the ten million pieces they have in a rocket, just before he'd answer. He looked puzzled, then he slumped forward. He was holding out his hand. . . ."

Jack raised his right hand toward his tousled hair just as a third bullet entered the back of his head. Blood and brains spewed into the air, creating a red cloud over his head.

"I've got his brains in my hands," Jackie shrieked. "My God, what are they doing? My God, they've killed Jack, they've killed my husband . . . Jack, Jack!"

She tried to hold the top of his head down, trying to keep the brains in. But there was nothing there. She jumped up and scrambled onto the trunk of the car. Later, she told Manchester that she was trying to retrieve a portion of her husband's head.

"The Secret Service behind us had closed in on our car and Mrs. Kennedy was climbing back on the back of the car," Nellie said. "When she was getting out of the car — maybe you would have tried to get out of the car. You don't know, because it's such a horrible thing that you can't blame anybody for anything."

"Clint Hill . . . was the first man in the car," Jackie told journalist Theodore H. White a few days after the assassination. "We all lay down in the car and I kept saying, 'Jack, Jack, Jack,' and someone was yelling, 'He's dead, he's dead!'

"All the ride to the hospital, I kept bending over him saying, 'Jack, Jack, can you hear me? I love you, Jack. . . .'

"When they carried Jack in [to the hospital], Clint Hill threw his coat over Jack's head. . . . It wasn't repulsive to me for one moment — nothing was repulsive to me — and I was running behind this big intern, I was running behind with the coat covering [Jack]. . . .

"I remember this narrow corridor. I said, 'I'm not going to leave him, I'm not going to leave him.' Then Doc Burkley [Rear Admiral George G. Burkley, U.S. Navy, personal physician to the president] came toward me, just shaking [with sobs]. He said, 'Mrs. Kennedy, you need a sedative.' I said, 'I want to be in there when he dies.'

"So Burkley forced his way into the operating room, and said, 'It's her prerogative, it's her prerogative.' And I got in.

"There were about forty people there. Doc Perry [Dr. Malcolm Perry, the operating room surgeon] wanted to get me out. But I said, 'It's my husband — his blood, his brains are all over me. . . . '

"There was a sheet over Jack. His foot was sticking out of the sheet, whiter than the sheet. I took his foot and kissed it. Then I pulled back the sheet. His mouth was so beautiful, his eyes were open. They found his hand under the sheet, and I held his hand all the time the priest was saying extreme unction."

Pageant

In Dallas, Lyndon Baines Johnson was sworn in as the new president of the United States. But it was Jacqueline Bouvier Kennedy who held the country together for the three days that followed.

Once back in Washington, she asked Bill Walton, her artist friend; Sargent Shriver, her brother-in-law; and Angie Duke to help with the funeral arrangements. They set up a working group in the West Wing and dispatched teams of people to the Library of Congress to do research on Abraham Lincoln's funeral. The Library was closed, and the researchers had to use flashlights to read the pertinent passages in the dark.

Jackie wanted the White House to be draped in black, just the way it was when Lincoln lay in state. Every detail of the Lincoln funeral had to be duplicated — from the riderless black horse and the horse-drawn caisson to the design of Lincoln's catafalque, the platform on which the coffin would rest.

First to last, Jackie made all the decisions for what would become the greatest pageant in American history. She had gotten her wish; she was the overall art director of the twentieth century. But her wish had been granted at the cost of her husband's life.

She was asked where Jack should be buried.

Cardinal Cushing spoke on behalf of the Kennedy family and the Irish Mafia — Kenny O'Donnell, Dave Powers, and Larry O'Brien. He suggested that Jack be buried in Boston in the Kennedy plot.

"Yes," Eunice chimed in, "we're all going to be buried around Daddy in Boston."

Jackie would not hear of it. Jack did not belong merely to Boston; he belonged to the entire nation. He would be buried at Arlington National Cemetery. And there would be an eternal flame.

"Won't people find that pretentious?" Sargent Shriver asked.

"Let them," Jackie said. Then she added: "And I'm going to light that flame myself."

* * *

Who was going to break the news to Caroline and John?

Janet Auchincloss raised the subject with Jackie at Bethesda Naval Hospital, while the autopsy was being performed on Jack.

"Jackie, are you going to tell the children, or do you want me to, or do you want Miss Shaw?"

What did her mother think?

"Well . . . John can wait," Janet said, "but Caroline should be told before she learns from her friends."

"Oh, yes, Mummy," Jackie said. "What will she think if she suddenly . . ."

She stopped and thought a moment, then continued: "I want to tell them, but if they find out before I get back, ask Miss Shaw to use her discretion."

Janet, as usual, took matters into her own hands. She telephoned Maude Shaw.

"How are the children?" she asked.

The children were doing better than she was, Miss Shaw replied honestly. It was a constant struggle for her not to break down in tears in front of the children. Caroline was four days shy of her sixth birthday. John would turn three in two days.

"Mrs. Kennedy wants you to tell Caroline," Janet said.

"Please, no," Maude cried. "Let this cup pass from me."

"You must," said Janet. "There's no one else."

"I can't take a child's last happiness from her. I don't have the heart — I can't destroy her little happy day."

"I know, but you have to."

"Please, *please,* can't someone else do it?"

"No, Mrs. Kennedy is too upset."

After she hung up, Maude put John to bed, then went into Caroline's bedroom. The little girl loved her nanny. Maude had brought the newborn Caroline home from the hospital in New York, and she had broken the news that baby Patrick — the brother Caroline had been looking forward to — had gone to heaven.

"Your father has been shot," Maude told Caroline. "They took him to a hospital, but the doctors couldn't make him better."

Caroline did not say anything.

"So," Maude continued, "your father has gone to look after Patrick. Patrick was so lonely in heaven. He didn't know anybody there. Now he has the best friend anyone could have."

Still, Caroline remained silent.

"God gives each of us a thing to do," Maude went on. "God is making your father a guardian angel over you and your mother, and his light will shine down on you always. His light is shining now, and he's watching you, and he's loving you, and he always will."

Caroline threw herself onto the bed, buried her face in the pillow, and cried.

Jackie refused to take a sleeping pill that night; she wanted to be clear-headed for the challenges of the coming day. But she did make one concession to her feelings of utter abandonment. As she walked toward her bedroom, she stopped and called to her stepfather, Hugh Auchincloss, whom she had invited to stay at the White House with her mother.

"Uncle Hugh," she said, "I don't want to sleep alone."

Hughdie took her arm, led her into the bedroom, and lay beside her all night long.

* * *

The next day after a family Mass,
Jackie returned to the Family Quarters.
Maude Shaw had dressed Caroline and
John in powder-blue coats and red
lace-up shoes. She added a black
mourning band for Caroline's hair.

Jackie came into the nursery carrying
blue stationery.

"You must write a letter to Daddy and
tell him how much you love him," she
told Caroline.

After Caroline had finished her letter,
she helped John scribble on his piece
of stationery.

Jackie then took the three notes —
hers and the children's — and put them
into envelopes. She found a pair of gold
cufflinks that she had given Jack and
a piece of scrimshaw bearing the presidential seal. With all these items in
hand, she went downstairs and entered
the East Room, where Jack lay in his
casket.

Together, she and Bobby kneeled by
the open coffin.

Bobby was wracked by unbearable
feelings of grief and guilt. He had been
informed that Lee Harvey Oswald,
Jack's assassin, had connections to

Castro's Cuba. It was Bobby who had approved the CIA-Mafia plot to assassinate Castro. And it was Bobby who had hounded and harassed the mob, especially Sam Giancana and his henchmen. Was Jack's death Castro's revenge? Had Jack been murdered by the mob? Was he, Bobby, personally responsible for his brother's death? He did not know the answers to these questions, but as he knelt by the coffin, he could not help but wonder.

Others were beginning to wonder, too. For in Dallas, Lee Harvey Oswald had just been shot in front of television cameras by Jack Ruby, a nightclub owner with connections to the mob. Even as Jackie peered inside the coffin in Washington, Oswald was undergoing an operation at Parkland General Hospital, where Jack had been taken the previous day.

Jackie told the author William Manchester that she had kept thinking, *This isn't Jack, it isn't Jack.*

She put the three letters, the cufflinks, and the scrimshaw in the coffin.

Bobby removed his PT tiepin.

"He should have this, shouldn't he?" Bobby asked Jackie.

"Yes," she whispered.

Then Bobby took out another memento — an engraved silver rosary — and slipped that in the coffin, too.

The coffin was wheeled out of the East Room and placed on a gun carriage.

"Mummy," John asked Jackie, "what are they doing?"

"They're taking Daddy out," his mother said.

"But why do they do it so funny — so slow?"

"Because they're so sad."

One hundred million Americans were tuned to their television sets as the gun carriage left the North Portico of the White House and made its way up Pennsylvania Avenue toward the Capitol. In homes across the country, TV images flashed back and forth, often so fast that people had a hard time absorbing their meaning.

There was Jackie, veiled and dressed in black, leading the funeral procession, walking the eight blocks from the White House to St. Matthew's . . . her brothers-in-law and Jack's cabinet members following her, trying to keep step to the slow, mournful beat of the muffled drums . . . and the world leaders, DeGaulle, Haile Selassi, and Prince Philip, all marching together in honor of the fallen young president. . . .

And then, suddenly, there was an instant replay of Jack Ruby shooting Oswald . . . NBC's commentator Tom Petit, standing five feet away from Oswald, gasping, saying, "He's been shot — Lee Oswald has been shot! There is panic and pandemonium! We see little in the utter confusion . . ."

But what everyone remembered was Jackie. She stood with her children, one in each hand, her eyes swollen, her mouth drawn up in grief, looking much as she had at her father's funeral six years before.

"The cameras were frozen on the motionless widow," Manchester wrote, "and omitting those who were reading newspaper accounts or talking to friends, nearly everyone in the United States was watching Mrs. Kennedy. [Ninety-five] percent of the adult population was peering at television or listening to radio accounts. To the Americans must be added all of Europe and those parts of Asia which were periodically reached by relay satellite. Even Russia had announced that the Soviet Union would televise the funeral, including the Mass in St. Matthew's. By Sunday noon, the U.S.A. and most of the civilized world had become a kind of closed-circuit hookup. Nothing existed except this one blinding spotlight."

And that spotlight was focused on Jackie.

Rising from the Ruins

Four days after Jack was buried at Arlington, Jackie showed up at Hyannis Port without any prior warning.

"I'm here to see Grandpa," she told Rose.

Jackie seemed distraught, and Rose tried to block her from going upstairs to Joe's bedroom.

"No, no," Jackie assured Rose, "I'm not upset. . . . Please, please, leave me alone. I'm fine. I just want to see Grandpa."

She ducked past Rose and ran up the stairs.

"Oh, Mrs. Dallas," she said to Joe's nurse, "I want to see Grandpa."

She handed Rita Dallas the folded American flag that had been draped over Jack's coffin and instructed her to give it to the ambassador later. Then she went into Joe's room.

"When Jacqueline finally gained access to the ambassador's room," wrote her cousin, John H. Davis, "she ran up to his bed, embraced him, and leaned her head against his shoulder. The aged patriarch, paralyzed and mute, tried to greet his daughter-in-law, but could only utter a little cry.

"Jacqueline then drew back, and sitting on the bed, gave the ambassador a full and detailed account of everything that had happened since she and the president left Washington for Texas and returned for the funeral and the burial. She had wanted him to hear the full story from her. After she finished, the ambassador nodded, closed his eyes, and fell back on his pillow."

While she was on the Cape, Jackie telephoned Theodore "Teddy" White, a worshipful Kennedy biographer, whose articles frequently appeared in *Life* magazine. She asked him to come see her immediately because there was something that she wanted *Life* to say to the country, and Teddy must do it.

As Teddy drove through a driving rainstorm from New York City to Hyannis Port, he wondered why Jackie needed to see him in such a hurry. Was she upset by all the newspaper accounts that said Jack had been cut down before he could achieve his promise? Did she feel guilty that, at times, she had wished her philandering husband dead? Or was she simply looking for a public way to say good-bye to Jack — one final farewell in the presence of *Life*'s 6 million readers?

Jackie was wearing a cashmere pullover, a wide belt, and slacks when she greeted Teddy. His reporter's notes say that she looked drained and white. She had asked him to Hyannis Port, she said, because she wanted him to make certain that Jack was not forgotten in history.

"History! . . . History . . . it's what those bitter old men write," Jackie said.

"What she was saying to me was: Please, History, be kind to John F. Kennedy," Teddy scribbled in his notebook.

"But there's this one thing I wanted to say," Jackie went on. ". . . I'm so ashamed of myself. . . . When Jack quoted something, it was usually classical . . . no, don't protect me now. . . . I kept saying to Bobby, 'I've got to talk to somebody. I've got to see somebody.' I want to say this one thing — it's been almost an obsession with me — all I

600

keep thinking of is this line from a musical comedy. It's been an obsession with me.

". . . At night before we'd go to sleep . . . we had an old Victrola. Jack liked to play some records — his back hurt, the floor was so cold getting out of bed . . . on a Victrola ten years old — and the song he loved most came at the very end of this record, the last side of *Camelot*, sad *Camelot*: . . . 'Don't let it be forgot, that once there was a spot, for one brief shining moment that was known as Camelot.'

". . . There'll never be another Camelot again. . . .

"Do you know what I think of history? . . . When something is written down, does that make it history? The things they say! . . . For a while, I thought history was something that bitter old men wrote. But Jack loved history so. . . . No one'll ever know everything about Jack. But . . . history made Jack what he was . . . this lonely, little sick boy . . . scarlet fever . . . this little boy sick so much of the time, reading in bed, reading history . . . reading [about] the Knights of the Round Table . . . and he just liked that last song."

* * *

The healing process was slow.

"I feel like a wounded animal," Jackie told Nicole Alphand, the wife of the French ambassador to Washington. "What I really want to do is crawl into a corner and hide."

"In the weeks after Kennedy was assassinated," Ben Bradlee said, "Tony and I spent a couple of emotional weekends at Atoka, the Kennedys' country house in Middleburg, Virginia, with Jackie, trying with no success to talk about something else, or someone else. Too soon and too emotional for healing, we proved only that the three of us had very little in common without the essential fourth.

"Only four weeks after the assassination, after the last of these weekends, we received this sad note from the president's widow."

Dec. 20
Dear Tony and Ben:
   Something that you said in the country stunned me so — that you hoped I would marry again.
   You were so close to us so many times. There is one thing that you

must know. I consider that my life is over and I will spend the rest of it waiting for it really to be over.

With my love,
Jackie

Eleven days after the funeral, Jackie moved out of the White House and into an elegant Georgetown house that had been made available to her by Averell Harriman, the millionaire diplomat. Dressed in black, she continued to receive visitors — cabinet officials, foreign dignitaries, the rich, the great, and the famous.

As the widow of the martyred president, she was expected to live a life worthy of imitation — commendable, exemplary, saintlike. She could not be seen going out for an evening, even to the ballet or a concert.

She considered her life to be in ruins. People thought that money was no problem, that Jack had provided for her. The truth was quite different: Jack had left an estate valued at $1,890,464 — perhaps $10 million in today's currency. Interest on that sum was not much for a woman of Jackie's tastes. Once again, she had no *real* money.

She had always depended on older men to protect her. But she suddenly found herself alone. Bobby tried to fill the role of protector, but in the end, it turned out that he needed her as much as she needed him. Other men did not dare approach her. She was no longer a woman; she had become a national monument.

"I'll tell you one thing," she said to Charlie Bartlett. "They're never going to drag me out like a little old widow, the way they did Woodrow Wilson's widow. I am not going to play that role."

Shortly after the turn of the year, she abandoned Washington and bought an apartment on upper Fifth Avenue in New York City, directly across from the Central Park Reservoir. She was pleased that the building had been designed by Rosario Candela, the leading architect of the 1920s and 1930s. She had lived in a Candela building before her parents were divorced, and the familiar details in the architecture held warm associations for her.

For a while after she moved to New York, she found it hard to be with people who reminded her of Jack. When friends tried to bring up the White House years, she would invariably stop them, and say, as she had once said to me, "Please, let's not talk about the past. I have to remain alive for myself. I don't want to dredge up the past."

Once an appropriate time had passed, however, she started going out in public in the company of men — friends like director Mike Nichols, Tiffany's design director John Loring, and journalist Pete Hammil. Then, in 1968, after Bobby was assassinated, she panicked and sought safety — for herself and her children — in the married arms of Aristotle Onassis, a move that shocked the entire world and seemed, at least for a time, to damage her image. Overnight, she had gone from being Saint Jackie to being Jackie O.

But Jackie had an unerring sense of her stardom, and a connoisseur's appreciation of her own persona. She continued to wrap herself in the mythic cloak of Camelot, and worked hard to raise millions of dollars for the I. M. Pei–designed John F. Kennedy Library outside of Boston. She began inviting friends who had worked closely with

Jack to come to her home and speak to her children about their father. Arthur Schlesinger Jr., Theodore Sorensen, and Robert McNamara were among those she invited. These private seminars for Caroline and John continued for years.

In 1973 — ten years after Jack's assassination — Jackie invited Pierre Salinger, JFK's press secretary, to fly to Skorpios, the Greek island owned by Onassis.

"Make some notes before you come," she told him.

"You know," Salinger told Jackie's children after he arrived, "your father was an extraordinary man. He had many parts, and no one knew him completely. The person who knew him best was your mother."

Notes

One: Woman of the Century

The description of Jacqueline Kennedy Onassis in the fall and winter of 1981 is drawn mainly from the author's eye-witness notes and from interviews with Jackie's friends, some of whom asked to remain anonymous. Extensive on-the-record interviews were conducted as well with Jackie's family members and friends, including Hugh D. "Yusha" Auchincloss III; Nina "Nini" Auchincloss Straight; Peter Duchin; Solange Herter, whom Jackie considered to be her "best friend"; George Plimpton; Oleg Cassini; Gloria Emerson; Jackie's Vassar classmate Ellen "Puffin" Gates D'Oench; Pete Hamill; Ken McCormick, who worked with Jackie at Doubleday; Abraham Ribicoff, who was among the first politicians to promote the idea of Kennedy for president; Lois "Casey" Ribicoff; Pierre Salinger; Samuel Pisar; and Aaron Shikler, the artist who did

Jackie's White House portrait.

Confidential interviews were conducted with Jackie's friends regarding her personal life, including her face lift by a Park Avenue surgeon, her visits to the Nardi Salon for periodic facial treatments, and her mixed feelings about holding a yearly Christmas party in her apartment. In each case, the author relied on two or more verifying sources.

The description of Jackie's Fifth Avenue apartment is drawn primarily from the author's eyewitness notes based on his personal visits there on two separate occasions. Further details regarding the apartment were supplied by a number of Jackie's friends, all of whom asked for confidentiality.

The architectural history of Jackie's apartment at 1040 Fifth Avenue comes from Paul Goldberger, the former architectural critic of *The New York Times* and currently that newspaper's chief cultural correspondent, and from Christopher Gray, an architectural historian.

Interviews were also conducted with Brigit Gerney, the wife of Arkadi Gerney; S. Carey Welsh; Sonny Metha; Grace Mirabella; Sylvia Whitehouse Blake; and Charles Whitehouse.

The author quotes a hand-written letter he received from Jackie dated May 22, 1981.

Accounts of the deranged California law-school graduate who stalked Caroline and Mark David Chapman's hit list come from articles in the *New York Post* (June 25, 1981) and *The New York Times* (December 22, 1981).

Books that were used in this section include Billy Baldwin's *Jackie Kennedy Onassis: A Memoir*, which was excerpted in *McCall's* in December 1974; and David Lester's *Jackie Kennedy Onassis: A Portrait of Her Private Years* (Birch Lane, 1994).

The author also quotes Stephen Spender's "I Think Continually of Those Who Were Truly Great" from *Collected Poems, 1928–1953* (Random House, 1955).

Two: Fawn in the Woods

The portrait of Jackie's years at Merrywood and her junior year abroad in France is based on interviews with dozens of family members and friends, many of whom were interviewed repeatedly. These sources include Hugh Auchincloss III; Nina Auchincloss Straight; the novelist Louis Auchincloss; Ellen D'Oench; John "Demi" Gates, one of Jackie's early beaus; Phillip Geyelin, formerly of the *Washington Post*, and his wife, Cecilia; Charles Bartlett; Martha Bartlett; Patricia Roche Wood; Taylor Chewning, a longtime Newport resident; Thomas Guinzburg; Solange Herter; Aileen Bowdoin Train; George Plimpton; Peter Duchin; Cass Canfield Jr.; and Nelson Aldrich.

The description of Jackie's romantic entanglement with John Marquand Jr. is drawn chiefly from interviews the author conducted with Marquand's friends, including George Plimpton, Peter Duchin, Cass Canfield Jr., and Thomas Guinzburg. Further interviews for this section were conducted with

Brigit Gurney; Nina Straight; and several sources who requested anonymity. Gore Vidal's *Palimpsest: A Memoir* (Random House, 1995) contains a brief passage about Jackie's intimate relationship with Marquand.

A description of Merrywood, the Auchincloss estate outside Washington, D.C., comes primarily from the author's eyewitness notes based on his visit there in September, 1995. The author also relied on *Historic Landmarks Survey*, published by Virginia's Fairfax County, and a number of interviews, including with Allan and Diane Kay, the present owners of Merrywood.

A description of Jackie's room was gleaned from interviews with family members, family photographs, and from the author's eyewitness notes.

Additional interviews were also conducted with Betty Jones, Brigit Gerney, Sylvia Whitehouse Blake, Elon Marquand, Timothy Marquand, Aileen Train, Blair Fuller, Peter Matheisson, John Train, Susan Martin, Gloria

Jones, Wilfred Sheed, Ellen Adler, Mary Bailey Gimbell, and Dr. William Cahan.

The author Marie Brenner kindly made available several essays that Jackie submitted for *Vogue*'s Prix de Paris contest in 1950. Ms. Brenner discovered the material in the *Vogue* archives during the course of her own research for an article she wrote for that magazine after Jackie's death. These documents have never been published before.

Other sources include letters Jackie sent from Paris in 1950; these were made available to the author by Hugh Auchincloss III.

Principal published sources include Nelson W. Aldrich Jr.'s *Old Money: The Mythology of America's Upper Class* (Alfred A. Knopf, 1988), Joseph Alsop's *I've Seen the Best of It* (Norton, 1992), George Carpozzi's *The Hidden Side of Jacqueline Kennedy* (Pyramid Books, 1967), Nigel Hamilton's *Reckless Youth* (Random House, 1992), Ralph G. Martin's *A Hero for Our Time: An Intimate Story of the Kennedy Years* (Macmillan,

1983), Anthony Summers's *Official and Confidential: The Life of J. Edgar Hoover* (Putnam, 1993), J. C. Suares and J. Spencer Beck's *Uncommon Grace: Reminiscences and Photographs of Jackie Bouvier Kennedy Onassis* (Thomasson-Grant, 1994), Mary Van Rensselaer Thayer's *Jackie Bouvier Kennedy: A Warm, Personal Story of the First Lady* (Doubleday, 1961), and Evan Thomas's *The Very Best Men: Four Who Dared: The Early Years of the CIA* (Simon & Schuster, 1995).

The following articles were also used: Michael Lewis's "The Rich: How They're Different . . . Than They Used to Be," which appeared in *The New York Times Magazine* (November 19, 1995); Camille Paglia's "A Horse, a Flame, a Rose," in *The Guardian* (June 9, 1994); and David Sheff's interview with Gore Vidal, in *Playboy* (December, 1987).

The song "Civilization" ("Bongo, Bongo, Bongo") was written by Bob Hilliard and Carl Sigman.

The National Weather Service Forecast Office in Sterling, Virginia, provided regional climatic data for Virginia in the spring of 1951.

Three: The Way of the World

The narrative of Jackie's trip to New York City to visit her father and to meet the editors of *Vogue* is drawn from interviews with Hugh Auchincloss III; Beverly Corbin, the current occupant of John Vernou Bouvier III's apartment on East 74th Street; Franklin D'Olier, Jack Bouvier's brother-in-law; Jane Hutchinson Ogle, a previous *Vogue* Prix de Paris winner; Carol Phillips, a staff writer at *Vogue* in 1951; Mrs. Iva Patcevitch, the wife of *Vogue*'s publisher in 1951; Kate Rand Lloyd, a staff writer at *Vogue* in 1951 and a previous winner of the *Vogue* Prix de Paris; and Dr. Michael Sheehy, the current president and medical director at Silver Hill, an exclusive sanitarium in New Canaan, Connecticut.

Background for Jackie's tenure at *Vogue* also comes from interviews with former *Vogue* staff members, including

Susan Oberstein, Despina Messinesi, Catherine di Montezemolo, Babs Simpson, Mary Jane Poole, Grace Mirabella, and Susan Train.

The author also made use of a previously unpublished letter, dated May, 1951, from Jackie to Mary E. Campbell, the personnel director of Condé Nast, and another previously unpublished letter, dated October 10, 1950, from Jackie to the editors of *Vogue.* Both letters were made available to the author by Marie Brenner.

For information on Jackie's *Vogue* Prix de Paris entries, see the notes for section two.

Principal published sources include Stephen Birmingham's *Jacqueline Bouvier Kennedy Onassis* (Grosset & Dunlap, 1978), John H. Davis's *The Bouviers* (Farrar, Straus & Giroux, 1969) and *The Kennedys: Dynasty and Disaster* (S.P.I. Books, 1992), David Halberstam's *The Fifties* (Villard Books, 1993); C. David Heymann's *A Woman Named Jackie: An Intimate Biography of Jacqueline Bouvier Kennedy Onassis*

(Lyle Stuart, 1989), Kathleen Bouvier's *To Jack With Love. Black Jack Bouvier: A Remembrance* (Kensington, 1979), and Ralph G. Martin's *A Hero for Our Time* and *Seeds of Destruction: Joe Kennedy and His Sons* (G. P. Putnam's Sons, 1995).

A full-page photograph of "the Misses Bouvier" appeared in the March 1, 1951, issue of *Vogue*. Igor Cassini's description of Jackie as "Deb of the Year" appeared under his byline Cholly Knickerbocker in the *New York Journal-American*.

Four: "These Charming People"

The accounts of Jackie's first meeting with John F. Kennedy, her brief employment at *Vogue*, and her trip to Europe are drawn from several dozen interviews, including those with Hugh Auchincloss III; Charlie Bartlett; Martha Bartlett; Taylor Chewning; Gloria Emerson; Phillip and Cecilia Geyelin; Mrs. William McCormick "Deeda" Blair; William Blair; Mrs. Minnie Farrell Cassat Hickman; Barbara Lafferty, Loretta "Hickey" Sumers's sister; Aubin Sumers, Loretta Sumers's sister-in-law; Robert Mossbacher; Kate Rand Lloyd; Carol Phillips; Jane Hutchinson Ogle; Mrs. Iva Patcevitch; Susan Oberstein; Despina Messinesi; Catherine di Montezemolo; Babs Simpson; Mary Jane Poole; Grace Mirabella; Susan Train; Nina Auchincloss Straight; Sharman Douglas; Garry Fishgall, the author of *Against Type: The Biography of Burt Lancaster*; and Patricia Roche Wood.

Published sources include Joan and Clay Blair's *The Search for J.F.K.* (Berkley, 1976), Jacqueline and Lee Bouvier's *One Special Summer* (Delacorte Press, 1974); Kathleen Bouvier's *To Jack With Love*; Davis's *The Kennedys* and *The Bouviers*; Halberstam's *The Fifties*; Hamilton's *Reckless Youth*; Heymann's *A Woman Named Jackie*; Martin's *Seeds of Destruction* and *A Hero for Our Time*; and Arthur Schlesinger Jr.'s *A Thousand Days: John F. Kennedy in the White House.* (Houghton Mifflin, 1965).

Dave Powers, a member of the Kennedy entourage who served as the president's special assistant, is quoted in the August, 1995 issue of *Life* that Jack once said of his first meeting with Jackie, "I've never met anyone like her. She's different from any girl I know."

See note in section three regarding Jackie's letters to Mary Campbell.

For a description of life aboard the *Queen Elizabeth*, the author drew on brochures given to passengers by the Cunard Line, available from the University Archives at the University of Liverpool, Great Britain, as well as the first-class manifest of the June 7, 1951, voyage on which Jackie and her sister Lee sailed. John Maxtone Graham, the author of *The Only Way to Cross*, a book on the *Queen Elizabeth*'s golden age, was also interviewed.

The author drew on accounts in periodicals for discussions of the cultural and political background of the times. These accounts include Charles Bartlett's articles about Senator Joseph McCarthy and Senator Estes Kefauver in *The Chattanooga Times* (April 30, 1951), and a nine-page photo essay by Irving Penn on 73 famous Washington personalities in *Vogue* (August 15, 1951). In addition, accounts of President Truman's dismissal of General Douglas MacArthur as United Nations commander in Korea appeared in *The New York Times* (May 13, 1951) and the *Washington Post* (May 11, 1953).

Five: A Rendezvous with Death

The account of Jack's medical condition is drawn from interviews with his friends and physicians, most of whom asked to remain anonymous. In addition, the author interviewed Abraham Ribicoff; George Smathers; Gloria Emerson; Jack Anderson; and a number of medical experts, including Dr. Richard Mahler, an Addisonian specialist at New York Hospital; Dr. George Thorn, who, as a leading authority on Addison's in the 1950s, was consulted by Jack's doctors; Dr. John Baxter and Dr. James B. Turrell at University of California at San Francisco; Dr. Marvin Siperstein, who was present at

Parkland Hospital in Dallas and administered high doses of steroids to Jack after he was shot; and Dr. John Bilezikian, at the Columbia Presbyterian Medical Center in New York.

The narrative of Jack's trip to Vietnam is based on several interviews with Edmund Gullion, the American chargé d'affaires in Vietnam in 1951.

The undated cablegram from General Matthew Ridgway to Congressman John Kennedy is published for the first time in this book. It was obtained from the John F. Kennedy Library.

Principal published sources include the Blairs' *The Search for JFK*, Davis's *The Bouviers*, Doris Kearns Goodwin's *The Fitzgeralds and the Kennedys: An American Saga* (Simon & Schuster, 1987), Hamilton's *Reckless Youth*; Heymann's *A Woman Named Jackie*; Peter Collier and David Horowitz's *The Kennedys: An American Drama* (Summit Books, 1984), Herbert S. Parmet's *Jack: The Struggles of John F. Kennedy* (Dial Press, 1980), Schlesinger's *A Thousand Days*; Robert Shaplen's *A Forest of*

Tigers (Alfred A. Knopf, 1956), and Theodore C. Sorensen's *Kennedy* (Harper & Row, 1965).

The author used transcripts from radio and television programs, including a November 14, 1951, address by Jack over the Mutual Broadcasting Network, and an appearance by him on December 3, 1951 on NBC's *Meet the Press.*

The author also quotes Alan Seegar's poem, "I Have a Rendezvous with Death."

Six: From This Moment On

Material for this section, which describes Jackie's turmoil over her engagement to John Husted, is drawn from interviews with John Husted; Hugh Auchincloss III; Louis Auchincloss; Martha Bartlett; Charles Bartlett; Robin Chandler Duke; Betty Beale; Gloria Emerson; Sidney Epstein, who, as city editor of the *Washington Times-Herald* in 1951, hired Jackie as the paper's inquiring photographer; John Gates; Phillip and Cecilia Geyelin; Solange Herter; Ormande de Kay, one of Jackie's early beaus; Wendy Burden Morgan; Nina Auchincloss Straight; Lisa Wright, the press secretary to Representative Rasco Bartlett, who, in 1996, occupied JFK's old office in Room 322 in the Cannon Office Building.

The scene in which Jackie meets Florence Pritchett Smith in Jack's office is drawn from interviews with several anonymous sources, who were given an account of the meeting by Florence Smith.

The description of Janet Auchincloss's striking Jackie across both cheeks was gathered from interviews with Louis Auchincloss and other family members who wished to remain anonymous.

A description of the Sulgrave Club, where the Dancing Class was held, comes from the author's eyewitness notes based on a visit to the club in 1994. Additional information on the Dancing Class is drawn from Maxine

Chesire's article, "Very Interesting People," which appeared in the *Washington Post* on June 18, 1967, and Scottie Smith's "Dancing Class Leaves Broken Hearts," which appeared in the *Washington Post* on November 26, 1967.

The description of Jackie's eyeshadow falling on Jack's shoulders comes from an interview with Gloria Emerson, who witnessed it happening.

Principal published documents include Louis Auchincloss's *Sybil* (Greenwood Press, 1951), Jackie and Lee Bouvier's *One Special Summer*; Heymann's *A Woman Named Jackie*; Kitty Kelley's *Jackie Oh!* (Lyle Stuart, 1978), and Evelyn Lincoln's *My Twelve Years with John F. Kennedy* (David McKay, 1965).

Jackie's Inquiring Photographer pieces ran in the *Washington Times-Herald* (February 10, 1952, and March 3, 1952).

The New York Times carried Jacqueline Bouvier and John Husted's engagement notice on January 21, 1952.

The words and music for the 1950 song "From This Moment On" were written by Cole Porter.

The weather data for May 17, 1952, was provided by The National Weather Service Forecast Office in Sterling, Virginia.

Seven: Out of the Shadows

The narrative of Jack and Jackie's courtship is drawn from interviews with Hugh Auchincloss III; Lauren Bacall, who attended the London ball at which Jackie was present; Steven Bogart; Letitia Baldrige, Jackie's friend from Vassar and later her White House social secretary; Art Buchwald; Morton Downey Jr., the son of Morton Downey, one of Joseph P. Kennedy's closest friends; Anne Downey; Clay Felker; Gloria Emerson; Sidney Epstein; Frank Waldrop; John Gates; John Husted; Henry Porter, the London editor of *Vanity Fair*, who provided some of the description of the London neighborhood where Jackie stayed during the coronation of Elizabeth II; George Smathers; Paul Fay; Evelyn Lincoln; Cass Canfield Jr.; Phillip and Cecilia Geyelin; Hélène Arpels; Charles Spalding; Pat Roche Wood; Nina Auchincloss Straight; and Aileen Bowdoin Train, Jackie's traveling companion to London and Paris in 1953.

The description of Joseph P. Kennedy's meeting with Jackie at Hyannis Port was provided by Morton Downey Jr., who was given a full account of the meeting by his father, Morton Downey, one of Joe's best friends.

The description of Hileah Park circa 1950 comes from an interview with Joe Hirsch, now the executive columnist for the *Daily Racing Form* in Miami.

The section "All Men Are Like That" is based on several interviews over the course of more than a year by the author and his research assistants with John Gates.

Published sources include Birmingham's *Jacqueline Bouvier Kennedy Onassis*; Collier and Horowitz's *The*

Kennedys; John Crittenden's *Hialeah Park: A Racing Legend* (Pickering Press, 1989); Goodwin's *The Fitzgeralds and the Kennedys,* Sam and Chuck Giancanna's *Double Cross: The Explosive, Inside Story of the Mobster Who Controlled America* (Warner Books, 1992); Ronald Goldfarb's *Perfect Villains, Imperfect Heroes* (Random House, 1995); Hamilton's *Reckless Youth;* Kelley's *Jackie Oh!;* Rose Kennedy's *Times to Remember* (Doubleday, 1974); Robert Lacey's *Majesty: Elizabeth II and the House of Windsor* (Harcourt Brace Jovanovich, 1977); Martin's *A Hero for Our Time* and *Seeds of Destruction;* Herbert S. Parmet's *Jack: The Struggles of John F. Kennedy;* Kenneth O'Donnell, and Dave Powers, and Joe McCarthy's *"Johnny, We Hardly Knew Ye": Memories of John Fitzgerald Kennedy* (Little, Brown, 1970); and Thayer's *Jacqueline Bouvier Kennedy.*

Jackie's bylined stories on the coronation of Queen Elizabeth II appeared in the *Washington Times-Herald*: "Crowds of Americans Fill 'Bright and Pretty' London" appeared on June 2, 1953; and "Nobility and Film Folk Strut at Perle Mesta's Clambake," appeared on June 9, 1953.

The following article was also used: Alistair Forbes's "Camelot Confidential," which appeared in *The Times Literary Supplement* (June 13, 1975) and *The New York Times* (November 5, 1952).

Eight: For Better, for Worse

The descriptions of the events leading up to Jack and Jackie's wedding, as well as their wedding day and honeymoon, come from interviews with Hélène Arpels, a friend of Rose Kennedy's; Hugh Auchincloss III; James Auchincloss, Jackie's half brother; Washington society columnist Betty Beale; Marion "Oatsie" Charles (Leiter), John Kennedy's favorite Washington socialite; Taylor Chewning; Phillip and Cecilia Geyelin; Sylvia Whitehouse Blake; Evelyn Lincoln; Chauncey Parker, a family friend of Jackie's; Ellen D'Oench; George Smathers; Paul Fay; Charles Spalding and James Reed, ushers at the wedding; and Nina Auchincloss Straight.

The account of Jack and Jackie's honeymoon is drawn from interviews with eyewitnesses, including Hal Boucher, the photographer at San Ysidro Ranch, and Carol Crowley, who was a saleswoman at the San Ysidro Pharmacy.

Principal publications include Birmingham's *Jacqueline Bouvier Kennedy Onassis*; Diana DuBois's *In Her Sister's Shadow: An Intimate Biography of Lee Radziwill* (Little, Brown, 1995); Collier and Horowitz's *The Kennedys*; Heymann's *A Woman Named Jackie*; Davis's *The Bouviers* and *The Kennedys*; Charles Higham's *The Life and Times of Rose Fitzgerald Kennedy* (Pocket Books, 1995); Kelley's *Jackie Oh!*; Lawrence Leamer's *The Kennedy Women: The Saga of an American Family* (Villard Books, 1994); Martin's *Seeds of Destruction*; and a book Joan Meyers edited for Atheneum Press published in 1965 called *John Fitzgerald Kennedy . . . As We Remember Him.*

Joseph P. Kennedy's reaction to the

Auchinclosses and to Hammersmith Farm comes from a number of sources, including a passage that appeared in the original draft of Paul Fay's *The Pleasure of His Company* (Harper & Row, 1966), which was excised prior to publication under pressure from Jackie. The unedited manuscript of this book is available in the Myrick Land Papers at Boston University's Mugar Memorial Library.

Nine: What Jackie Knew

Accounts of the trials and tribulations of Jack and Jackie's first months of marriage and of Jack's brush with death during his back operation come from interviews with Hélène Arpels; Charles Bartlett; Kenneth Battelle, Jackie's hairdresser; Evelyn Lincoln; Father John Flannagan; Marion Charles; Ellen D'Oench; Robin Chandler Duke; Gloria Emerson; Nigel Hamilton, the author of *JFK: Reckless Youth*; Solange Herter; Paul Fay; J. C. Irondelle, who was the reception manager at the Hotel du Cap in 1955; Priscilla Johnson McMillan, who had once worked in John Kennedy's senate office as a researcher; Catherine Van Older, the director of physical therapy at the Rusk Institute; Myer Feldman; J. Paul Molloy, who served as minority counsel on the Senate Commerce Committee and who drank at the Carroll Arms; Chauncey Parker; George Smathers; Evan Thomas, the editor of *Profiles in Courage*; and Dr. Atilla Toth, a New York Hospital specialist in the relationship between venereal infections and infertility.

Further material on Jack's back operation is derived from "Management of Adrenocortical Insufficiency During Surgery," which was accepted for publication July 28, 1955 in the *American Medical Association Archives of Surgery.* The authors are James A. Nichols, M.D., Charles L. Burstein, M.D., Charles J. Umberger, Ph.D., and Philip D. Wilson, M.D. "Case 3 — Example of a Patient with Adrenal Insufficiency Due to Addison's Disease Requiring Elective Surgery" is now accepted by medical researchers and Kennedy scholars as an account of John Kennedy's surgery in 1954.

* * *

The narrative of Jack's trip from the New York Hospital for Special Surgery to Palm Beach is taken in large part from "NBC White Paper, The Age of Kennedy: The Early Years," which was broadcast May 29, 1966.

The description of the F Street Club is based on interviews with William Merriam, the nephew of the original owner of the club's building; Richard Howland, a board member and co-owner of the club; and Sandra McElwaine, a Washington journalist.

The description of Bill Thompson's escapade with unnamed women on board a Florida-bound train, as well as the bacchanalian atmosphere at the Carroll Arms, comes from several interviews with friends and business associates of Thompson, all of whom wished to remain anonymous.

Principal publications include *The Uncommon Wisdom of Jackie Kennedy Onassis: A Portrait in her Own Words*, which was edited by Bill Adler (Citadel Press, 1994); Collier and Horowitz's *The*

Kennedys; Davis's *The Kennedys*; DuBois's *In Her Sister's Shadow*; Goodwin's *The Fitzgeralds and the Kennedys*; Heymann's *A Woman Named Jackie*; Kelley's *Jackie Oh!*; Arthur Krock's *Memoirs: Sixty Years on the Firing Line* (Funk & Wagnalls, 1968); Leamer's *The Kennedy Women*; Martin's *A Hero for Our Time*; Hamilton's *Reckless Youth*; Lincoln's *My Twelve Years with John F. Kennedy*; Parmet's *Jack: The Struggles of John F. Kennedy*; and Richard Reeves's *President Kennedy: Profile of Power* (Simon & Schuster, 1993).

The letter from Theodore Sorensen to Jackie when she was in the hospital with a broken leg is at the John F. Kennedy Library in the Pre-Presidential Papers, Box #503.

The words to the 1953 song "No Other Love" (From "Me and Juliet") were written by Oscar Hammerstein II; the music was written by Richard Rodgers.

Ten: Hitting Bottom

The description of Jack's failure to win the 1956 vice presidential nomination, the near collapse of his marriage to Jackie, and Joseph Kennedy's intervention to save the marriage come from interviews with Morton Downey Jr.; Ann Downey; Alistair Forbes, a friend of Lee Radziwill; Nigel Hamilton; Letitia Baldrige; Wendy Morgan; Timothy Horan; Evelyn Lincoln; Marion Javits; Grace Warnecke; Phillip and Cecilia Geyelin; Solange Herter; Ronald Kessler, the author of *Sins of the Father;* Evelyn Lincoln; Laurie Macdonald, the daughter of Torbert Macdonald, Jack's college friend; George Smathers; Myer Feldman; Dr. Hanna Meiland, a New York gynecologist; Charles Spalding; and Nina Auchincloss Straight.

Jack Anderson, the Pulitzer Prize–winning Washington columnist, kindly interviewed several sources on the author's behalf.

The description of the weather on the day Jack and Jackie's stillborn baby was buried comes from Carl Sawyer, a state climatologist in Rhode Island.

Principal publications include Carpozzi's *The Hidden Side of Jacqueline Kennedy*, Collier and Horowitz's *The Kennedys*, DuBois's *In Her Sister's Shadow*, Goodwin's *The Fitzgeralds and the Kennedys*, Heymann's *A Woman Named Jackie*, Higham's *The Life and Times of Rose Fitzgerald Kennedy*, Kelley's *Jackie Oh!*, Rose Kennedy's *Times to Remember*, Ronald Kessler's *Sins of the Father: Joseph P. Kennedy and the Dynasty He Founded* (Warner Books, 1996), Leamer's *The Kennedy Women*, Lincoln's *My Twelve Years with John F. Kennedy*, and Martin's *A Hero for Our Time*.

John Kennedy's passport renewal application is at the John F. Kennedy Library in the John F. Kennedy Personal Papers, Box #6, "Souvenirs, 1941–1958: Passport Application File."

The *Washington Post* (August 25, 1956) carried a front-page account of how Robert Kennedy tried unsuccessfully to contact Jack after Jackie's stillbirth.

A description of the Le Pavillon restaurant comes from Alvin Kerr's "Specialities de la Maison," which appeared in *Gourmet* (February, 1967).

Eleven: Big Casino

The narrative account of Jack's campaign for the presidency is drawn from numerous sources, including Jack Anderson; Charles Bartlett; Lillian Brown, who worked on Jack's television makeup; Meyer Feldman; Janet Des Rosiers Fontaine, Joseph Kennedy's former mistress and the stewardess aboard the *Caroline*; Phillip and Cecilia Geyelin; Sam Giancana, the nephew and namesake of Chicago Mafia boss Sam Giancana; Albert Hadley, an associate of Mrs. Henry "Sister" Parish, who was Jackie's interior designer for the N Street house and later for the White House; Solange Herter; Jacques Lowe, the photojournalist who took the portrait of Caroline chewing on Jackie's pearls; Priscilla Johnson McMillan; Joseph Shimon, an associate of Sam

Giancana's; Theodore C. Sorensen, Jack's speech writer; and Nina Auchincloss Straight.

The columnist Liz Smith kindly interviewed Judith Campbell Exner on the author's behalf; she also provided valuable editorial insight.

The description of Langdon Marvin's bringing a woman into Jack's hotel room prior to the first Kennedy–Nixon debate comes from an interview with Jack Anderson, who discussed the incident with Langdon Marvin.

The description of Max Jacobson's injecting Jack with amphetamines prior to the Kennedy–Nixon debate is drawn, in part, from Richard Reeves's *President Kennedy: Profile of Power.* Other sources for this incident wished to remain confidential.

The account of Lee Radziwill's sleeping with Jack is derived from several interviews the author had with Nina Auchincloss Straight. In addition, Gore Vidal refers to Jack and Lee's sleeping together in *Palimpsest* (page 19), quoting Michael Canfield as telling him: "There were times when I think [Lee] went perhaps too far, you know? Like going to bed with Jack in the room next to mine in the south of France and then boasting about it." Vidal also writes in *Palimpsest* (page 311), "As Lee had gone to bed with Jack, symmetry required her [Jackie] to do so with Bobby."

Principal publications include Kathleen Bouvier's *To Jack With Love*; Ben Bradlee's *A Good Life: Newspapering and Other Adventures* (Simon & Schuster, 1995); Davis's *The Kennedys*; Judith Exner's *My Story* (Grove Press, 1977), as told to Ovid Demaris; Giancana's *Double Cross*; Heymann's *A Woman Named Jackie*; Kitty Kelley's *His Way: The Unauthorized Biography of Frank Sinatra* (Bantam, 1986); Kessler's *Sins of the Father*; Lincoln's *My Twelve Years with John F. Kennedy*; O'Donnell, Powers and McCarthy's *"Johnny, We Hardly Knew Ye"*; Maud Shaw's *White House Nannie: My Years with Caroline and John, Jr.* (New American Library, 1965); and Sorensen's *Kennedy*.

Remarks by Jack at the fifty-first annual meeting of the Mississippi Valley Historical Association on Friday evening, April 25, 1958, in Minneapolis are available at the Kennedy Library.

Some of the description of the first Kennedy–Nixon debate is drawn from Christopher Matthew's book, *Kennedy & Nixon: The Rivalry That Shaped Postwar America.* (Simon & Schuster, 1996.)

Twelve: Queen of the Circus

Material relating to Jackie in the White House, Jack and Jackie's trip to Paris and Vienna, and Joe's stroke is based on dozens of interviews with family members, friends, and New Frontiersmen, including Nina Auchincloss Straight, Hélène Arpels, Letitia Baldrige, George Ball, Charles Bartlett, Phillip and Cecilia Geyelin, Alistair Forbes, Kenneth Battelle, Betty Beale, Oleg Cassini, Taylor Chewning, Ellen D'Oench, Angier Biddle Duke, Robin Chandler Duke, Myer Feldman, Pierre Salinger, Janet Des Rosiers Fontaine,

Solange Herter, George Smathers, Albert Hadley, Janet Jeghelian, Evelyn Lincoln, George Plimpton, and Dave Powers.

The account of Dr. Max Jacobson's visit to Jackie's suite at the Quai d'Orsay in Paris is based on an interview with a member of Jackie's entourage who requested anonymity.

The description of Joseph P. Kennedy's involvement with Ann Gargan after his stroke is based on an interview with Janet Jeghelian, his physical therapist.

The author also quotes Jack C. Davis's February 3, 1966 interview with Sister Parish.

The publisher of *Women's Wear Daily*, John Fairchild, provided the author with invaluable insights into Jackie's approach to style while she was in the White House.

Albert Hadley of Parish-Hadley Associates kindly made available to the author Sister Parish's files relating to the restoration of the White House, including an undated memo, "Suggested Changes for the White House From a 'Report of Henry du Pont, Chairman,' The Fine Arts Committee and Mrs. John F. Kennedy"; a memo dated May 18, 1961, "Concerning Gifts to the White House, Henry du Pont, Chairman, The Fine Arts Committee for the White House"; a letter dated June 28, 1961, to Sister Parish from Jayne Wrightsman, a member of the Fine Arts Committee; letters from Jackie to Sister Parish, dated July 16 and July 17, 1961; and Letitia Baldrige's confidential memo, "Notes for Mrs. Kennedy on meeting Mary Jayne McCaffree at White House on November 23," dated November 24, 1960.

Letitia Baldrige's letter to Janet Des Rosiers, then the secretary to the American ambassador in Paris, asking her to deliver an order of Givenchy clothes to the air attaché for shipment to the White House, is dated September 19, 1961, and was kindly made available to the author by Janet Des Rosiers Fontaine.

Jackie's letter inviting Ellen D'Oench

to the Senate ladies' lunch is dated April 6, 1961, and was kindly made available to the author by Ellen D'Oench.

Henry du Pont's letter asking Jackie to "put back between the windows the little Baltimore desk with Dr. Franklin's mirror above it" and David Stockwell's account of Jackie's keeping du Pont waiting come from Elaine Rice's master's thesis, "Furnishing Camelot: The Restoration of the White House Interiors 1961–1963, and the Role of H. F. du Pont," which was submitted to the faculty of the University of Delaware in the fall of 1993, and was kindly made available by Elaine Rice.

Principal published sources include Oleg Cassini's *One Thousand Days of Magic* (St. Martin's Press, 1995) and *In My Own Fashion* (Pocket Books, 1987); Heymann's *A Woman Named Jackie*; Kelley's *Jackie Oh!*; Kessler's *Sins of the Father*; Leamer's *The Kennedy Women*; Martin's *A Hero for Our Time* and *Seeds of Destruction*; O'Donnell, Powers, and McCarthy's *"Johnny, We Hardly Knew Ye"*; Richard Reeve's essay, "John F.

Kennedy, 1961–1963," which appeared in *Character Above All: Ten Presidents from FDR to George Bush* (Simon & Schuster, 1995); Thomas Reeves's *A Question of Character*; James Reston's *The Artillery of the Press: Its Influence on American Foreign Policy* (Harper & Row, 1967); Truman's *First Ladies*; and J. B. West's *Upstairs at the White House* (Coward, McCann and Geoghegan, 1973).

The account of Jack's demanding that Jackie buy only American clothes appeared in *Women's Wear Daily* (September 1, 1960). A letter that Jackie sent to *Women's Wear Daily* about her approach to dressing was paraphrased and appeared virtually word for word in *Women's Wear Daily* (November 23, 1960).

Jackie's comment that the White House looked like Moscow's dreaded Lubyanka Prison appeared in Mary Van Rensselaer Thayer's "Jacqueline Kennedy's Years in the White House," in *McCall's* (January, 1968).

Thirteen: The Abyss

The narrative of the fateful years 1962 — including Jack's troubling relations with Judith Campbell and Marilyn Monroe, Jackie's relations with Gianni Agnelli, and the impact of the Cuban missile crisis on Jack and Jackie's marriage — is drawn from scores of interviews, including George Ball, deputy secretary of state under President Kennedy; Angier Biddle Duke; Taylor Chewning; George Smathers; Charles Bartlett; Kenneth Battelle; Paul Fay; Mario d'Urso, a socialite investment banker and a friend of Gianni Agnelli; George Griffen, an American consular officer in Italy in 1962; Alan Friedman, the author of *Agnelli: Fiat and the Network of Italian Power* (New American Library, 1988); Curtis Bill Pepper; Courtney Evans, J. Edgar Hoover's chief liaison with Robert Kennedy; Cartha Deloach, the number-three man in the FBI under Hoover; and James Spoto, author of *Marilyn Monroe: The Biography* (Harper Paperbacks, 1993).

* * *

The writer Sally Bedell Smith kindly provided the author with confidential material that was incorporated into this chapter.

The scene of Jackie, Dave Powers, and the president in Glen Ora was related to Stephen Corsaro, the researcher for Nigel Hamilton's *Reckless Youth,* by William Johnson, the chief archivist at the John F. Kennedy Library.

Principal publications include Alan Friedman's *Agnelli: Fiat and the Network of Italian Power* (New American Library, 1988); Kelley's *His Way*; Leamer's *The Kennedy Women*; Martin's *Seeds of Destruction*; Richard Reeves's *President Kennedy*; Thomas Reeves's *A Question of Character: A Life of John F. Kennedy* (Prima Publishing, 1992); Donald Spoto's *Marilyn Monroe: The Biography* (Harper PaperBacks, 1993); Anthony Summers's *Goddess; The Secret Lives of Marilyn Monroe* (Onyx, 1986); Margaret Truman's *First Ladies: An Intimate Group Portrait of White House Wives* (Random House, 1995); and West's *Upstairs at the White House.*

* * *

For further descriptions of Jackie's visit to Ravello, Italy, in 1962, the author made use of articles that appeared in the Italian daily *Corriere della Sera* (August 8, 1962) and the magazine *Gente* (August 24, 1962).

Fourteen: Love Lies Bleeding

The account of Jack and Jackie's last year together is drawn from interviews with Anne Truitt, a close friend of Mary Meyer's; Jack Anderson; Charles Bartlett; George Ball; Angier Biddle Duke; Robin Chandler Duke; Charles Spalding; Phillip and Cecilia Geyelin; Kenneth Battelle; Blair Clark, Jack's friend from Harvard; Paul Fay; Evelyn Lincoln; Brigit Gerney; Nigel Hamilton; Mario d'Urso; Douglas Burden; Stanley Tretick, a *Look* magazine photographer; Theodore H. White; William Manchester; Taylor Chewning; Peter Duchin; Gloria Emerson; Ellen D'Oench; Diane Dubois, author of Lee Radziwill's biography, *In Her Sister's Shadow*; and Nina Auchincloss Straight.

* * *

The author gratefully acknowledges the invaluable guidance he received from Anne Truitt, the soul of discretion, on the subject of Jack's relationship with Mary Meyer.

Principal publications include Bradlee's *A Good Life*; Davis's *The Kennedys*; Dubois's *In Her Sister's Shadow*; Heymann's *A Woman Named Jackie*; Lincoln's *My Twelve Years with John F. Kennedy*; William Manchester's *The Death of a President* (Harper & Row, 1967); Martin's *A Hero for Our Time* and *Seeds of Destruction*; Frank Ragano's *Mob Lawyer* (Scribners, 1994); and West's *Upstairs at the White House.*

Theodore White's "The Camelot Documents," 1963–1964, were obtained from the Kennedy Library.

For insight into Jackie's life in New York, the author is indebted to Pierre Salinger, Abraham Ribicoff, George Plimpton, and many of Jackie's friends, who requested confidentiality.

The following people kindly agreed to

be interviewed on the record:

Eller Adler
Patrick Ahern
Nelson Aldrich
Dr. Patricia Allen
Cicely Angelton
Durie Appleton
Hugh D. Auchincloss III
James Auchincloss
Louis Auchincloss
Wayne Auterman
Lauren Bacall
Dr. Michael Baden
Letitia Baldrige
George Ball
Charles Bartlett
David Bartlett
Martha Bartlett
Kenneth Battelle
Dr. John Baxter
Betty Beale
Warren Bechtel
Marilyn Bender
Michael Beschloss
Dr. John Bilezikian
William Blair
Sylvia Whitehouse Blake
Steven Bogart
Clarence A. Boonstra

Arnaud De Borchgrave
Hal Boucher
Lillian Brown
Art Buchwald
Wendy Burden
Douglas Burden
Horace Busby
Dr. William Cahan
Cass Canfield Jr.
Jim Cannon
Ann Cassidy
Oleg Cassini
Marion Charles
David Chavchavadze
David Chesnoff
Taylor Chewning
Steven Citron
Janice Clapoff
Blair Clark
Judith R. Cohen
Robert Colacello
Shirley Connell
Elise Constable
John Cooney
Bev Corbin
Stephen Corsaro
Patricia Coughlan
B. B. Crespi
John Crittenden
Carol Crowley

Bernard Crystal
Helen Dalrymple
John Davis
Lorraine Davis
Peter Davis
Mary de Limur
Ormande De Kay
Cartha Deloach
Ovid Demaris
Theodore Desloge
Catherine di Montezemolo
Anne Downey
Morton Downey, Jr.
Diana DuBois
Peter Duchin
Angier Biddle Duke
Robin Chandler Duke
Mario d'Urso
Ellen D'Oench
Franklin D'Olier
Mel Elfin
Gloria Emerson
Sidney Epstein
Courtney Evans
John Fairchild
Paul "Red" Fay
Myer "Mike" Feldman
Clay Felker
Richard Finn
Stanley Fisher

Gary Fishgall
Francis Fitzgerald
Father John Flannagan
Janet Des Rosiers Fontaine
Alistair Forbes
Marian Fourestier
Alan Friedman
Blair Fuller
Lynn Garafola
John Gates
Jeoffrey Gates
Brigit Gerney
Phillip Geyelin
Cecilia Geyelin
Sam Giancana
Mary Bailey Gimbell
Lucianne Goldberg
Paul Goldberger
Ronald Goldfarb
Barak Goodman
Allen Goodridge
John Maxtone Graham
Christopher Gray
George Griffen
Sydney Gruson
Tom Guinzburg
Todd Gustavson
William Haddad
Albert Hadley
Pete Hamill

Nigel Hamilton
W. Bradford Hatry
Ed Hayes
Bonnie Hedges
Dr. William Heimdahl
Isaac Herschkopf
Seymour Hersh
Solange Herter
Minnie Hickman
Joseph Hirsch
William Hitchcock
William Holt
Walter Hopps
Timothy Horan
Anne Marie Houston
Richard Howland
John G. W. Husted
J. C. Irondelle
Marion Javits
Janet Jeghelian
Betty Jones
Gloria Jones
Helen Kaplan
Allan Kay
Diane Kay
Peter Keating
Kitty Kelley
Robert Kennedy Jr.
Ronald Kessler
Jennifer King

Mary Louise King
Phillis Kirk
Rochelle Knoler
Barbara Lafferty
Dr. Michael Lavyne
Patrick Lawlor
Lawrence Leamer
Timothy Leary
Evelyn Lincoln
Dan Link
Karen Lichtman
Kate Rand Lloyd
Louise Lorrah
Jacques Lowe
Robert Maheu
Dr. Richard Malher
Elon Marquand
James Marquand
Timothy Marquand
Ralph G. Martin
Susan Martin
Peter Matheisson
Sandra McElwaine
Mary McFadden
Mary McGrory
Priscilla Johnson McMillan
Marianne Means
Kay Meehan
Dr. Hanne Meiland
William Merriam

Despina Messinesi
Sonny Metha
David Michaelis
Melody Miller
James Mintz
Grace Mirabella
Betty Monkman
James Morely
Wendy Morgan
Robert Mossbacher
Edna Murray
Gay Mutino
Barbara Newman
Kenneth Noland
John B. Oakes
Susan Oberstein
Jane Hutchinson Ogle
Mel O'Rourke
Ann Owen
Christina Oxenberg
Chauncey Parker
Mrs. Iva Patcevitch
June Payne
Beverly Pepper
Curtis Bill Pepper
Dr. Ethel Person
Dr. Frank Petito
Carol Phillips
Rifield Phyllis
Nick Pileggi

Samuel Pisar
Warren Platt
George Plimpton
Mary Jane Poole
Henry Porter
Dave Powers
Consuelo Quiroz
Theron Raines
James Reed
Richard Reeves
Abraham Ribicoff
Lois Ribicoff
Elaine Rice
Donald Ritchie
Frank J. Sackton
Pierre Salinger
Peggy Reeves Sanday
Susan Sandler
Marianne Schelsinger
Julie Schieffelin
Charlie Schieppes
Carlotta Schuster
William Seibert
Wilfred Sheed
Dr. Michael Sheehy
Mimi Sheraton
Aaron Shikler
Joseph Shimon
Babs Simpson
Dr. Marvin Siperstein

Sara Slavin
George Smathers
Amanda Smith
Liz Smith
Sally Bedell Smith
Walter Sohier
Theodore Sorensen
Charles Spalding
Donald Spoto
Wendy Stark
Jean Stein
Mae Stone
Nina Auchincloss Straight
Chris Strong
Arthur Stryker
Aubin Sumers
Phillip Talbot
Virginia Thaw
Connie Bradley Thayer
Evan Thomas
Helen Thomas
Jason Thomas
Michael Thomas
Dr. George Thorn
Dr. Atilla Toth
Robert Towbin
Aileen Russell Train
John Train
Susan Train
Stanley Tretick

Anne Truitt
Francesca Stanfill Tufo
Dr. James Turrell
Craig Unger
William vanden Heuval
Frank Waldrop
Grace Warnecke
William Warner
Estha Weiner
S. Cary Welsh
Tom Werblin
Richard Whalen
Charles Whitehouse
Cherie J. Whitney
Tom Wicker
Gerry Wilson
David Wise
Robert Wolders
Patricia Wood
Lisa Wright
Phyllis Wright

Acknowledgments

A journalist who chooses to write a book about the courtship and marriage of Jack and Jackie Kennedy runs into a vexing problem. He finds that a number of his subjects' best friends and closest associates — those who should feel a moral obligation to bear witness — are often the very same people who try to prevent him from discovering the truth.

Apparently, any F.O.K. (Friend of the Kennedys) who dares to speak out about Jack and Jackie still runs the risk of being banished from what is left of the Kennedy royal court. To this day, many of Jack and Jackie's acolytes continue in their misguided effort to cloak the Kennedys — and, it must be added, their own reputations and livelihoods — in the mindless myths of Camelot.

A journalist also finds that the Kennedy Library, which is run at taxpayers' expense by the National Archives and Records Administration, frequently seems more interested in promoting a positive Kennedy image than in fostering historic accuracy.

Since Jackie's death in the spring of 1994, however, more and more people have been willing to talk to a fair-minded reporter. Of the more than 325 people who agreed to speak on and off the record for this book, the following deserve special thanks for their willingness to be quoted directly: Solange Herter, Hélène Arpels, Hugh D. Auchincloss III, Abraham Ribicoff, Charles and Martha Bartlett, John Husted, Gloria Emerson, Nina Auchincloss Straight, Janet Des Rosiers Fontaine, Morton Downey, Jr., Phillip and Cecilia Geyelin, and Janet Jeghelian.

I owe my appreciation to Peter Salber and Ted Slate at the *Newsweek* library; Dr. Robert Batscha and Karen F. Lichtman at the Museum of Television and Radio; Etta Froio and Merle Thomason at *Women's Wear Daily*; Elaine Rice at the Maryland State Archives; Ann Morfogen at Sony America; Jane Hutchinson Ogle, formerly of *Vogue*; Allan and Diane Kay, the current owners of Merrywood; Cherie J. Whitney at DACOR, the Diplomatic and Consular Officers Retired organization; Beverly and Curtis Bill Pepper in Italy; and Samuel and Judith Pisar in France.

The book's narrative was significantly strengthened by Marie Brenner, who generously gave the author unpublished material written by Jackie when she applied for the *Vogue* Prix de Paris in 1950.

Writer Ronald Kessler graciously introduced the author to Janet Des Rosiers Fontaine, a source who would not have been otherwise available.

Jack Anderson kindly interviewed several sources and gave richly of his experience and wisdom.

Columnist Liz Smith also interviewed a source on the author's behalf and was a font of knowledge and much encouragement.

Similarly, Sally Bedell Smith, Kitty Kelley, Nigel Hamilton, Richard Reeves, and Ralph Martin were extremely generous with their assistance.

John Fairchild, the chairman of Fairchild Publications, provided much historical insight and wisdom.

Significant contributions were made by Maura Sheehy (who conducted a number of interviews), Isabel von Fluegge (who read the manuscript and weeded out its more egregious flaws), John Mikulenka (who helped the author launch the project), Alfred Fariello (who transcribed hundreds of hours of interview tapes), and researchers Peter Keating, Kristina Cordero, Robert Sieczkiewicz, Peggy Loftus, Nadine Witkin, Derek Skepper, Peter Turvey, and Richard McGowen. Stephen Corsaro suggested ways to approach research at the Kennedy Library.

Katharine O'Moore-Klopf was an inspired copyeditor, and Cecilia Hunt did a meticulous job verifying facts.

Daniel Okrent and Bobby Burrows at *Life* magazine suggested the best sources for photographs.

Ann Schneider and Mia Dilorio added a great deal to the book with their photo research skills.

My associate and friend, Sandeep Junmarkar, directed the research for this book, and accompanied me on every step of the project. His passion for the subject always equaled mine, and his contribution can be felt on each page of the finished book. I owe him a special debt of gratitude.

Graydon Carter, the editor of *Vanity Fair*, provided me with the time and assistance that made this project possible. His enthusiasm for the book was always a restorative tonic.

Walter Anderson, the editor of *Parade*, lent the kind of steady encouragement and wise perspective that lightens a writer's burden.

Jack Scovil, my agent, was unflagging in his patience and inexhaustible in his friendship. He and I spoke practically every day on the phone.

Walter Bernard and Sandy Carlson, well-known art directors, gave unstintingly of their time, and their suggestions were incorporated into the design of the book's cover.

Miles Chapman, Mark Gill, Patricia Matson, Anita Goss, and Arthur Gelb put on their formidable thinking caps, and came up with possible titles.

At Pocket Books, I owe thanks to many talented people — Emily Bestler, Gina Centrello, Liz Hartman, Cindy Ratzlaff, Antoinette Lefebvre, Paolo Pepe, Jeanne Lee, Robin Kessler, and their former colleague, Bill Grose, who was the first to share my vision.

On a personal note, I would like to

thank Dr. Michael Sacks and Irwin Sloan, both of whom helped turn what could have been an onerous task into a creative experience. I also feel very grateful for the support I received from my family — Karen and Alec Klein and Rob and Melissa Barrett.

No words can express the gratitude I feel toward my wife, Dolores Barrett, who sustained me, loved me, and made it all worthwhile. This book is dedicated to her because I am dedicated to her.

Further Acknowledgments:

Excerpt on pages 26–27 from COLLECTED POEMS 1928–1953 by Stephen Spender. Copyright © 1934 and renewed 1962 by Stephen Spender. Reprinted by permission of Random House Inc. and Faber and Faber Ltd.

Excerpt on page 154 from "I Have a Rendezvous with Death" by Alan Seeger. Reprinted with the permission of Scribner, a Divsion of Simon & Schuster, from POEMS by Alan Seeger. Copyright © 1916 by Charles Scribner's Sons. Renewed 1944 by Elsie Adams Seeger.

Excerpt on page 459 from "That Old Black Magic" by Johnny Mercer and Harold Arlen. Copyright © 1942 by Famous Music Corporation. Copyright © renewed in 1969 by Famous Music Corporation.

The employees of Thorndike Press hope you have enjoyed this Large Print book. All our Large Print titles are designed for easy reading, and all our books are made to last. Other Thorndike Large Print books are available at your library, through selected bookstores, or directly from us.

For information about titles, please call:

(800) 223-2336

To share your comments, please write:

Publisher
Thorndike Press
P.O. Box 159
Thorndike, Maine 04986